D0069312

MORE FAR-REACHING ACCLAIM FOR OUR NATION'S FIRST FAMILY OF AMERICAN ANTIQUE FURNITURE

"An exciting compilation of extraordinary memories and information."

> Wendy A. Cooper
> Director, Wallace Gallery
> The Colonial Williamsburg Foundation

"Will be the standard text in connoisseurship and conduct. . . . A masterpiece!"

> Edward L. Stone
> The White House Preservation Fund

"A very readable account on the development of the antiques business in this century. . . . As time passes the importance of this book will increase since it records an important aspect of the development of so many great museum collectors."

> Michael K. Brown,
> Associate Curator
> The Bayou Bend Collection
> The Museum of Fine Arts, Houston

"It is a joy to read Harold Sack's *American Treasure Hunt*. Readers of his book can't help feeling that they are 'listening' to an insider providing invaluable information about specific examples of American furniture and individual collectors."

Charles F. Hummel,
Deputy Director for Collections,
The Henry Francis du Pont
Winterthur Museum

"Harold Sack knows so much about American Antique furniture — and his love for it is so great — that when I hear him talk about a specific piece, Harold Sack *becomes* that piece of furniture."

Bill Cosby,
Collector

"Quite simply the most interesting book about the antiques trade in a long time . . . amazing in its frankness."

Maine Antiques Digest

AMERICAN TREASURE HUNT

Harold Sack and Max Wilk

DKB Publishing
New York

ISBN: 0-9638464-0-X

Designed by Jeanne Abboud

Manufactured in the United States of America

First DKB Publishing Edition: October 1993
10 9 8 7 6 5 4 3 2 1

Dedicated to the memory of my parents,

ANNE AND ISRAEL SACK

*"In the Olden Days of art
Builders wrought with greatest care
Each minute and unseen part
For the gods see everywhere."*

— ANON.

" 'Look at this,' he says. 'It's a beautiful old Windsor chair. I bought it at an auction. We needed some more chairs for the house, so I gave this to a chair maker down the road to copy. Now, he never had anyone who taught him how to make this kind of chair. It took him 20 years of working on different chairs, reading books just to learn how to make a Windsor. So there you have a thousand years of knowledge breaking down. That knowledge disappeared in the 20th Century.' "

— DAVID MAMET

(The New York Times Magazine, April 1985)

Contents

Foreword

HAROLD SACK, the *summum bonum* among scholars of American antique furniture and the senior statesman of dealers, transcends all others today in the pantheon of American antiquarians. In *American Treasure Hunt*, Harold Sack gives us a frank, provocative, amusing history, with vigorous intelligence, of the great Augustan age of antiques collecting in America. He provides not only a vivid personal account of dramatic moments in the quest for masterpieces of American cabinetmaking, but also an admirable tale full of lively anecdotes and closely observed portraits of great American collectors over the last half century.

The structure of the book is like a great Victorian country house, replete with curious antiquarian details, rambling corridors, innumerable rooms decorated in a variety of styles, capacious closets, grand staircases, and noisy plumbing, an imposing house, well adapted to its complex functions. With *American Treasure Hunt*, Harold Sack has fulfilled our obsessive ambition: to get inside the antiques trade, to step beyond the door and down the corridor. What a rewarding view awaits!

— Wendell Garrett
Editor and Publisher
Antiques

AMERICAN
TREASURE HUNT

ONE

The Remarkable
Discovery Syndrome

WHEN I was about nine or ten years old, my father began to bundle me up and the two of us would go off to spend Saturday afternoons together. Back in those early 1920s, other fathers might be taking their sons to a Fenway Park ball game, or downtown to the movies or to a vaudeville show, or even camping or fishing along some sparkling New England trout stream.

Not my father, Israel Sack. He had me beside him in the front seat of his long, open Buick touring car, on its black leather upholstery, and in those pre–seat belt days, we careened our way down rutted back dirt roads, calling on a Mr. Littlefield, or Mr. Tuck, some farmer, or a rural entrepreneur who'd lately become a dealer in local antiques.

It may not have seemed so to me at the time, as I bumped and rolled on that drafty front seat, but in truth, we were on a far more romantic mission than any of my school classmates those Saturdays. We were treasure hunting.

My father was a man with a mission, as he hurried hopefully on to unearth some piece of fine, early American craftsmanship that had perhaps been tucked away for years in the back room of a farmhouse, or a family heirloom, down from the attic, covered with a century's worth of dust. A New Hampshire chest, or a Massachu-

Israel Sack, 1953.

setts desk, a highboy . . . or perhaps some primitive family portrait, encrusted with its years of grime.

Once we got to our remote destination, I would listen as he dangled a high price as bait. I can remember the owners wincing and squirming, reluctant to sell, but up and up would go my father's offer, and rarely was his bait refused. Dangle a dollar sign in front of most Yankees, and they will usually jump through the hoop.

On most days, my father was successful, and we'd return to Boston, weary but triumphant, with another fine antique piece, "in the rough," perhaps, but ready to be carefully restored and polished for his Charles Street shop. On other Saturday forays, he might not be so successful, and we'd pitch and rock home with nothing to show for the day's travail.

But throughout his long life, my father continued searching for those buried treasures, those temporarily forgotten masterpieces of furniture and silver. "Crazy" Sack my father might be to others in the trade, but the prices he paid back then were only relatively high. What he gave for those marvelous antiques were 1920s' "hard" dollars, and time — which he was far ahead of — has proved him correct. Present-day prices for these items make what my father paid then seem ridiculous indeed.

But it was never merely commerce and profit that impelled him, day after day, to unearth the next . . . whatever. Israel Sack was a man truly possessed by a deep love for antiques, and those early American craftsmen who created them.

It's decades later, but since I and my brothers were all infected by our father's taste and enthusiasm at a very early age, we have all been possessed by the same drive. We continue to search for treasures. In this, we're far from unique.

Everyone who collects, be it furniture, silverware, antique china, or even ephemera (that new catch-all word which covers such a multitude of heretofore trivial items), is driven by the same fantasy.

Call it the Remarkable Discovery Syndrome.

You may be a buyer, or a dealer, a museum curator or a knowledgeable browser in an out-of-the-way antiques show, on your way to a flea market, or to a neighborhood tag sale . . . but you live with this fond dream always ticking away in your subconscious. Each and every day, it motivates you.

Its scenario goes something like this.

You will wander into an antiques shop in a backwoods village or on a quiet city side street. There, in one of the rear rooms, covered by a slight coating of dust, is a piece of furniture. Or a piece of silver. Some old china. A desk, a chair, a card table, a pitcher, a bureau, a tapestry, a framed piece of primitive art, it doesn't matter specifically what. For the sake of this scenario, it will be graceful, well proportioned, a bit shabby perhaps. But most important, this item will be so anonymous that no one will know its monetary value.

Eventually, then, you will buy it for a smallish price, bring it back to your home, dust it, polish it, and set it in a corner where it will be admired. Then it will quietly lapse into its new role as a member of the family. Nobody will pay it much attention, but there it will sit, like some sleeping princess, waiting to be discovered.

Time passes, and then, one day, someone with a sharper eye will come into the house, spot the Something, and ask its origin. Careful research will turn up the fact that this may not be just another early American Something . . . no indeed. *Eureka!* This may be even a unique piece, signed, perhaps, by its maker, one of the fine early American craftsmen, a furniture maker, a silversmith, an artist — and —

Now the excitement builds. Museum people will examine the Something and pronounce it, in their wisdom, authentic, and they will guardedly hint at a more exciting aspect of this Something. Because of its rarity, it is extremely valuable. For how many other such examples of early American craftsmanship can exist?

In the antiques business, such news spreads rapidly, and soon there will be phone calls from auction houses, who wish to send their representatives in an effort to snag this Something for a forthcoming sale. Dealers, bearing checkbooks, will arrive on the doorstep. Numbers will be quoted, thousands, or more, mind-boggling amounts, and the climactic scene of this fond and lovely fantasy we all share will come when that Something, that same Something discovered in that darkened back room hiding beneath its coating of dust, finally changes hands again . . . for a six-figure price.

I understand this fantasy very well. It goes back to the days when my father and I knocked on New England farmhouse doors. So I realize that's all it is, a fantasy. It almost never happens.

Except when it does.

People come into our 57th Street showrooms quite often with snapshots or pictures of pieces they wish to sell. They're usually recommended, either by knowledgeable friends, or even by museums, because they know that our firm has always paid top prices for good early American pieces. And they also know that should we buy, the item has to be authentic. We screen out fakes, or pieces of dubious worth.

About six months ago, we had a visitor, an attractive gray-haired lady from Essex, Connecticut, call her Mrs. White; she brought with her a photograph of a tea table she had in her home.

Her table appeared to be similar to a Goddard table that had been sold, years back, in the depths of the Depression, 1930, at the Philip Flayderman sale, at the American Art Galleries. In those dark days following the 1929 crash, that Goddard-Townsend tea table brought the then-astronomical price of $29,000 when it was purchased by Henry du Pont, the collector responsible for amassing the great antiques collection at Winterthur, in Delaware.

The furniture created in the workshop of those two Quaker craftsmen, John Goddard and John Townsend, is especially notable for its superb artistic craftsmanship. One soon learns to recognize among other details their unique design treatment of the ball-and-claw foot, a motif prevalent in America and England during the eighteenth century.

In Colonial America, the ball-and-claw differed in design from one region to another, so identification of the origins of such a piece can be based in great part on the differences in the way the feet are carved.

On the Goddard table sold at the 1930 auction, the talons are open, so that one can see through the space where the talons reach the ball, an extremely difficult piece of work for a wood-carver, but also a very interesting design feature. It is quite beautiful and extremely rare.

I know of only three such tea tables, from the period 1750–1760, truly the golden years of the Goddard-Townsend workshop in Newport, Rhode Island. Two of them are in the Winterthur collection, and the third is in a private collection in Providence, Rhode Island. Then, there is an identical form of this table in which the claws of the foot are *not* open. There are only three of this version of the Goddard-Townsend table extant. Total, six tables of this form known to us.

And now, this pleasant lady from Essex, Connecticut, arrived in our showroom with a snapshot of — could it be? — the seventh.

Where had she acquired her table?

The scenario was almost eerily the same as that of the Remarkable Discovery Syndrome. It seemed she had purchased it some thirty or so years back, from a decorator, a lady who had found it in Seattle, Washington. And that was its entire provenance.

Now, after all this time, someone had recently told her that her tea table seemed to be an old and valuable piece of early American furniture. There are antiques dealers everywhere, knowledgeable dealers, but rather than consult them, Mrs. White had gone to a library and done some research on her own. In the course of studying she'd come across photographs of the two Goddard-Townsend tea tables in the Winterthur collection. By this time, she had gotten the idea that perhaps her table might be similar, but it was only that,

Townsend open-talon mahogany tea table, Newport, Rhode Island, circa 1760. This is one of seven known examples of the ball-and-claw foot form of tea table with voluted sides attributed to the Townsends and Goddards of Newport, R.I. This example illustrates the use of open talons on the otherwise very distinctive design of the Newport ball-and-claw foot with elongated talons grasping an elongated ball. Interestingly, this table is the only one of the group attributed by its carving to John Townsend rather than John Goddard.

so far: an idea. Most people — correctly, I might add — would not assume that sitting in a living room in Essex, Connecticut, quietly minding its own business, there could be a masterpiece of early American craftsmanship, a museum piece equivalent to its mates in Winterthur. The odds against such a possibility are staggering.

Now, Mrs. White had come to see us, to determine whether her fantasy was fact. Since our firm is considered the final authority in establishing authenticity in early American furniture, could we please provide her with some information about her table?

My brother Albert made an appointment to go up to Essex and examine her table, but unfortunately, through a combination of circumstances, he wasn't able to keep the date.

A few days later, we discussed Mrs. White and her table, and although the temptation to dismiss the lady as merely another wishful thinker was quite strong — especially when one considers the number of wild goose chases we embark on to examine so-called authentics — we decided Albert had better go up to see her forthwith.

He telephoned to make a second appointment. By then, Mrs. White was a touch reluctant, and who can blame her? Since Albert had canceled his first date, she had probably decided that she was getting short shrift from Israel Sack, Inc. Albert prevailed, however, and he went up to see her.

Mr. and Mrs. White are a pleasant couple in their early seventies, who live in a charming small house on an Essex side street. She ushered Albert inside to see her table.

When he'd finished examining it, he was convinced the impossible had occurred. Here, in an Essex living room, where it had been hidden away for all these years, was the *fourth* Goddard-Townsend tea table with the intricate open ball-and-claw feet.

True, there was one problem: the finish. When Mrs. White had originally bought it, the wood had varnish on it, and in trying to remove that old varnish, somebody had cleaned it off a bit too hard. Obviously no one had recognized the table as a valuable antique. But outside of the finish, the piece was flawless.

And it certainly had been bought by Mrs. White for a fair price: $180.

My brother told her, "I believe this to be 'right,' and we could pay you a good deal of money for this piece, but you must understand, we don't want it shopped around. We'd even be willing to pay a premium for this piece, if the situation is kept private."

Mrs. White was obviously startled, then pleased, but she kept her cool and promised Albert she would think it over. "Could you give me some idea of a price?" she asked.

"All I can tell you," he said, "is that it's probably very valuable, but until you're ready to talk about whether or not you'll sell it, we can't discuss price."

Mrs. White promised to get back to him.

Albert went back to the daily round of commerce here in our showroom, and we waited. Suddenly, almost two weeks had passed since Albert's visit to Essex, and he realized he had not heard from Mrs. White.

He called her to ask whether she'd decided to go any further with her tea table, and had she perhaps decided to sell it?

Indeed, she had. She told Albert that since he'd been there, she'd been in touch with Christie's auction house, here in New York, and they had given her table their immediate attention. When their expert had come up to examine it, he'd put a very high estimate price on it, should she decide to consign it to auction.

What price? Business being business, Mrs. White wouldn't reveal their estimate. Furthermore, Mrs. White had decided that putting her table up for auction would probably be the most advantageous way of disposing of it.

Albert is certainly an expert on furniture, but in this case he deferred to my — we hoped — persuasive abilities. "Would you have any objection if my brother Harold came up to examine your table and talk to you about it?" he asked.

"Not at all," said Mrs. White. "I'm not sure it will do him any good at this point, but he might as well come."

My father, who was a shrewd appraiser not only of early American furniture, but of people, had taught me a rule early on. "Everyone likes to deal with a rich man," he'd say. So the following day, I hired a chauffeured limousine and had myself driven up to Essex.

The stretch limousine deposited me in the Whites' driveway, and I was shortly in the company of two very nice people, quite warm and hospitable. We had coffee, and I soon found out Mr. White had retired from his position in a Hartford insurance company, where he'd specialized in finance. Was he by any chance acquainted with my old Dartmouth friend Bill Morton, who'd once been with American Express? He certainly was, and soon we were deep in pleasant conversation about Bill, Dartmouth, and various other related matters.

On and on we rambled, chatting amiably away, but always on social subjects — nothing to do with antiques. Soon, it was past noon, and the question came up of what we would do about lunch. Then, somewhat reproachfully, Mrs. White said, "But, Mr. Sack, you haven't even *looked* at the table yet."

Which wasn't quite true. When I'd entered her house, I'd glanced at her table out of the corner of my eye. I already knew it had a refinished top surface, and even though I'd only caught a glimpse of the table, my first thought was *That is a goody.*

Let me explain about my reaction.

There are many ways that experts and connoisseurs look at furniture. To some, it's an art form. Others love construction, and are interested only in how a piece is made. Then, there are those who look at early American furniture and want to understand only its provenance. History, especially family history, is what turns them on.

I respond to the aesthetics. I call it *aspect,* and for me it's vital. I have always found, in judging authenticity, that first glimpse is always my best guide. The first impression is the most important; for me it's the only right one. Where I can go wrong is later: when I go back over a piece, and if and when I start to rationalize, to make excuses for possible flaws, and equivocate about other aspects that may be perhaps odd, or unacceptable.

That very first look, however — it's the most sensitive, and for me, it's a wonderful guide. I rely on it.

What Mrs. White didn't know was that I'd intentionally avoided going over to get down and examine the table more carefully, no matter how tempting it was to do so.

It was a calculated move on my part, for I realized I was in a somewhat ambiguous position up there in her home. It was obvious that after a good deal of painful soul-searching, Mrs. White had decided to part with a cherished piece of furniture; she'd already been in touch with Christie's, and had for all intents and purposes made up her mind to put the piece up for auction. Now, here I was, in her living room, and I represented a disturbance which might upset her plans. And what is more, she owed me and my firm nothing.

So simple psychology dictated I spend time becoming friends with her and Mr. White, before any discussion of business took place.

But now, Mrs. White had given me a definite signal to get on with it.

"Well, Mrs. White," I said, "I have seen it. I'd want to examine it a little bit more after we're through talking. I'm enjoying my stay with you so much, we'll get to the table later. But first, may I ask you a question? Has anyone else seen it besides the man from Christie's? Have you perhaps approached Sotheby's?"

No, she had not. It seemed once before she had been treated at Sotheby's in a very high-handed manner. "But when I went to Christie's," she told me, "I was treated very nicely. So I did not go back to Sotheby's with this table."

"Fine," I said. "Anybody else?"

She hesitated, and then said, "I know I promised your brother I wouldn't shop it around, or anything like that, but I must confess one thing. I did call up the Metropolitan Museum — but only to get an estimate on how valuable such a table as this might be."

"And what did they say?" I asked.

"Well," she said, "when I spoke to the curator there, he was very uninterested. He told me they don't put values on furniture, that it's against their policy. However, when I mentioned that this piece was very much like the Goddard table in Winterthur, the one with the open-taloned feet, which originally was sold with a bill of sale signed by John Goddard, he suddenly seemed very interested." (I could certainly understand why.) "He wanted to know if he could come up to see me," said Mrs. White.

"*And* your table," I said.

She smiled. "Yes. I didn't want to break my promise to your brother, but I couldn't resist having him come up to our house and look at my table, could I? So he arrived, and spent several hours going over it, and said he wanted it for the Metropolitan."

"As a gift, of course," I suggested.

Mrs. White glanced at her husband. Mr. White smiled benignly, but said nothing. Then she nodded.

"I told him we weren't in a position to make such a gift," she said. "Then he said he would like it to be down there so he could get hold of various people who might be able to raise the money to *buy* my table for the Metropolitan."

"Did anyone mention a price?" I asked.

She shook her head. "But I do feel," she murmured, "it should go to a museum."

I nodded. "Well, we haven't negotiated anything on your table yet," I said, "but I can assure you if my firm is successful in buying the piece, it will eventually go to a museum. One other thing I'm absolutely sure of: it will only go to a buyer who loves it and cares for it. At today's prices, it has to be bought by someone with knowledge, and with real taste. And it will probably be left by such a person to a museum, where good things always end up."

"I admit I've developed an attachment to the table," she sighed. "We've had it here for so long it truly has sentimental value. However," she conceded, "I know you have the best clients. When I read about your buying that Goddard-Townsend kneehole desk, with the shell carving, at Sotheby's for $685,000 — well, then I knew you qualified as a serious buyer."

On such a point, I certainly couldn't argue with Mrs. White. We'd set a new record for the price of any early American piece two years earlier, in 1983, which took care of our qualifications as a buyer. But so far as Mrs. White's position as a potential seller was concerned, I had a problem. She, being no fool, was certainly not about to reveal to me at what price Christie's had estimated the value of her table.

Our minds were on the same wavelength. "Tell me, Mr. Sack," she asked, "why *shouldn't* I send it to auction?"

"Good question," I told her. "If you do, several things can happen. At Christie's, the price could go through the roof, if and when a lot of excited competitors bid on it. On the other hand, it has been refinished, and that finish should be partially restored. That might cause its price to suffer. Remember, you're dealing in a very small business arena, where all the various dealers know each other. If they decide to bad-mouth your table because of its finish, they can easily knock its price way down. So, while Christie's can estimate you a price, remember that it's no guarantee the table will fetch that price."

Mrs. White shrugged. "In that case," she told me, "I can always have it back."

"Ah, yes," I reminded her, "but then, please remember, it will have been shopped."

"That wouldn't matter," she said, firmly. "Because I could keep it here for ten years more, and then my children could have it."

"Connoisseurs have very long memories about such matters," I warned her. "So do dealers. *And* if you wait ten years, none of us has any idea what market conditions will be like then. However, if you decide to sell to us, and we agree on a price here and now, you do know that the bird is in your hand, and the money we pay over to you will have at least doubled in ten years. Your husband is a financial man. Ask him how much these dollars will compound over a decade."

Mr. White had long been silent, but now he stood up. "Mr. Sack," he said, "enough business. Let's go out to lunch."

"First, let him look at the table," said his wife.

I agreed. It was time.

My first glimpse of her table had been correct.

My father used to say, when he saw some elegant piece of early American craftsmanship, "It speaks to me." Mrs. White's table spoke to me.

Then I examined it more carefully. My detective work turned up certain clues. When I turned the table upside down, I discovered a crosspiece, a structure used only on Goddard-Townsend tables. I could see the piece of wood was maple, and it was speckled with wormholes. Now, we know in the midyears of the eighteenth century, the worms attacked the maples in and around Newport, Rhode Island, which is where the Goddard-Townsend workshops flourished. So when I found that particular brace, with its traces of long-gone worms, I had a strong indication my initial instinct about the table being "right" was correct.

And as for the discoloration on its finish, when I checked the table top, I could see it had been removed at one time. Beneath it, there was a small canvas inset; so at one point, there'd been a shrinkage of the wood, and someone had actually filled it in a bit, to compensate. Another good sign, for when a piece is this old, we like to see traces of its usage over the past two centuries, or of some kind of repair of minor damage.

Finally, the carvings on the legs seemed to me to be identical to the Goddard-Townsend designs of that period, not only on these card tables and tea tables, but also on their highboys and lowboys.

Mrs. White's table was, as Albert had originally assessed it, certainly authentic. As well as being rare.

How rare it was, even I didn't realize. Not yet. But I knew I had to buy it.

We went to lunch at a pleasant local restaurant. The food was excellent, and we continued chatting. I thought this might be the appropriate time to tell Mr. and Mrs. White something pertinent about Israel Sack, Inc.

It happened during my fiftieth reunion at Dartmouth, back in 1982. I was up in Hanover, enjoying the festivities, while at the same time a Goddard-Townsend Newport kneehole desk was due to come up for sale at Christie's.

We'd had a lot of discussion about the sale, but we'd decided that although this was a major piece, we were committed to other things, and we were undecided whether to purchase the desk. Not that it wasn't a fine piece; it simply was not on our agenda at the moment.

However, up in Hanover, as I sat listening to our speaker, I realized his speech wasn't diverting my subconscious, which was reminding me that at this exact time, the Goddard-Townsend desk was due to come up for sale down in New York, and maybe I had better bid on it after all, and not let it get away too cheaply.

So I excused myself from the lecture, went over to the Hanover Inn, called Christie's in New York, and they said yes, the piece would be up in about ten minutes or so. I gave them my telephone number and instructed them to call me just before the lot came up. "I may decide to bid," I told them, "but I want to be in at the end, because I haven't quite made up my mind on it."

After the piece came up, the bidding promptly rose to $350,000. I figured that was enough, and I passed. The desk ended up being bought by a very wealthy Texan from Houston.

Later on, however, word got back to this gentleman that none of the Sacks had attended the sale, and nobody had bid for them on this particular kneehole desk. Which made him quite nervous. Why were the Sacks, who were noted for buying up every available major piece in the country, not present? Could something possibly be wrong with his purchase? Perhaps it needed further authentication, and should something be proved wrong with it, why then, he would forthwith return it to Christie's.

Before things went any further, Christie's, in utmost confidence, revealed to the Texas gentleman that while the Sacks had not been visible at the sale, Harold had definitely bid by telephone from Hanover, while at his reunion, and he had ended up the underbidder. Would this fact serve to reassure and satisfy the Texas collector?

It would, and it did, and he promptly paid for and brought home his superb Goddard-Townsend kneehole desk, convinced it was "right."

"I told you this story only because I wanted to explain the power we seem to have in the marketplace," I told the Whites. "Not that we would ever boycott your sale, or anything as underhanded as that. But it does show how, if you turn this power around, the name Sack in the provenance of an antique piece seems to move the price upward. The fact is, over the years, we've come to the point where we can almost create a market."

"I can understand it," said Mrs. White, "but doesn't it seem rather a closed circle?"

"When prices get to this level," I told her, "there aren't too many sellers, and even fewer buyers."

She smiled. "I must also tell you the man from Christie's and the gentleman from the Metropolitan both gave you the highest praise, and said if any dealer buys my table, it should go to Sack."

"Nice to hear," I said, "and I must say, I agree with them."

It was time to talk price. I made an educated guess. "I'm thinking that the estimated price Christie's told you your table would bring at auction would be somewhere between two and three hundred thousand dollars."

Neither of them answered, but they both smiled politely.

The next move was still mine.

"I can tell you what I'll offer," I said. "I'm prepared to give you three hundred thousand dollars."

Mrs. White kept absolutely poker-faced. But for the first time, her husband spoke up. "Very interesting, Mr. Sack," he said. "But what about taxes?"

"Well," I said, "you're going to be hit with a capital gains tax, certainly, since your wife bought this table for one hundred eighty dollars. But I don't see how you can avoid that, do you?"

We sipped our coffee, while I waited for an answer.

Mr. White turned to his wife. "I don't really think we're that far apart," he said. "I think we ought to talk further about the price, dear, don't you?"

I understood what he meant. If I raised my price, it would serve to make up a good deal of the capital gains tax she'd be incurring.

Mrs. White nodded, and waited for me.

"All right," I told her. "I'll stretch it a little bit. But I'm getting up to my limit now, because when I come to sell this piece, I'll have to make an entirely new market for it. I'll buy it now for three hundred twenty-five thousand."

I could tell from their reactions my offer was much better than Christie's estimate. Mrs. White turned to her husband, then she said, softly, "Dear, what should I do?"

"Darling," he told her amiably, "it's your table."

"Yes, it is, but I want your advice," she said. *"Please?"*

It was obvious what had kept their marriage solid for all these years was a fine balance of mutual trust.

Mr. White cleared his throat. "Mr. Sack," he said, "I'll recommend my wife sell you her table if we can settle this deal at three hundred fifty thousand."

All around us, polite people went on quietly eating their lunches, oblivious to the three of us at our table, as we sat over coffee cups quietly discussing a six-figure price for a Goddard-Townsend table with as little excitement as if this were an everyday experience. For all three of us.

I thought about Mr. White's counteroffer.

I thought, *Lord, how few of these tables exist, and how rare the opportunity to buy one.*

"If I say yes, would you shake hands on the deal?" I asked.

"Oh, Lord," sighed Mrs. White. "What will I tell the man from Christie's? He'll be so disappointed!"

"You can merely tell him you sold it to Sack, who was crazy enough to pay such a high price for it that you couldn't turn it down," I said.

Mrs. White smiled finally, although a bit weakly. *"Yes,"* she admitted. "That would be the sensible answer, wouldn't it?"

"Then we have a deal?" I asked. I held out my hand.

We shook.

"Oh, Mr. Sack," she sighed. "I know you'll find a good home for it, and I hope you do very well with it, but I am going to miss my tea table very, very much!"

I could understand exactly how she felt. The money I would pay her for that beautiful piece of early American craftsmanship, truly a work of art, no matter how large the sum, could never replace it. She'd originally bought it because she loved it. As my father would have said, it had spoken to her. . . .

Luckily, I could help her solve that problem. A year or so previously, by coincidence, Albert had bought a reproduction of one of those Goddard-Townsend tables in Boston. It was a good reproduction, part of another group of authentic pieces. "Why don't I send it up to you, and you can have it sitting in your living room?" I suggested. "Won't that help?"

She thanked me for being so thoughtful.

But now I had another problem. So far, all we had was a handshake. We'd made a deal, but we were still in the restaurant, without a bill of sale. How could I arrange for one? It was a moment that called for diplomacy and tact.

Mr. White solved my problem for me. "Look here," he said, the pragmatic businessman, "you own my wife's table, and it's obviously just gone up considerably in value."

Quite an understatement.

"So what about insurance?" he asked.

"Ah!" I said. "*We* have insurance. A blanket policy. The minute you sign a bill of sale to me, that table will be insured for the full amount of its price to Israel Sack, Inc."

"In that case," said Mr. White, rising, "let's go right back to our house, and we'll draw one up and sign it immediately."

Which we did. He drew up a proper bill of sale, Mrs. White and I both signed it, and in a matter of several hours, the Goddard-Townsend tea table had become our firm's property.

Several days later, the table arrived safely in our New York showroom.

The first person I called in to see our new prize is a young professor, Michael Moses, who was working on the definitive history of Messrs. Townsend and Goddard, whose genius has become so apparent.

He hurried in to see our prize, and we spent time carefully examining it. In so doing, we found out more about this tea table. Since John Goddard's carved designs hardly varied, we had concluded that those other tea tables from the Goddard-Townsend workshop — all six of them — must have all been made by him. But this particular piece, since it had carvings exactly the same as a few signed John Townsend pieces, has to be the *only* such table made by John Townsend! This Michael Moses definitely established.

Making it the ultimate in Remarkable Discoveries.

Michael was as exultant as we were. He insisted this great new find be immediately photographed, so he might have his publishers insert the picture as the frontispiece of his forthcoming book. No matter if it meant changing the format of his book — this was too important a find not to be so honored. "The only John Townsend open-talon ball-and-claw foot tea table of this form ever located — it deserves a place of honor!" he insisted.

My first impression had served me well.

The table went off to the shop where our specialists in refinishing could see what they might do about the discoloration.

When it came back, they had done a superb job. The discoloration had magically vanished. In its place was a warm, golden mellow color, and we had ourselves a magnificent, unblemished masterpiece.

Now we were plunged into a situation I hadn't foreseen.

Thanks to my ability to persuade Mrs. White to part with her treasure, Israel Sack, Inc. had acquired a tiger by the tail.

We owned one of the rarest pieces of early American furniture I'd ever seen, created by one of the finest of the early American craftsmen. Irreplaceable.

To whom were we going to sell this magnificent Townsend table?

It was a ticklish problem. We have our own group of knowledgeable and affluent collectors, people with whom we do business on a regular basis, many of whom have been relying on our expertise for years. Others are more recent visitors to our showrooms, but nonetheless equally as devoted to our early American inventory. If we sold this great table to one customer, without offering it to any of the others, wouldn't we instantly make enemies of those unlucky ones? Wouldn't each of the rest be entitled to ask us, later, and with justice, "Why didn't you let *me* know?"

We spent a good deal of time agonizing over the exact way to sell the table. Perhaps we could simply put it on display in our showroom. Without a price on it, merely as an exhibit. Thus, all our customers could see it.

Then, perhaps, we might hold a silent auction, at which all potential buyers might bid.

. . . No, that was not the way we do business. So much, perhaps all, of our trade is based on close personal relationships with our buyers. A silent auction would be far too impersonal; again, one or more of our customers might be offended by such a procedure.

Meantime, we decided it was prudent to discuss our new problem with one or two of our best customers, and to ask them their advice on how best to proceed. Supposing, we suggested, we put out this Townsend table and finally did set a price on it. Then, should only one of our customers decide he wished to meet that price, no problem — it would be his. If, however, more than one buyer wished to pay that sum, then he and whoever else wanted it could draw lots. My brothers and nephew concurred with this plan. How did that sound?

Customers to whom I spoke didn't relish that suggestion at all.

"Put a price on it, and then show it," said one. "*You* decide. Otherwise you'll merely tantalize everyone!"

We went into a huddle and priced that lovely table at $675,000.

A tremendous markup? Indeed. But let me respectfully point out that such unique items do not come down the pike every day. Most of our inventory is sold at a very reasonable markup over our cost. But that extensive inventory has to be maintained every day, whether it's sold or not. Remember, we own and operate a business

The Sack brothers and nephew: Albert, Harold, Donald, and Robert.

with as high an overhead as any other 57th Street establishment, and by the end of the year, any year, our profit, after expenses, is no more than that of, say, B. Altman's furniture department. But that is where the similarity ends. B. Altman can reorder and restock a popular item. We, on the other hand, can only sell such a Goddard-Townsend masterpiece once.

Then we called the two or three most logical possibilities on our list of customers, the people we knew who not only could afford that table, but would want it and love it. We told each one that whoever would pay our price first could have it.

I was careful to arrange it so they all had precisely the same time in which to make up their minds.

One of them, a gentleman from Virginia, promptly sent his wife up to see the table. It was love at first sight; she went home to ask him to buy it. We had several others who came in to see it but decided to think it over.

While they thought, I had a call from Virginia.

"I haven't seen the table," said my Norfolk customer, "but my wife has, and she loves it. I'd like to buy it, and I'm going to have to rely on you. What do *you* think about this?"

What did I think?

I thought exactly what I'd thought when I first stepped inside the Whites' house in Essex, and caught a glimpse of John Townsend's magnificent tea table, with its elegant proportions and its superb ball-and-claw carved feet. *It spoke to me.* After two centuries of anonymity, there it was. Magnificent.

So I told my Virginia customer, "I love it as much as your wife does, and I'm sure you will, too."

"Good enough," he said. "I'm not only buying a table, I'm buying you. So I might as well take it."

The table is now in his Virginia home, where I'm certain he has come to cherish John Townsend's work of art as much as his wife does, as much as we did, and as much as Mrs. White, of Essex, Connecticut, did when she first saw it, all those years ago, and bought it for $180.

My only regret is that my father, Israel Sack, who taught me so many years ago how to recognize a masterpiece, is not still around so that he, too, could enjoy having John Townsend's table speak to him.

And so far as that tantalizing fantasy, the Remarkable Discovery Syndrome — which we all carry around with us in the subconscious — is concerned, it is very much alive and well.

Who knows where — or if — the next one will turn up?

TWO

Israel Sack's Early Years

I N our home in Roxbury, Massachusetts, there weren't too many antiques around the house, and those that were there had a peculiar habit of abruptly disappearing. There were times when it was a bit like being an actor in a constantly changing stage set. In those days, the world of antiques was far smaller and more personal than it is today. Collectors, dealers, and customers all knew each other on a casual, intimate basis, and there was considerable socializing. Thus my father would bring home often, usually unannounced, a dealer, or a customer, to share dinner. My poor mother would then have a scant hour or so in which to improvise a proper meal sufficient for the newcomer.

Then, the following day, there could be a knock at our front door, and she'd open it to find Mr. Stone, our trucker from Charles Street, waiting on the doorstep. "Mrs. Sack," he'd announce, "I have your sideboard here."

"What do you mean, you have my sideboard?" she'd reply. "I *have* my sideboard!"

"No, you don't," Mr. Stone would explain. "Mr. Sack sold that one last night. We're here to take it away, and we've brought you a substitute."

That guest my father had brought home for dinner had perhaps fallen in love with our dining room sideboard while enjoying our hospitality and listening to my father's biblical parables. Eventually, after the customary haggling and give-and-take, my father and he had struck a deal. Good-bye sideboard.

My dear mother would be furious at having to empty out her linens and silver — again — and to stock another piece, so precipitously, and without ever having been consulted. And where was my father? Why, conveniently off somewhere, unreachable, scouring the New England countryside for another family heirloom with which to begin the whole process again.

Small wonder my mother grew to resent having her home furnished with such vanishable antiques. She was uncomfortable living in a showroom. Since she never knew which item would be the next to depart from her home, no one could blame her for that basic insecurity.

Not so my father. Such daily activity, both in his home and in his Charles Street shop, was his meat and drink. He thrived on it. Newly arrived in this country, he had found his calling. In a few short years, he had already become well established as one of the leading dealers in early American antiques. He enjoyed the complete confidence of most of the blue-blooded Boston families, and his stock was considered as choice as the roster of his customers.

Along Charles Street, he was known to all the other newly established antique dealers as "Crazy" Sack, a name he'd earned because of the rapidity of his decisions, the high prices he cheerfully paid, and the even higher prices for which he would then proceed to sell.

He had developed his passionate love affair with early American antiques, which continued for the next half century, after he'd arrived in Boston in 1903, an eager immigrant cabinetmaker from far-off Lithuania.

His was a classic saga of the convert, who comes to love and cherish his acquired faith with a fervency far outweighing that of those who were born to it.

He had been born in 1883 in Kovno (now known as Kaunas, in Lithuanian Soviet Socialist Republic), then a small *shtetl,* a bustling center of craftsmen who specialized in cabinetmaking. But my grandfather Sack was actually a merchant, whose family was, according to the standards of those times, fairly prosperous. In the normal course of events, his young son Israel would have gone into the family trade and remained a merchant.

But life for the Jews of that era, even those who had created small businesses, was oppressive and dangerous. Legal barriers maintained by the Czar's minions, and the bloody pogroms sporadically carried out by his ruthless Cossacks, were the order of the day. Where could a young student, well versed in the Bible and the Talmud, dream of going to avoid being drafted into the Czar's vast army? Only to America, that Golden Land.

Early on, young Israel reasoned that in order to emigrate across the Atlantic, it was vital to learn a trade. To be able to work with his hands would always provide him with a decent living. So, at fourteen, he apprenticed himself for two years to one of Kovno's many cabinetmakers. In the Sack family, to become a cabinetmaker would be a disastrous loss of status. Years later, he would remember, "In our town we had the greatest and most efficient grapevine telegraph system in the world. In less than five minutes, all of Kovno knew about it. I was too young to understand that I'd broken my poor mother's heart, but I was determined, and I stuck to it."

Apprenticeship was a mean and difficult life, one step removed from Dickensian slavery. Most who were apprenticed to a trade were boys whose parents could not afford to support them. They would start at the age of ten to twelve, and serve not less than four to six years. The unfortunate apprentices slept on straw pallets, huddled against the cold nights in ragged blankets, in some corner of that same shop where they performed their endless hard days' labor. The food was poor and barely sufficient to keep adolescent boys from starvation. Any trade which was learned under such circumstances had to be worth the effort.

Young Israel was determined; he also continued his studies, especially of the Bible; for the rest of his life, both educations, of his hands and of his mind, would serve him in good stead. Surrounded by the furniture in his shop, he would quote the words of the biblical prophets to us. "The prophet Jeremiah was my teacher's favorite," he'd tell us. "One passage I always remembered was when he said, '. . . the fathers have eaten a sour grape and the children's teeth are set on edge.' " My father agreed with his teacher. Years later he told us, "Isaiah said, 'The time will come when God shall judge among the nations and rebuke many people, and they shall beat their swords into plowshares, and their spears into pruning hooks. Nations shall not lift up swords against nations; neither shall they learn war any more.' " Then my father would shrug and sigh, holding up a cautionary finger. "But," he would always observe, ". . . He didn't set a *date*."

The young Talmudic scholar quickly developed his talent for woodworking and mastered the intricate fundamentals of cabinet-making. After several years, he would receive his diploma as a full-fledged artisan, a test passed only when he had made a complete piece of furniture by himself, which would then be passed on by a critical panel of veteran Kovno craftsmen.

By this time, he was eighteen, and subject to Russian military draft. Having saved up enough money for passage to London, he prudently decided not to wait any longer. To escape from the Czar's foraging recruiters was primary. Israel bought passage from a local agent who specialized in smuggling Lithuanians across the border. He bade his parents and family a tearful farewell, and set off on the first leg of his long and perilous journey.

During the first night, the small party was locked up in a barn. The next leg of the trip would take them across the border. "I was getting a little worried because we lingered there a little too long," he remembered, years later. "And sure enough, that night, we were discovered! Russian soldiers pounced on the door, yelling at us to let them in. When we wouldn't, they began to break down the door! Every time they tore off a board, the sound of those rusty nails could be heard for miles. I'd been sound asleep, but now I was wide awake and terrified. Somebody beside me in the pitch dark was wailing that we were all captured, and doomed! In the midst of all that commotion, I instantly began to think of the best way to escape. I wasn't going to let myself be captured. In Russia in those dreadful days, if you were caught anywhere without a pass, they'd send you off in a convoy, guarded by soldiers, like some convict, on foot. You could be thousands of miles from your final destination. You could march for days.

"That wasn't for me," he told us. "I figured the safest way was to dig a hole under the barn, through the dirt floor, and try to escape. I kept on digging desperately, with my hands. Already, they'd torn off the barn door, and I could hear the soldiers commanding 'Women and children first!' I kept on digging until I'd finally made myself a passage big enough to get out of there, and to escape into the night. I squeezed myself into it, and as I got out through the dirt, I could hear the soldiers in front yelling 'Lead 'em off!' "

Israel hid until daybreak, and then began to walk through the strange countryside. Finally, he came to a farm. There, kindly peasants escorted the young immigrant-to-be up to the German border, and showed him a path across. Once he had made it safely to the offices of the agency where his passage had previously been guaranteed, he was on his way. By steamer, he made the journey down to England.

Once in Liverpool, his earlier decision to master a trade served him well. Within hours of landing in that great British city, he had been hired to work in a cabinetmaker's shop.

Compared to his struggles in Lithuania, the young Israel's difficulties in England were relatively mild. He was the greenest of greenhorns, and thus subject to the customary harassment in his new place of employment. "We had straight-grain mahogany, the worst kind of mahogany you ever saw," he recalled. "It was hairy. In the first place it had some strong odor to it. Your nose would swell up twice its size, and your fingers would, too. That wood was so hairy, you could only sandpaper it one way, with the grain, and even that was thin. I was the greenhorn, so I got it all the time. You see, wood is very expensive and scarce in England. They'd put me to work on drawer bottoms, for which they used the cheapest mahogany. You had to get used to it, and whatever they gave me to do, I worked on it."

Early on, the "greenhorn" began to display his abilities. "My boss found out I was very good at dovetailing," he told me. "In England they made special dovetails to hold little shaving-glasses, and it's quite a trick to do it right, so that got to be my specialty."

Two weeks after the young immigrant had gone to work, there was a strike. In those days of the early twentieth century, there was no such movement as communism. Socialism was the rallying cry of the workers. The shop where he worked was full of socialists, who spearheaded the strike. Even though my father didn't believe in the cause, he went out on strike with the others. "It satisfied the other men," he recalled. "To them, I was a hero. And as for my boss, since I'd already told him what I was going to do, and promised him it wasn't anything personal, he understood why I did it."

Later on, when the strike was settled, one of the leaders tried to convert my father to socialism. His proselytizing efforts fell on barren ground. "Socialists have nothing," my father countered pragmatically. "What have they got to divide?"

My father maintained his studies of the Talmud throughout his life. "Money doesn't mean much to an orthodox Jew," he told me. His favorite saying, one which he was fond of quoting to us, and to his customers, whether they be Jew or gentile, all his life, was ". . . Money is not the root of all evil, it is the *getting* of money that is."

A year or so later, he had saved up enough money to buy himself passage to America, a steerage ticket on the Cunard Line. He had also learned enough English to be able to speak, albeit with a decided accent, to the authorities at Ellis Island.

"When we came to Ellis Island," he recounted, "and we went through a turnstile there, one at a time, I didn't have anybody to meet me. They asked me if I had five dollars cash. I didn't have quite that much, but I said, 'Yes, sure!' Then, one of the officials asked me, 'What can you do?' I said, 'I'm a cabinetmaker.' The man patted me on the back and said, 'My boy, you go right in. You're just the kind of fellow we need in this country!' Believe me," sighed my father, years later, "those wonderful words were sweet music to my ears."

The optimistic comment of that long-gone immigration functionary would prove to be far more prophetic than even he might have imagined. Israel Sack had arrived in the Golden Land, and from then on, he would never look back, except to discover earlier American craftsmen and their work.

My father made his way up to Boston. "I had a friend in Kovno who'd left for America before I did, and he went to Atlanta, Georgia.

He'd been there a couple of years, and I'd written him a letter asking him what conditions were like in America. He wrote me back: 'In this country, God helps those who help themselves.' That became my motto."

It was 1903, a very dark year. There was a depression on, jobs were scarce, and men, thousands of them, walked the Boston streets desperately looking for work. Luckily, my father had a kindly distant relative, a lady who had a spare room and who would extend him hospitality and credit for two weeks.

Miraculously, he would also shortly find himself a job as a cabinetmaker with a Mr. Stephenson, who owned a shop. Satisfied with my father's credentials, Stephenson asked how much he wanted in pay, per week.

Father's immediate response showed the bold and original quality that would characterize his business dealings for the rest of his life. "Nothing," he said.

The startled Stephenson asked for an explanation.

My father promptly supplied it. "You don't know me," he said, "and you don't know what I can do for you. Let me work for you two weeks, and when I'm to be paid at the end of the two weeks, you give me whatever you think I'm worth to you, and I'll be satisfied."

Eventually, the arrangement was sealed with an eight-dollar salary — in those days, a handsome weekly sum — and my father's business career in America had begun. But he was not yet involved with authentic early American furniture. His new employer, it seemed, was a specialist in creating imitations.

"In his makeup, it seemed he had an allergy for genuine things," my father recalled. "Everything we made was concocted right there. They had an 'ammonia room' where they'd bring newly made chairs, and put them all inside that room, and the ammonia fumes were used to age them. Whenever a new boy, such as I was, would come to work, they'd tell him to go open the door, and of course, those fumes would come boiling out, they'd hit him, and he'd fall flat on his back!"

His education continued rapidly. ". . . After a while, I became his right-hand man. I was his greatest concocter. You always had to use your intelligence in that sort of work. You had to meet the questions you knew would be asked by people who'd examine your concocted furniture later. We'd make up such monstrosities!" he remembered, years later. "There wasn't anything that was good. Oh, we'd concoct something that was beautiful — if you didn't know anything. I remember, once we made a writing table that was a showpiece. We used very old boards as the basis of it, and they were the structure— then we simply built the case around them, see? They're perfect for such a project. It took us two or three weeks, and we inlaid that writing table from top to bottom — all around that original case of wooden boards. By the time we were finished, we had a showpiece— and if you checked, those old boards inside were what sold you on its authenticity. Believe it or not, some fellow came in who had a Beacon Street store, he saw the table, he had to have it. He paid five hundred dollars for it — a very stiff price for those days. The table went into his store window on Beacon Street and he ended up selling it for a very big profit. Why not? He sold it as an old one because it had been sold to *him* as an old one. He couldn't see that anyone could possibly have faked it. But *we* had."

The "ammonia room" and the central core of authentic old boards were, and still are, two of the mainstays of that vast and shadowy "fake" industry, where pieces of so-called Chippendale design, or butterfly tables, as well as highboys, sideboards, or slant-top desks, could be fabricated on demand, in out-of-the-way shops, to pass scrutiny among eager and greedy uneducated buyers, and produce an ever-rising price as the years passed.

Assemblages made up of odd pieces of old furniture, cunningly joined together with new fronts, soon became the speciality of such "fakers." The newly constructed pieces could be buried in convenient backyard lime pits, to induce instant aging. A deftly wielded keyring, in the hands of a skilled concocter, would leave varied "authentic" dents and marks of wear on wooden legs and feet. "Wormholes" could be faked with specially created tools. Artificers would go to the extreme of firing fusillades of rock salt from shotguns at a twentieth-century piece of work, thus transforming it instantly into its eighteenth-century ancestor.

Why, you may well ask, would such an industry spring up right there in New England, an area where so many authentic pieces of early American furniture were so easily available for discovery in the homes and farmhouses surrounding Boston and Providence, and which abounded in the farther northlands of Maine, New Hampshire, and Vermont?

The simple answer is cupidity. Making fakes was — and is — easier than buying originals.

In order to get those authentic pieces, one would have to journey out to the rural areas and buy from stony-faced Yankees. Long and arduous trips over rutted dirt roads, and then, endless bargaining and argument, until the weary dealer might succeed in taking away some treasured family piece.

Far simpler and more efficient, then, for a cabinetmaker to create antiques. Especially if he had skilled craftsmen such as young Israel Sack working in his shop, available to turn out an acceptable "concoction" that would pass muster under the sharpest eyes of any potential buyer, and thus bring in a very rapid profit.

After several years in Mr. Stephenson's shop, my father had saved up enough money to consider going into business for himself. But his ambition was to repair authentic antiques — not to continue creating those spurious works his boss favored.

"I asked myself, 'What am I doing for him I couldn't do better for myself?' " said my father. "I took a vacation, and when I came back, I didn't come back to Stephenson. I had some cards printed, had a place hired for eight dollars a month, and I went to the lumberyard. I had thirty dollars left. With that kind of capital, you certainly couldn't afford to pay fifteen dollars for a workbench, so I walked to the lumberyard in Charlestown, which was about five miles away. I bought a plank, and carried it all the way from the yard on my shoulder to my new place, took my tools, and *built* myself a workbench."

Then the budding entrepreneur returned to his first boss. "I told him I'd started in business for myself, and if he'd give me work, I'd guarantee I could do it for less money in *my* shop than I could do it working for him. I told him why — I was a young fellow, strong, ambitious. I didn't have to get in at eight-thirty in the morning and work only until five-thirty. No. I could get in at five in the morning, and work till *ten!*"

Greedy Mr. Stephenson enthusiastically agreed to such a proposal. Who wouldn't? So Israel Sack was immediately launched in business for himself, in an enterprise which would rapidly flourish.

"Charles Street, where my shop was, was near Beacon Hill, where all the early Boston collectors of antiques lived. They knew me from Mr. Stephenson's shop, where we'd taken care of their furniture, so it was easy enough for me to get their business."

The proper Bostonians were difficult taskmasters. "They'd stand in my shop and watch while I worked," he remembered. " 'Don't touch this — don't touch that!' God forbid, you shouldn't take off a tiny bit of dirt, or anything. You see, these were very early Pilgrim pieces, and they were very precious to their owners. Early American — the best — and I repaired them. That's where I first became fond of the real old, honest-to-goodness antiques. . . . Not my ex-boss. He'd come to them when he was too old, I guess."

In those early years of his career, the emphasis on collecting by pioneer Bostonian collectors was on the very earliest forms of American antiques — not only the severe Pilgrim pieces, but the more complicated William and Mary and Queen Anne styles.

The simple elegance, durability, and personality of the American pieces captivated young Israel, and he began to deal in them. "As soon as I got a little money, I'd go out and buy old furniture on my own, and then repair and sell it," he told us.

From then on, the transition from cabinetmaker-repairer to dealer was rapid. Fairly soon, he had worked up a large wholesaler's business on Charles Street, and from the very beginnings, his sights were set high. "I sold in quantity," he said, "and I'd buy the same way. Junk never appealed to me. Right from the start, I had a flair for good things. One of the nearby Lowell Street dealers had a couple of basements with three or four pieces he'd gotten from the 'pickers' I wanted to buy, and he wanted fifteen hundred dollars. In those days, that was a huge sum. I offered him a thousand dollars, and finally I said to him, 'How much will you take for all you've got in those two cellars?'

"He had two partners, and they went in the back of the room and came back, and he said, 'Three thousand dollars.' "

Eventually, the price was settled at $2,500. "I said, 'Boys, I have no money. I can't pay you cash.' "

There was another conference, while the brash Israel waited for the response to his daring offer. Finally, the other dealer returned again. "Okay," he said. "Your credit is good. Will you give us notes?"

My father promptly signed five notes of $500 each. And called a moving man.

"I took out their goods, cleaned everything up, and started to sell," he recalled. "It was a wonderful batch of material for stock. Every month I paid them back — out of their own money. I got so much ahead every month, I was able to pay them back ahead of time. And that was the beginning. You know dealers — if they find another dealer where they can buy good merchandise at reasonable prices, they'll flock to him like bees around honey. It got so my place was a beehive. Dealers from all over New England used to come in, and there wasn't a day in the year when I didn't have lunch with either one, two, three, maybe even four dealers!"

Even those early Charles Street dealers, attracted by their confrere Israel Sack's amazing success, could not imagine the future which lay ahead for the young man. Soon, he would rocket into dizzying status, as adviser and confidant to collectors of the highest rank; he would become a connoisseur and trusted authority who would be consulted by museum curators and millionaire collectors.

Only a few short years after landing in this Golden Land, "Crazy" Sack had unearthed his own rich vein of gold, the crafts of those native early Americans who had preceded him to these shores. Never again, throughout his life, through good times and disasters, wild affluence and near-bankruptcy, would the immigrant boy from Kovno be swayed from his newfound love. His passion for American antiques and their creators would never flag. From those earliest Charles Street days on, he would always look back, into the riches of the American past.

❧ THREE

Charles Street and My Youth

MY mother may have been less than fascinated by antiques, but not I. Very early on, my father began to take me downtown to his shop at 85 Charles Street.

Charles Street is a short thoroughfare through which there have passed more American antiques than any other similar area in the country. Number 85, the modest building which was my father's first shop, and which still stands, was a four-story structure, not more than fifteen feet or so wide, and almost forty feet deep.

I was born in 1911, which means my first introduction to my father's daily world would have been in the post–World War I days; in those early 1920s, Charles Street was no longer the dirt road it had been when my father first opened up his premises. The city had widened and paved it, and in so doing, the Boston authorities had paid my father several thousand dollars for the land in front of his store, which had been condemned. Since my father, vigorous and confident, had promptly used all that municipal cash to expand his collection of fine antiques, it could be said that the City of Boston was partially responsible for the future success of "Crazy" Sack.

Charles Street was far from imposing; it is a short thoroughfare which winds up toward Boston Common, and the shops which

lined the crowded pavement were small and jammed tightly against each other.

There, on Charles Street, in that series of stores, I spent my Saturdays amid a community of antiques dealers, most of them new American citizens like my father, who'd made that street their own turf, and spent their days arguing, bargaining, wheedling, and cajoling their customers — or each other — into buying or selling.

The entry level was on Charles Street, and so was the noise.

Today, most of those shops are long gone, replaced by boutiques, bookshops, or posh little gourmet food shops. But I know, from having seen them myself, how through those early modest Charles Street antiques shops there passed, each day, so many early American masterpieces. It was, as it had been for my father, my personal academy. From each piece he'd encountered, he learned.

After all, my father's basic education in early American furniture, and its creators, was largely self-acquired. It had to be. He and all those other dealers on Charles Street learned their trade as they went along. New Americans went to night school. My father's school was open seven days a week, all day. How else was he to learn about the various pieces of furniture he'd acquired from reluctant New England families?

Today, we have at our disposal vast, well-documented collections in our public museums, with all the literature and the catalogues from innumerable loan exhibits adding to our knowledge. We have stacks of textbooks and elegantly illustrated works on specific periods, and specific makers; we can refer to scholarly articles which began in 1922, with the establishment of *Antiques* magazine. Such a body of structured history, factual and visual, serves to provide the present-day curator, collector, or dealer with considerable backup for his daily judgment.

Not so for my father, or for any of his fellow dealers on Charles Street, in the years before World War I.

True, local collectors and customers helped him recognize and understand the grace and beauty of early American furniture, which they'd been raised with in their own homes, but the young immigrant from Kovno would acquire the major part of his vast knowledge through his own sharp eyes and empathetic responses. As, eventually, did I.

In my father's busy hours in and out of Charles Street, each piece which came through the doorway brought with it a history lesson. If "Crazy" Sack encountered some piece of native American furniture which appealed to his eye, or "spoke" to him viscerally, then he would hurry about to learn more of its maker and his origin, or which Colonial workshop it had been fashioned in, years ago.

Once kindled, his passionate love affair with early American styles never flagged. He responded to the individual creativity which those long-gone American craftsmen, once they were freed of the English guild system, so brilliantly demonstrated by their works. Since my father had worked in England, he was well versed in the guild system. Those early American pieces which passed through Charles Street were precisely the opposite of the opulent and overdecorated English furniture he'd labored over for long hours.

Remember, English furniture was cradled in the tradition of pomp and ceremony, and it was designed strictly for the use of the nobility and the very upper classes. Since it was produced by a rigid guild system, apprentices were trained to perpetuate a tradition of design and craftsmanship without ever altering the slightest detail, unless the master craftsman of the shop had approved the change beforehand.

That guild system was also predicated on the fact that the excellence of the finished product should be judged only by its embellishment. So those great English carvers and inlay specialists had to become adept, not in *creating* design, but in constantly adding more and more decorative flourishes to the basic furniture. None of them was ever permitted to function as a creator of the whole piece. The English process evolved into an elegant assembly line, studded with expensive options.

Here in the American Colonies, freed from that stifling English guild system, pure ornamentation became the secondary issue. Luxurious detail wasn't the whole piece; it would merely be an integral part of the design. Inevitably, the form and proportion of a chair, a table, a desk, or a sideboard, created in a Colonial workshop at the hands of a skilled craftsman free to express his personal vision and taste, would become the basis for the great early American pieces. In the shops of such free craftsmen as Benjamin Frothingham, the Charlestown, Massachusetts, furniture maker, Paul Revere, the silversmith, Simon Willard, the clockmaker, and all their other great contemporaries, creativity thrived.

And after my father began to encounter such masterpieces, his quest for them would continue all his life. Years later, he summed it up. "All the important furniture in America was made by important craftsmen who will go down in history as famous. These people were geniuses, not ordinary people. A man like Benjamin Randolph, he was a great master. Consider Thomas Affleck, of Philadelphia. David Rittenhouse, with his clocks. They were people of distinction, people who mingled with the best society. They were members of the congregations of all the wealthy people. In other words, in the olden days, if a man were a distinguished craftsman, not only was his work recognized, but he himself was revered. Notice that a man like John Singleton Copley did a portrait of Paul Revere. He didn't make pictures of ordinary people; he picked out the best."

"The best to the best!" he would insist. "The best man buys the best thing. I don't mean best by how much money he's got in the bank, or how much money he's made in the pickle business. That has nothing to do with it. I mean, some background of quality. Quality is in furniture, like everything else . . . the best. *Nearly* as good, is not good."

It was that passionate belief which was to vault my father into the forefront of the Charles Street dealers.

But when I first began to visit his shop on Saturdays, I had none of his passion for antiques. Not yet. All I knew was that I was entering a strange and wonderful, constantly changing arena, where I watched my father in the midst of his cramped inventory of serpentine chests and blockfront bureaus, arguing, cajoling, and joking with customers, or carrying on a rapid-fire conversation in some unintelligible private language with another dealer — it was years before I could learn to decipher this strange mixture of code words, shorthand, and often Yiddish. The first rule I learned was *Be quiet, and listen.* I obeyed.

Downstairs, on the first floor, was the cabinet shop, in which repairs and restorations were done. I especially liked the strange smells of various polishes and stains which filled those rooms, and I always headed for them first. There I would get a big greeting from the three or four cabinetmakers who labored long hours downstairs. They were all immigrants, one of whom was my father's brother, and they were full of boundless energy and enthusiasm. While I stood around, watching them repair various pieces, I inhaled all the odors of the magic potions they used, mingled smells which were both aromatic and heady. I learned to admire and respect their craft, and I would always marvel at the speed and thoroughness with which some old piece could be disassembled by their deft hands. Then its old glue would be dried out and scraped away, and patches of newer wood carefully inserted, which stood out smooth and white against the older wood before it was touched up. Under their loving ministrations old gooey varnishes were carefully removed with the exact right blend of varnish remover, and I would watch as the ultimate alchemy took place, from which the final gold was created. The old wood's finish was skillfully matched with finishing shellac, and then carefully rubbed down. When it was done, there stood that fine antique, its patina lovingly restored to its century-old beauty by the magic hands of those new Americans.

Then I would go upstairs to wander through the rooms filled with various early American pieces which my father had acquired on his long trips into the countryside and brought back to Charles Street for sale to Boston collectors.

They had begun to gravitate in steadily increasing numbers to this cheerful, gregarious dealer from Lithuania. Daily, he struggled to separate Bostonians from their Yankee dollars, in return for their own generic treasures, no mean feat.

He developed into a brilliant salesman. He had to be, in order to survive. Extracting a fair price from those crusty Bostonians took not only the utmost patience and ingenuity, but a thorough understanding of psychology.

My father's customers were invariably male, who would arrive in his shop without their wives. To me, a meek ten-year-old boy, they seemed so tall and imposing, so implacable, that I would tremble in their presence. Not so my father. Every so often he would remind whatever Brahmin from Beacon Hill he was dealing with that he, Israel Sack, was descended from a long line of learned rabbis.

Thus he would work very hard to sell them great New England masterpieces of unquestioned authenticity. Most of them were, in the language of today's commerce, the toughest of sales. Even after they'd come to realize that in Israel Sack, of 85 Charles Street, they had that rarity, an honest expert who not only was possessed of a great eye for authenticity and beauty, but who was also a dealer who could be trusted to produce the goods, their early American Puritan genealogy would always prevail: *Waste not, want not* (under any account) . . . and *Don't enjoy yourself too much.*

It was part of an education for me to watch as their heritage came to the fore. Their self-discipline in not purchasing the most remarkable treasured piece of furniture should they even suspect its price was excessive always amazed me. The Bostonian gentleman would leave the shop having stubbornly denied himself the pleasure of owning the piece. My father, exhausted, would shrug. Disappointed, yes, but optimistically willing to wait for the next customer . . . someone, perhaps, who had funds and wasn't a Bostonian.

How much he must have suffered, all those years on Charles Street, with his daily battles and duels, dealing with that parade of customers who loved everything about Israel Sack's furniture, except his price.

Perhaps it was just as well my father's old customers haven't survived to see the prices being paid these days, here in our showroom or at the auction houses, for all those pieces of early American furniture, their own New England heritage, in fact, which they so stubbornly denied themselves years ago on Charles Street.

Since I was a sensitive and rather shy young boy, and while my father dealt with those various Bostonians who would stop in to inspect his stock, I would stand by, trying to appear tall and pleasant. Every so often, one of them would take notice of me and ask, "Well, my boy, what do you plan to be when you grow up?"

I would look chagrined and try to hide my embarrassment. Then I'd stammer out something inconsequential. The Bostonian would turn to my father and somewhat sardonically remark, "Well, at least I hope you don't plan to make an antiques dealer out of him."

I remember being quite annoyed at that. How could that dignified Bostonian be so distrustful toward a profession my father conducted with such honesty? Why should there be the inference that the profession of antiques dealer was somehow synonymous with gypsy, thief, peddler, or fly-by-night . . . far outside the pale of the uptown legitimate New England Brahmins?

As a group, those Charles Street dealers were hardworking, resourceful, and extremely keen. In retrospect, it is astonishing to note how the instinctive taste and acumen of my father, and that small, tight group of his fellow dealers in and around Boston, managed to unearth and preserve so much of our American past. Bless him and the other Charles Street dealers, so many of them lately arrived in this country, for their acumen and daring. Their drive to turn an honest daily dollar from those treasures which they unearthed in New England farms and houses has had enormous benefits. Future generations have been provided with a bountiful share of our American heritage because Charles Street dealers went in pursuit of New England family heirlooms. Their daily foraging was vital to their existence, for in those days there was no such thing as a floating supply of antiques. Each and every piece had to be discovered, bargained for, and brought down to Charles Street for sale, either from one dealer to another, or to potential collectors.

*   *   *

I traveled up and down Charles Street every week, and so I began to know each one of those dealers well. There was Mr. Grossman, for one, a sober-faced gentleman who sat in a chair in the front of his store, who never smiled at me, and who never seemed to leave that chair throughout the entire day. I never could understand where he got his pieces of furniture, but he always did, and some of them were wonderful. He was a careful businessman. He never gambled, always played his cards close to his chest, and consequently he never had to sell anything quickly in order to make ends meet, a generic problem in the antiques business. Whenever my father tried to buy a piece from Mr. Grossman, it always seemed to be more difficult than with other dealers; Mr. Grossman always held out for the very best price, and if he didn't get it, he shrugged and sat back in his chair, unperturbed.

That prudent style of business served him well. It was in sharp contrast to my father's more daring modus operandi. After the 1929 crash, other dealers, including my father, had good reason to rue their more flamboyant operations. Not so Mr. Grossman. He sailed blithely through the Depression, and today, half a century later, his son Hyman and Hyman's wife, Sanka, both in their eighties, are still operating that same store on Charles Street. Their own private collection, some of which has remained tucked away in the upstairs regions of the shop all these years, has been the source of several splendid antique pieces which we have been proud to sell.

Across the street was a dealer named Fred Finnerty, who handled the more rustic or "country-style" primitive antiques. At 80 Charles Street was Leon David, whose son Ben was to become my partner, years later, in a summer store in Ipswich. Mr. David was a fine merchant, and while he'd originally begun dealing in furniture, he moved into hooked rugs, which he secured on his many trips to Maine and Canada.

When B. Altman's department store in Manhattan opened an antique rug department in the 1920s, Mr. David became their largest supplier. Every so often, he would locate a fine piece of early American furniture, and I can remember how he and my father would battle strenuously over the price, again arguing in that strange dealer-shorthand private language they used. But despite their commercial set-tos, the two men were firm friends. During the dire Depression years, Mr. David's capital, which he'd derived from his prudent real estate investments, served to sustain our family's business.

Around the corner, on Beacon Street, was a man named Mr. Stainforth, who dealt in prints and antique ship models. He and I became friendly, and he would often take me sailing. Years later, in the opulent late 1920s, my father bought a half-interest in Mr. Stainforth's business.

But in the early years on Charles Street, there were few dealers capable of challenging my father's rising position. One was Philip Flayderman. Philip and his son Benjamin were not only active dealers in early American furniture, but were both extremely bold in their drive to acquire fine pieces. As their capital increased, the Flaydermans traveled far and wide, scrambling madly to acquire the best available. The two men were reckless buyers, but always with a flair for the extraordinary, either in form or in historical background.

Benjamin Flayderman was an imposing, burly chap, whose nose had once been broken in a street fight. Neither he nor his father had the finesse which my father developed, nor did they have his ability to deal with customers. I can vividly remember times when actual fistfights took place between Ben Flayderman and such rough-and-ready types as "Red" Jacobs, a wholesaler, over who was entitled to such-and-such particular antique piece which had emerged on the market.

But beneath that rugged, formidable exterior, Ben Flayderman was inherently a very decent man. A few years later, he demonstrated it to me when I first decided to go into business for myself and become an adolescent salesman of Realsilk hosiery. Up and down Charles Street I trudged, doggedly showing my father's friends and associates my sample case of Realsilk. Not one of them deigned to make a purchase, and I would have been a complete failure at the trade had it not been for Ben Flayderman. Whether it was out of good-heartedness or simple pity, I am uncertain; but the fact is, he took me into their shop and bought a collection of Realsilk which, in retrospect, I'm certain he did not need.

The culmination of the Flaydermans' activities during the bustling 1920s resulted in one of the most important auctions of that era: in

January 1930, the Philip Flayderman Sale, held at the American Art
Galleries, the forerunner of today's Parke-Bernet.

Another dealer I remember was the leading auctioneer in Boston
at that time, an Englishman named Louis Joseph, who imported
pieces from England and who then ran large auction sales of such
"antiques" which would not in any sense pass the eye of an educated buyer. England always provided a steady supply of reproduction pieces, and the American market was a fine place in which to
dispose of them. Everything the doctor ordered was available at
Joseph's auctions: plenty of sets, also plenty of pairs, a steady supply
of precisely the correct "solid" furniture, for the unwary buyer.
When any purchaser might become nervous about his new acquisition and would bring it to be analyzed by a professional dealer,
such as my father, his awakening would be rude. My father never
went out of his way to hurt anyone, but his love for authenticity was
strong, and when called on for his advice, he believed it was his duty
to give it, truthfully, without equivocation, and clearly. Thus, Mr.
Joseph and my father at a very early period of their acquaintance-
ship developed a healthy mutual antipathy. If Mr. Joseph expected
my father to demonstrate professional courtesy in the face of all
these obvious reproductions he passed off on his customers, he was
mistaken. Father continued to tell Mr. Joseph's unwary customers
the truth, adding, "If you can't tell the difference between skunk
and mink, why buy the mink?"
"Crazy" Sack was a man dedicated to mink. He was also to become the ombudsman of the collecting public, and as time passed,
his word came to be final. Such expertise created quite a responsibility for him, and indeed for us, his sons. Somehow the public
began to assume, and still does till this day, that it is the Sack
family's duty to share our accumulated knowledge for the protection of all.

Those Charles Street dealers I've cited were already well established. They were not to be confused with the relatively new class of
subdealer operators on whom they relied so basically for their steady
stream of goods — the "pickers."

The "picker" usually operated from a Lowell Street basement. He was the smallest of businessmen, and the most nervous. Such busy entrepreneurs were self-adaptors of the highest order, whose survival was based on equal parts of wit, sharp eyes, keen determination, and above all, the gambler's instinct. All such attributes were needed to survive in what was essentially a low-capital, high-risk daily lottery.

"Picking" is now an old, established profession. Even today, antiques dealers, as my father and his Charles Street fellows did then, rely on the picker's "finds" as a source. But in those early days of this century, a successful picker had to be a meld of prospector, secret agent, medicine-show salesman, and flimflam man, with no assurance that his labors would ever earn him a dollar.

Consider the picker's lot. Early each day, he would venture forth from his premises, some low-rent Lowell Street basement, a dingy and dank headquarters lit by candles, to go forth on a foraging mission, to scour suburban streets and tiny outlying towns, where he would dodge angry dogs to knock on doors, much as a second-hand dealer, or a used-clothing buyer. "Pardon me," he would ask the sullen householder, "but is there any old furniture for sale here?"

His would be a daily spin of the roulette wheel — hopefully to pry out of an unwilling and suspicious housekeeper some piece of dusty furniture, an old painting, or a batch of knickknacks, which could promptly be turned over to any Charles Street dealer whose cash would reward the tired picker for his daily persistence and shrewdness.

The picker operated on the slimmest base of capital, was constantly in a state of indecision as to whether he had struck gold (or merely iron pyrites), and if one of his latest acquisitions did not sell promptly, he would justifiably be thrown into a panic.

They were a hardy breed, those early Lowell Street operatives. They flew strictly by the seat of their well-worn pants, without illustrated reference books by Wallace Nutting, nor any Sotheby's or Christie's auction catalogues to refer to as a value index. They put up with hostility, ran the gamut of suspicion, anti-Semitism, local authorities, and even the perils of daily weather. I was a very young boy in the early 1920s, but I can still remember when one of the old-timers, a dealer named Alpert, along with his partner, was struck and killed by a train at a New Hampshire crossing in their horse and wagon, as they brought back a full load of antiques they had picked up along their rural route. It was a devastating blow to their Lowell Street colleagues; even those who never previously had a kind word to say for either of them joined in bemoaning their fate. Not to mention the loss of their load. . . .

By the early '20s, the pickers were switching to primitive autos and trucks, which presented an even more complex set of hazards. Constant flat tires, balky engines which had cranks instead of self-starters, open touring cars with ever-leaking roofs, and those flimsy celluloid side windows which did little to keep out the chill New England winds. The picker's range of travel may have widened with the coming of the combustion engine, but his life did not change. It would still be an obstacle course for the hardy picker as he endured the bad food, and those endless, primitive, pre-motel overnight accommodations, doggedly making his way from farmhouse to farmhouse, jouncing along rutted dirt roads with hardly enough room for another vehicle to pass by without one or both going off the road. And hopefully knocking on a door, avoiding the angry watchdog, to ask the householder, "Pardon me, ma'am, but is there any old furniture for sale here?"

Later on, as I grew up, I can remember one of the prize pickers of those days, a man named Joe Epstein. At that time, we were living in Roxbury; many times in the early mornings my father would get on the telephone and call Joe. "I have a job for you, Joe," he would say. "Mrs. X in Newburyport has a blockfront bureau which is not for sale. Get it."

Joe was probably the ugliest man I've ever met. He was tall, rangy, stoop-shouldered, with black unruly hair, small beady eyes which needed thick glasses, tremendous bushy eyebrows, and large, sensuous lips. He seemed always to need a shave, and wore clothes almost as antique as the furniture he pursued. I can still wonder what reaction such an apparition induced when he appeared on Mrs. X's doorstep and rang that Newburyport doorbell.

Yet he always got the piece. It could have been hypnosis, charisma, or perhaps he induced pure fear, but whatever Joe Epstein's secret was, it was effective. Later that same day, he'd arrive at my father's shop, bringing in Mrs. X's blockfront, to be handsomely rewarded by my father.

Joe's success became a challenge. Other pickers, fascinated by his techniques, would often bet him a hundred dollars that he couldn't get a piece from a certain difficult owner. Joe would take up the gauntlet. While the others parked nearby to watch him, he'd case the place. If the owners had a dog, he would borrow another mutt, and just happen to be strolling by. Then he'd strike up a conversation with the hapless object of his pursuit. Ten minutes later, he and the mutt would be indoors. That was only one of his tricks. And he always won the hundred dollars.

Not that my father relied on pickers for his source of supply. He made constant trips on his own out of Boston to search for furniture, and I sometimes accompanied him.

I remember one of those trips was to the rural home of Mr. Littlefield, where my father and that crusty Yankee farmer-turned-dealer got into a heated negotiation over a lovely three-section sat-inwood bowfront desk, a particular New Hampshire style of antique which customarily turned up in those areas north of Boston. My father was trying very hard, because the piece was truly a beauty, and he knew it would be an asset to his Charles Street stock in trade. The argument over price continued on and on, with Mr. Littlefield laconically turning down my father's offers, the two men hammering away at each other like determined rams, each of them intent on outdoing the other.

As for me, I soon became thoroughly bored, so I wandered off to the barns behind the main house. I loved barns, with their rows of stalls filled with large horses, snorting and stamping their feet, munching on feed. I prowled around them, and then I began to wander in and out of the stalls. Evidently I began to worry one of those huge horses, for he picked up his heavy foot, stepped on mine, and wouldn't lift his leg!

I couldn't release myself from that heavy hoof, and I became panicky. I let out such a terrified yell that Mr. Littlefield and my father came rushing out to see if I'd been killed.

When Mr. Littlefield saw what had happened, he roared with

laughter, quickly tapped the horse's leg, and released my bruised foot. But my pride had also been bruised, and I was so humiliated, I wouldn't let my father stay around that farmhouse another minute. Chagrined, and probably somewhat frightened by the danger he thought I might have been in, my father heeded my tearful requests to leave, and away we went in his Buick, back to the safety of urban Boston.

I was too confused and upset to know whether or not my father eventually did buy that beautiful three-section satinwood bowfront desk. But if I had to venture a guess, I'm sure he was back there, the following day.

Even now, sixty-odd years later, whenever I encounter one of those satinwood bowfront bureaus, I feel a pang of echoing nostalgia, and my foot, in true Pavlovian fashion, begins to tingle.

My father had a great sense of humor, and a store of anecdotes and humorous stories that were part of his stock in trade. Much of his humor was wry and self-deprecatory, leavened with a strong philosophic strain, obviously developed from his early Talmudic studies. Once, in New York, a friend introduced him as "Israel Sack, the leading expert on American antiques." My father shrugged. "What's to be an expert?" he said. "You make several serious financial mistakes, and right away you've become an expert!"

He had a knack of thawing out those sober and cold-blooded New Englanders which came into play whether he was selling or buying. I recall being with him at a house somewhere in the north of Boston, when I was about fifteen. My father was seated in the living room with the lady of the house, a rather prim, middle-aged matron. They were in the midst of one of those intense bargaining sessions, this time over one of her choice pieces, a Sheraton Salem sofa.

It had been going on for quite some time, and I got up and wandered away, this time to browse through some of the lady's house. Her collection was first-rate, and I spent time carefully studying the various other pieces she owned. When I returned to the living room, they were still at it. He wanted the sofa, she was willing to sell, but neither could agree on a a price.

Suddenly, my father pointed at me and said, "All right, why don't we let my son put a price on it?"

I was stunned and somewhat embarrassed, but I remember recovering, and I got into the spirit of it by saying, "Why put a price on the sofa alone? I saw so many other nice things here."

My father burst out laughing, slapped his knee, and said, "My sentiments exactly! Why don't you take a piece of paper, write down what you think each piece is worth, and I'll do the same. Then we'll compare."

The lady of the house fell right in with his proposal, and for the next few minutes, we both proceeded to make notes on what we thought her collection of fine furniture was worth.

Then, when we'd finished our estimates, I'd arrived at a total figure of $7,800.

Beaming, my father revealed his figures. His total was $7,500.

Remarkable! My father was pleased as punch with my precocious acumen. I basked in his approval. The lady of the house was delighted with the results of my father's ploy. So delighted, in fact, that shortly afterward, she and my father had agreed on a price for her sofa. What the final figure was, I was too dazed to remember, but my father never forgot that incident. So proud of my budding aptitude was he that he chuckled and referred to it for years.

Around the corner from Charles Street there was a shop run by Katrina Kipper, a tall, charming woman with bright red hair and a very dignified manner. She had the confidence of some of Boston's best families, and she handled fine decorative accessories and very good quality furniture. Miss Kipper's fiancé had been killed in World War I. He was the son of a Boston Brahmin, Mr. Herbert Lawton, a woolen merchant, the epitome of the successful businessman, and in my case, an inadvertent teacher who gave me a pragmatic lesson in human nature.

Mr. Lawton was a typical rough-and-ready Yankee, who wore a monocle and affected a beard, and was always alert to any opportunity for profit. *Ask and give no mercy — the world is for the strong —* that was his motto, as I was to discover.

Mr. Lawton knew full well how to get my father's fighting blood up, and the discussions between the two of them were often vehement. But they both respected each other highly, and continued to do business. Mr. Lawton had quite a flair for great American silver, and some of the best passed through his hands, always for his eventual gain. When he bought from my father, he would keep a piece for a while, trade it, or sell it back to my father at, of course, a handsome profit.

In his seventies, Mr. Lawton would swim a mile daily in season, and on the occasions I would meet him in the store, he would have me feel his biceps, which were as hard as any prize fighter's. He was slightly hard of hearing, and when he asked my father for a price, and got it, he would cup his ear as if he hadn't heard the figure, and say, "Come again?" It was a ploy that inevitably led to a sustained argument.

I remember vividly an incident in my father's shop from which it took my pride quite a while to recover.

I must have been sixteen, when one Saturday my father had to leave on a sudden errand. He instructed me to look after the store while he was gone. By this time, he had moved from his original shop at number 85 to a wider building next door, at number 89. In those new premises, there were eight steps which led from the street up to the first floor. Everything that came in or went out had to be brought up or down those stairs.

That Saturday afternoon, I was under strict instructions from my father not to tell anyone where he had gone, when he'd left, or why, nor even when he might return. In those days, such cloak-and-dagger secrecy was vital for survival in the antiques business. Absolute silence was the best insurance that none of one's Charles Street competitors could beat one to the punch.

Dealers had many other little tricks. If, after a long argument, you couldn't manage to separate some choice piece from an unwilling owner, you proffered an absurdly high figure, far beyond any possible price. Nowadays, this is called "high-balling," and psychologically, it is very effective. You floated that impossible figure into the owner's mind, leaving it behind as you went out the door. If and when any of your competitors would arrive, in pursuit of the same item, he would be confronted by an owner who, in all honesty, could rock him with that absurdly high (and totally mythical) price which had already been offered by an unsuccessful dealer. Spite work, true, but effective.

There was a sudden pounding on the outer door, and when I opened it, I found outside, staggering beneath the weight of a large piece of furniture, two of the neighborhood pickers. One of them I recognized; he was Mr. Rubin, a young and aggressive fellow who had headquarters in a nearby basement.

The two lugged their burden past me into my father's shop and set it down in the front hallway. When Mr. Rubin had regained his breath, he demanded, "Where's your dad?"

I was staring at what they'd brought. Even I could see it was certainly a prize piece. A large Chippendale mahogany serpentine-front desk, with beautifully sculptured ball-and-claw feet. To this day, I can recall it vividly, right down to the large willow brass handles, and the mellow tones of the wood. Who knew how they'd managed to separate this beauty from its owner? What mattered was that they had it now, and since pickers always operated on a very small amount of ready cash for capital, they had to turn over any new acquisition promptly. That was vital to their survival.

"Is he around?" demanded Mr. Rubin. "Where is he?"

Both men stared at me with serious and eager faces.

I wanted to tell them he'd be back soon; I knew it couldn't be more than an hour or two, but my father's orders were orders, and must be obeyed. "Sorry," I said. "I don't know."

They glanced at each other, shrugged, and reluctantly moved to heave the heavy desk up and out again.

"Wait!" I said. "How much do you want for this?"

Mr. Rubin hesitated, scratched his chin, and promptly said, "Seven hundred fifty dollars."

I had no idea whether that was fair, outrageous, or cheap. All I did know was that there, in front of me and imminently about to vanish from my father's premises, was this beautiful Chippendale desk.

I took a deep breath and blurted out, "That's a good price, and I know my father will buy the desk. Leave it here until he gets back."

It was a wild gamble on my part, and I began to pray it would be justified.

Mr. Rubin hesitated again, and went into a brief, muttered consultation with his partner, then turned back to me. "Okay," he agreed. "We'll leave it here for an hour, and if he's not back, we'll take it away then."

Impatiently, nervously, I waited for my father to return. It was a very difficult, uncertain time for a teenager who'd taken it upon himself to make such an expensive decision, and was waiting, praying, indeed, to be proved correct.

The store door opened. In came, not my father, as I fervently hoped, but Mr. Herbert Lawton.

Upon hearing that my father was not in, he was about to turn and leave when his sharp eye caught a glimpse of that Chippendale desk. He advanced on it, giving it a careful once-over.

"What is this, if you please?" he demanded.

Foolishly, I blurted out what had happened. I violated the first rule of the antiques business, but I had a desperate need to confide in someone what I had done. By the time I was finished, he'd learned it had been brought in by Mr. Rubin, for what price, and the circumstances of its having been left here in the shop.

"Don't you think I did right in hanging on to this desk until my father gets back?" I asked Mr. Lawton.

Mr. Lawton went on staring carefully at the desk for a long moment. Then he muttered something to the effect that I was indeed a bright lad, and strode out the front door.

I was greatly relieved. Obviously Mr. Lawton, a man of taste, agreed with my decision.

Time passed. I waited for my father to return, but still, there was no sign of him.

Suddenly the front door was pushed open, and in came Mr. Rubin and his partner. Without a single word to me, they picked up that beautiful Chippendale desk and toted it down the stairs.

When the door closed behind them, I was a completely confused teenaged storekeeper.

My father finally returned, an hour or so later, and said, "What happened while I was gone?"

I blurted out the whole story.

Without another word, my father promptly departed, to find Mr. Rubin.

When he returned a second time, his face was stony. Very quietly, he explained to me what had happened. That beautiful Chippendale desk was now the property of Mr. Herbert Lawton, his good customer.

My father, bless him, masked his frustration, and didn't take it out on me, although he had ample cause. He must have sensed how embarrassed and contrite I was, how furious at my own error in ever believing that an adult could be trusted, or treated as a confidant.

He didn't need to lecture me on the topic *silence is golden*. I'd already learned that lesson well.

The Golden 1920s

B y the mid 1920s, "Crazy" Sack had traveled quite a distance
from those early days in his shop on unpaved Charles Street.
His business had expanded at an amazing rate, and through the
doorway to his shop came a daily procession of customers, collectors, and, yes, a new breed, museum curators specializing in early
American antiques.

My education continued, both at Boston Latin School during the
week, and every Saturday in the shop.

By now, my father had summed up his accumulated wisdom into
ten major commandments, and in 1927, they would be published in
an advertisement in *The Antiquarian*.

That statement is still on the wall of our office today, and bears
rereading. What my father said then makes as much sense now, if
not more, than it did more than half a century ago:

> *Twenty-five years ago there were only about one thousand buyers
> of American antiques in the whole United States. Today there are at
> least one hundred thousand buyers of Americana. Out of every one
> hundred buyers there are less than 10% that would pay the price for
> a genuine American antique.*
>
> *As a rule people who buy "made over" pieces either know what*

they are buying or do not want to know. The antique game is no different than any other game. The problem of getting genuine antiques is no problem if one is willing to pay the price.

The following points may be of interest:

1. Never try to beat an antique dealer.

2. Remember that a dealer knows more about his own merchandise than you do.

3. Treat the dealer right and you will be treated right in return.

4. Molasses catches more flies than vinegar.

5. The friendship of a good dealer is a valuable asset to a collector.

6. Bargains in antiques are sometimes fatal.

7. If you desire a genuine piece ask for it by name and be willing to pay for it.

8. If you want preference put yourself on the preferred list.

9. If you can afford the best, buy the best.

10. The slogan ''A good antique is a good investment'' is absolutely true.

But from the very beginnings, my father's insistence on dealing only in the best had earned him the friendship and respect of knowledgeable collectors.

One of my father's earliest customers was a lawyer named Eugene Bolles. The two became good friends, as well as sturdy business acquaintants, swapping information and experience with each other. Bolles would often accompany my father on his frequent trips outside Boston, where they would spend their days foraging among local families for antique treasures.

Bolles, a quiet, unassuming New Englander, had been imbued with a passion for collecting since the 1880s, and over the years had amassed a huge collection of choice antique pieces, nearly six hundred in number, some of which dated back to the earliest Colonial period. One of his prizes was a chair-table, made of white oak, with a pine top, which had belonged to Peregrine White, who had been born aboard the *Mayflower* in 1620. It, as well as the rest of Bolles's collection, is now at the Metropolitan Museum, and how it came to be there is a story in itself.

Bolles's collection overflowed his home on Quincy Street, in

Dorchester. The historic Hudson-Fulton Exhibition was held in New York in 1909 to commemorate the discovery of the Hudson River three hundred years earlier, and Robert Fulton's first successful steamboat trip on it in 1807. At the exhibition, American antiques were put on display at the Metropolitan, and for the first time Americans were given an overall view of their own heritage. Bolles's huge collection was an integral part of that show, and Mrs. Russell Sage promptly offered to buy all of it for the Metropolitan Museum, if the museum would provide a wing in which to house it. Her generosity sparked enthusiasm from many other donors, and as a result, by 1924, the American Wing was completed. Ever since then, the Bolles collection has been preserved there for future generations to wonder at and to study.

There were others, less famous but nonetheless dedicated as collectors, who gravitated to my father's store. One of the early collectors was a Mr. Davis, a postal clerk in Concord, who had a deep love of and appreciation for Colonial pieces. Since he had access to local houses, he could coax such antiques from their owners for whatever his limited means might allow. He was obviously a determined and tasteful collector; when he died, his collection was left to the Concord Historical Society, where it is still proudly on display.

Herman Clarke and Hollis French were two truly great connoisseurs of Americana. The French collection of silverware was later donated to the Cleveland Museum, and the Clarke collection became the basis of a definitive, scholarly tract on American silver. There were also Albert Whittier, a real estate broker, Elmer Bright of the Boston Stock Exchange, the Long family of Cohasset, Colonel and Mrs. Fearing, and Mr. Batchelder of the Batchelder Coal Company. All of them, and many others, had learned to deal with Israel Sack, who by reputation was already known to be the most expensive dealer on Charles Street, but who also bought and sold only the real McCoy, no small accolade, indeed. For already, there was rampant fakery.

According to my father, one of the hottest collectible items of the day was the butterfly table, which became the first piece to hit a price of over $1,000 by the early 1920s. Naturally, as butterfly tables flew upward in price each year, they became the first American antique pieces generally to be faked; the supply of such sought-after items began to flood the market. Skillful craftsmen soon learned how to fill the demand. The frame of the butterfly table is very much like that of the far more common tavern table. Thus, hidden away in a back-street workshop, the artisan could use the legs and frame of an ordinary tavern table, convert the hinged top, and fabricate a pair of butterfly wings out of the old wood.

An astute collector would avoid such newfound "treasures." But the bargain hunters, as always, would be delighted to encounter what they assumed to be an unwary dealer, on some side street or in a small-town barn-shop. They would end up triumphantly bringing home a butterfly table of, alas, highly dubious ancestry.

Another local collector was a Mr. Jopp, whose specialty was antique clocks, but more importantly he was a high official in a Boston bank. I remember him as a lean man, with sharp eyes and a quiet manner. But he was truly unique; he was willing to act as a banker to antiques dealers, and to lend them capital.

The fact is, in those days antiques dealers were not in any commercial sense recognized as good solid businessmen, nor even as fair credit risks. Working capital was thus always a problem. Since any piece a dealer purchased involved an outlay of hard cash on the spot, when he needed funds, no one except, say, some sympathetic relative would lend him that vitally necessary capital. Antiques dealers traveled constantly, had constant expenses, and families to feed. Those who survived without financing needed ingenuity and an oversupply of optimism.

Mr. Jopp, bless him, had faith in antiques. He was a true connoisseur and loved what he collected. Since he was willing to lend local dealers hard cash from his bank, he promptly became a godsend to the Boston community. Needless to add, the local dealers developed an undying gratitude to the only friendly banker in town, and because of their goodwill, Mr. Jopp was able to build up a small but extremely choice personal collection. I remember with pleasure some of his fine Willard banjo clocks.

There were other State Street bankers and investment brokers who were not as generous as Mr. Jopp, but just as shrewd about the investment potential of choice antiques. I remember one in particular, Mr. Elmer Bright, whose investment firm, Elmer Bright & Son, would be my employer one summer, at the munificent wage of thirteen dollars per week, sans deductions. I didn't last much longer than that first summer; the investment business, dry and mechanical, did not hold the same fascination for me as the arguments and competition and discoveries that went on six days a week on Charles Street.

Nor was I to become a classical musician, even though my father had as customers Mr. Mollenhauer, the conductor of Boston's Handel and Haydn Society, and also Carl and Reinhold Faelten, two brothers who operated Boston's famous Faelten Pianoforte School.

I happened to be in my father's shop one day when they both appeared, two stately and dignified German musicians, both of whom resembled Kaiser Wilhelm. After my father introduced me, Mr. Carl Faelten asked my father if he would care to make a musician out of me. My father did not bother to consult me. "Why not?" he replied amiably. He was obviously more interested in concluding the sale he was involved with than any musical career I might have. But for the following seven years, I took the trolley from Roxbury to Huntington Avenue, where I had my piano lessons. In the end, I proved to Mr. Faelten that antiques, not music, was definitely my field. I have not touched the piano since, but I often wonder where the Faeltens' collection of antiques is now, including that piece my father sold which caused me seven long years of practicing.

There were many other early collectors who came to rely on my father's abilities in those early days, but none as typical a Bostonian as Mr. Samuel Gelston King. A refined and gentlemanly businessman, Gelston King was quite the opposite of such a dedicated and scholarly collector as Eugene Bolles. He was more typical of the wealthy upper-class men of commerce who would form the backbone of my father's clientele during the next decade, the roaring '20s. He was a member of the Union and Exchange clubs, had a summer house at Nahant, and sailed under the proud pennant of the Beverly Yacht Club.

He and my father first began to do business in 1912, when Mr. King visited the shop at 85 Charles Street. Up to that time, the King mansion on Marlborough Street had been furnished with pieces custom built by a noted firm of Boston cabinetmakers. That solid decor soon began to change.

His first purchase was a beautifully inlaid Hepplewhite sideboard my father had picked up outside Portsmouth, New Hampshire. The piece was "in the rough," which means that layers of varnish or dried shellac had left a crud, or deposit, on it, which obscured the underlying grain of wood and inlay. Mr. King liked the sideboard — he responded to its lovely proportion, design, and construction — but he was totally unused to its "in the rough" aspect.

He came back to see it several times, and on one occasion in the shop, he ran into Hollis French, even then considered an authority. French advised him to buy it, assuring him it would restore beautifully. Mr. King took the advice, and when the Hepplewhite sideboard was restored to its original handsome state, he was very pleased with his purchase. From that time on, he became a valued customer and friend. He went on to form a very distinguished collection.

My brothers and I had a thrill recently when a Queen Anne blockfront lowboy came into our hands. We had been told it came from one of Mr. King's descendants. Since we well knew Mr. King purchased his pieces exclusively from my father all those years ago, or had them authenticated by him, we felt certain this piece had once been in my father's possession, or had at least passed through his hands. We were quite excited subsequently to find an old illustration of the same blockfront in our early photographic files, with a note attached to it reading *"Present whereabouts unknown."* After half a century or so, it had indeed returned to the fold. It is now privately owned and is on loan to the Museum of Fine Arts, Boston.

In 1914, Mr. King had bought a Chippendale blockfront lowboy from my father, a different piece, for $750, which in those days was a fantastically high price. Our records show that in 1928, my father repurchased the same lowboy for $7,500, and sold it to Mr. Henry Francis du Pont, who had begun his career as the supreme collector of Americana. That lowboy can today be seen at Winterthur, the museum in Delaware which houses Mr. du Pont's splendid collection, a unique institution which not only affords the public a vast array of high-quality pieces, but is also a research center, busily engaged in collecting material on American craftsmen, their lives and their creations.

Mr. King's lowboy, which is illustrated in the Winterthur book on Queen Anne and Chippendale furniture in America, has today an appraisal value in excess of $250,000. Could Samuel Gelston King, or my father, or any of the other early Charles Street antiques dealers back then have ever imagined how Americans would awaken to the value of their past history, and to the treasures of their ancestral craftsmen?

In the 1920s, my father was one of the very few dealers who began to spend money having many of the fine antiques he handled being photographed, professionally, for the record. Later on, of course, when Wallace Nutting published his famous two-volume Furniture Treasury, in 1928, it would promptly become the indispensable archive of the history of American antiques, but until then, photographic records of rare early American treasures were, at best, haphazard.

Today, we carefully record and number and index every single item which is part of our stock. Fortunately, we have retained all my father's earliest records and photos, but often we come across old photos which, maddeningly, have no information attached. Where are those treasures now? Who knows? We can only wait, and hope, for them to reappear.

Which brings me to the story — one of my father's favorites — of Colonel Fearing, a tall, young Boston gentleman, and his sideboard. In 1926 my father had rented a house on Beacon Street; his stock was overflowing the Charles Street quarters, and he reasoned, quite sensibly, that the proper place to display his fine pieces was in their customary setting. So he opened up the Beacon Street house as a showroom for his customers, and the results soon justified that expansion. Sales were brisk.

One day a very imposing man strolled in. His name was Fearing, and he was already famous as a star member of one of the Harvard crews.

He strode over to a large sideboard, eyed it, and then asked the price, which was $7,500.

"I'll take it," he told my father. "How much do you want for the mirror hanging over it?"

The price was $2,500.

"I'll take it, too," said Colonel Fearing. Then after a few moments' browsing, he pointed to another antique table. The price? $1,200.

"I'll take that, too," said Colonel Fearing, briskly. He gave my father his address and left instructions for the delivery of his purchases.

"It was a good sale," my father remembered, years later, "because a big sideboard is not easy to sell — and that was an extremely large board."

An hour later, the telephone rang, and it was an irate lady, Colonel Fearing's wife. "Mr. Sack," she said, briskly, "I've got a bone to pick with you."

What seemed to be her complaint?

"You sold my husband a sideboard and a mirror and a table, and you had no business to sell them to him because *I'm* the buyer in the family," said Mrs. Fearing.

"I've learned," commented father, "if anybody kicks and you're going to do something about it, do it instantly. Don't hesitate, or you're lost. So I said, 'Mrs. Fearing, you've got it all wrong. I didn't sell your husband a thing.' "

"You didn't?" she asked. "Didn't he *buy* the things?"

"Yes," said my father, "he bought them, but I didn't sell them to him. He asked me the price of the sideboard, and said he'd take it. He asked for the price of the mirror, and said he'd take it. The same with the table. So you tell your husband for me if this is going to be a bone of contention in your family, he doesn't have to take them."

My father's psychology was excellent. Mrs. Fearing promptly became very friendly, her bruised feelings had been soothed, and everything returned to normal.

An hour later, Colonel Fearing came striding back to the Beacon Street showroom. My father, assuming he had come to cancel his order, quickly explained to his customer that his wife had called up and berated him. "She said she isn't going to let you put those things in the house," he told Fearing.

"Mr. Sack," said Fearing, "*I* bought those things, and I'm going to pay for them right away." And he added, "I do not care if my wife puts them in the woodshed!"

"I could have kissed him," said my father. Moments later, he had Fearing's check in hand, and that ended that.

The large Federal sideboard went off to the Fearing home and very soon afterward was completely accepted by Mrs. Fearing for the fine inlaid piece that it was. Some years later, my father recalled that he'd been in touch with the Fearings to find out if they'd be interested in selling him that massive Federal sideboard.

The Fearings were definitely not.

That however, is not the end of the saga of Colonel Fearing and his sideboard. The next act took place half a century or so later.

In the antiques business, such lengthy intermissions are quite customary. We Sacks have learned to cultivate patience.

Out of the blue, there came a telephone call from California, and a gentleman introduced himself to me as a Colonel Fearing. "I have in my possession a sideboard purchased from Israel Sack, in the 1920s," he said.

"Of course," I said. "I know who you are, and I know all about that sideboard."

"You know me, *and* the sideboard?" he asked, obviously surprised.

"In our family, the name Fearing is legendary," I said. "You were the star of one of my father's favorite anecdotes. We grew up hearing it."

I repeated the story as I'd heard it, and we both chuckled over it.

Now, what was there I could do for him?

After all these years, it seemed he wished to sell the sideboard because his present home in California was not large enough to house it properly. I asked him if he would send me a photograph, and when it arrived, I checked the picture with what we'd retained in our earliest files. Sure enough, it was the exact same piece as shown in one of my father's early, unmarked photos!

I called him to say it was indeed a very fine piece, and we'd be very much interested in repurchasing it.

"Well now, antiques have gone up a great deal lately," he said, which was something of an understatement. "I ought to get a very good price, shouldn't I?"

The vagaries of the antiques market are always fascinating. The price Colonel Fearing had paid for that Federal sideboard was indeed substantial, for the time. But consider. A blockfront bureau circa 1760–1770 during the same period might have cost him a mere $300 to $400 back then. Today, that big Federal sideboard of his has risen to perhaps $30,000 to $40,000, true, but that other neglected blockfront would bring much, much more — say $150,000.

But we both agreed, Colonel Fearing should get a good price for his sideboard. "After all," he commented, "it cost me eleven thousand, two hundred dollars originally."

"Excuse me," I said, "but the price of your sideboard was seventy-five hundred dollars."

"Are you sure?" he asked.

"Believe me, I'm sure," I told him. "I've heard that story over and over from my father to the point where I know it by heart."

There was a brief silence. Then the Colonel said, "You're right. I'm checking the original invoice, and I see there was also a Chippendale mirror for twenty-five hundred dollars and a table for twelve hundred dollars, all from your father. That accounts for my error."

We did not take long to negotiate an agreeable deal.

Colonel Fearing's sideboard was carefully crated, shipped back East, and arrived here at the Sack showroom where, after an absence of half a century, it went back on display.

And now for the coda.

A year or so later, it was purchased by an astute young Boston collector, and that beautiful sideboard was returned to a locale in Louisburg Square, not far from the very spot on Beacon Street where the entire saga began.

There were other collectors who made the 1920s vital, and their names are now well remembered because of their superb collections. Mr. George Horace Lorimer was the editor of the *Saturday Evening Post,* and he and his good friend Edwin Le Fevre actively pursued choice antiques. Le Fevre concentrated on glassware, and Mr. Lorimer went after furniture and fine china.

Mr. Le Fevre was a regular visitor to our Roxbury home, where I would listen to him and my father chatting for hours, discussing all sorts of different aspects of American collecting. Soon afterward, there would appear an article in Mr. Lorimer's magazine. I would read it and promptly recognize various threads of information I'd heard my father pass along to Mr. Le Fevre, as well as choice anecdotes he'd told Mr. Le Fevre about various antiques.

I often wondered whether my father was doing the right thing by being so free with *his* information, all of it hard earned and self-taught, especially since *I'd* been so carefully instructed to keep my own mouth tightly closed.

Down in New York, Wanamaker's department store had opened an antiques department, and their buyer began to come to Boston to purchase many pieces from my father. Other New York dealers had long since begun to use his sharp eye for quality as a dependable source of supply for their own customers.

One of them was a courtly gentleman named Henry Weil, and another firm was Collings & Collings. Mr. and Mrs. Collings were a couple whose regular visits to our house I remember well. They were addicted to bridge; they spent most of their days playing the game, but on Sundays, they would travel up to Boston to visit and buy from my father. They did not have many customers, but the ones they had were willing to pay Mr. and Mrs. Collings's enormous markups for their high-quality pieces. One of their major customers was young Henry du Pont, already embarked on his own brilliant collecting career.

In the very early days of his purchases, Mr. du Pont was not that certain of his own innate good taste. Often, he had seen pieces in my father's shop at 89 Charles Street, but he hadn't had the confidence to buy them there. Later, Mr. and Mrs. Collings would have purchased them and brought them to New York. Seeing them there in their premises, he must have had more confidence in their taste; he would end up buying from them at two to three times my father's original asking price.

That pattern soon ended. Mr. du Pont must have caught on to what was happening. His confidence in my father's good taste rose to the point where he came directly to the source, and from then on, he became one of my father's most loyal and valued customers.

In the late 1920s, my father took the plunge, and bought his first major collection in toto. It was an outstanding group of American pieces, which came from the Arthur Kelley family in Massachusetts, the contents not of masterpiece level, but as fine a collection as an upper-middle-class family would have amassed as a livable selection.

Unfortunately, it sold well.

I use that adjective advisedly, because the ultimate success of that first deal gave my father a keen taste for doing things on a much bigger scale. The rapid disposition of an entire collection such as the Kelley pieces seemed to solve his ever-present supply problem. As a lone operator, no longer would he have to use his valuable time seeking out individual pieces, a time-consuming process for the dealer, who also thereafter had to make each and every sale to his customers personally.

In this case, my father reasoned, more would mean less. Less detail, less harassment. And certainly, more for his ever-growing clientele.

In retrospect, however, dealing in large collections would prove to be one of my father's fatal errors. Heretofore, the purchase of individual pieces, or of smallish groups, could be handled financially out of his current sales and cash flow. In the case of purchases he'd made from other dealers, which was a regular occurrence, he could use what were called trade notes. But to purchase a large collection called for a much larger amount of ready, hard cash. To close such deals promptly, ahead of any competitive dealer, such as the Flaydermans, one needed bank credit.

On his previously smaller scale of operations, each and every week all outstanding bills had been paid. Had my father continued to deal in such a businesslike fashion, without investing large amounts of capital borrowed from the obliging banks, he might have gone through the bleak post-1929 crash period with, if not complete liquidity, at least sufficient financial assets to survive those difficult years.

But that is twenty-twenty hindsight.

*   *   *

In the 1920s, optimism was the battle cry. My father had gone off in the early part of the decade to visit England. His transatlantic trip must have been based on an amalgam of wanderlust and nostalgia, for was he not returning in triumph to the country where not so long ago he had worked an arduous twelve-hour day, shaping hard mahogany in that busy cabinet shop? Now he was an affluent American citizen, a very successful antiques dealer with a roster of gilt-edged clients, riding the crest of a successful wave.

All that loose money he had accumulated must have burned quite a hole in my father's pockets, for when he returned, he had brought with him large quantities of amber, pigs' bristles, and a stock of brass antique furniture hardware. The amber was eventually to be given away to various friends and relatives. The pigs' bristles? I am not certain what happened to his supply; about it, he was always secretive. But the furniture hardware was quite a different story.

Dealers from all over soon heard about "Crazy" Sack's newly acquired stock. Since most of the antiques dealers of that era were involved in cabinet repair, or one step removed from that type of work, in short order my father had sold most of the antique brass fittings he'd imported, to other dealers who'd use them on their own stock, or on pieces they had in for repair. So enthusiastic was the response to his stock of brass that he was encouraged to order more.

He ordered and reordered brass until, finally, a thriving trade was established, in a shop next door on Charles Street, to be known as the Sack Hardware Company. Eventually, he added a foundry in Cambridge, where brass hardware could be designed and cast to order. Although that enterprise was to be run haphazardly by some of our relatives, it would grow into a very large business. Later on, during the Depression, it would be sold to the sons of two prominent Boston families.

Then my father took the plunge, and in the late 1920s opened his first New York branch, at 383 Madison Avenue. For some time, it had become obvious that the center of the antiques business was beginning to shift away from quiet Charles Street to midtown Manhattan, where other dealers and the auction galleries were thriving.

Such affluent collectors as Miss Ima Hogg of Houston, Texas, Francis Garvan of Long Island, and Mrs. J. Insley Blair and Mrs. J.

Amory Haskell of New Jersey were all actively amassing large collections of fine early American furniture, china, and silver. In short order, my father was well established in the middle of the New York scene. He had also opened a quaint little side-street shop on Chestnut Street, in Boston, where he had a good stock of primitive furniture, he had a half interest in an antiques shop on Beacon Street, and he acquired his own warehouse. He also restored a fine old mansion in Marblehead, the King Hooper Mansion, which he stocked with fine pieces from his inventory, and then opened as a summer shop. By that time, I was enrolled as a student in the Boston Latin School, but my education continued during the summer when he stationed me at the King Hooper Mansion, to serve as a guide and (hopefully) as a salesman.

My father's empire was thriving, but within the structure, there were rapidly growing problems. In order to help him bring some sort of order into his operations, he hired people from the Harvard Business School, but they didn't last very long. A corporate-minded M.B.A. simply could not cope with the vagaries of a business built on one-of-a-kind antiques, with rapid-fire arguments on the sales floor, and split-second decisions involving four-figure sums of sales or purchases.

One of the major problems of such an unstructured business, one which dogs antiques dealers even today, is the inability of any one man to be in thirty places, all at one time. Even if my father had wanted to (and he did not, being very much his own man), he found he could not delegate his responsibilities to others.

Thus his office phone rang constantly, with callers, usually potential customers, impatiently demanding to make an appointment, not with any lesser personage, but with Israel Sack himself. In a one-of-a-kind business, they relied on a one-of-a-kind dealer.

My father's days and nights were taken up with constant travel; not only were his potential purchases scattered all over the landscape, but so, too, were his customers. His trips to Detroit, Washington, Williamsburg, or Philadelphia were long and arduous treks by rail or by car. Commercial air travel was years ahead, and the end result was that very often Israel Sack was not around, and since valued customers who'd come in to see him personally weren't

about to commit large sums to purchase items from lesser function-
aries, many sales were lost.

In time, the overhead from our expensive stock in trade would
thus become unproductive. I vividly remember those days going
over our financial statements with Mr. Stewart, our harried Boston
accountant. Even in the lush 1920s, that serious-minded man would
complain that my father's operations were dangerously loose. We
lacked sufficient organization, and while our volume was large, the
eventual profit derived from it was minuscule. It was then that I
began to have trepidations and forebodings about our future. Alas,
Mr. Stewart's alarums would prove to be accurate only a few years
later. With a vengeance.

But despite his accountant's muttered warnings, Israel Sack sailed
on through the decade, thriving, with steady cash flow. Collectors
were busily "swapping" with each other, and a new market had
opened up among American museums, all busily developing "American" rooms, to become permanent displays. My father dealt with
such institutions as the City Museum of St. Louis, the Minneapolis
Institute of Fine Arts, the Rhode Island School of Design, and the
Rockhill Nelson Gallery of Art in Kansas City. When the Rockefellers
began to restore Williamsburg, he devoted a good deal of time in a
search for choice pieces for that enterprise. All of these customers
meant more prestige; they also meant more and more travel on his
part, plus a great deal of his time and effort.

But the results were worth it. In the 1960s, while visiting one of
my sons at the university, I took a side trip to the City Museum of
St. Louis. I'd never visited that institution, and since my good friend,
Charles Buckley, who had been director of the Currier Gallery in
Manchester, New Hampshire, had lately been made director in St.
Louis, it created an added inducement for my visit. I was pleasantly
surprised to see so many choice antiques in St. Louis, and, in going
over the museum files with Charles, to find so many of those pieces
had originally come from my father.

We also discovered, ironically enough, that Meyric Rogers, then
the curator at St. Louis, found himself being castigated back in 1931
by the trustees of that institution for buying so many pieces from
Israel Sack!

Little did those myopic gentlemen realize that Mr. Rogers should have been paid a tribute, along with my father, for prescience.

And if, as the trustees seem to feel back in 1931, the prices Meyric Rogers paid for those antiques were high, I can only quote one of my father's comments: "Cheap is not necessarily a bargain. I have yet to see a successful collection, unless it's junk, accumulated in a bargain basement."

FIVE

Mr. Henry Ford
of Detroit

I N 1923, my father made the acquaintance of a man who was to become one of his major customers. The historic Wayside Inn, in Sudbury, Massachusetts, the very same building which had been immortalized by Henry Wadsworth Longfellow in his *Tales of a Wayside Inn*, came on the market, and was purchased by a wealthy, and already legendary, mechanical genius from Detroit, Michigan, Mr. Henry Ford.

As my father remembered their first meeting, it had come about after he himself had attempted to buy the Wayside Inn from its owner, a Mr. Lemon, and had been informed by Lemon that an option had been taken by a prospective buyer, as yet unknown.

My father accepted the turndown with good grace, and shortly thereafter, the newspapers carried the story that Mr. Ford, the father of the mass-produced Model-T, had invested in the historic Sudbury property.

His purchase of the Wayside Inn induced considerable anxiety and consternation among native New Englanders. Was this automobile tycoon from far-off Michigan planning to turn the historic structure into a popular restaurant, or some other gaudy roadside attraction?

"At that time, very few people knew Henry Ford," recalled my father. "No one knew what he looked like because his pictures weren't in the paper very often. Actually, I wouldn't have known Henry Ford if I'd met him on the street."

My father returned from lunch to his Charles Street shop one day, and as he walked in the door, he encountered a tall man, and a shorter one, who'd been waiting and now were ready to leave. The tall man introduced himself.

"He said, 'I am Henry Ford.' He shook hands with me. 'This is Mr. Campsall, my secretary. You know,' said Mr. Ford, "I just bought the Wayside Inn.'

"I said, 'The whole country knows you bought the Wayside Inn.'

"Mr. Ford said, 'I just want to know how to furnish it.'

"He was all excited," remembered my father. "Happy, in an exhilarated mood, like a child with a new toy. Why he'd come to me, I couldn't yet figure out, but it had probably been Mr. Lemon who owned the place who'd told him about me."

Mr. Ford wanted to know if my father had lunched.

"Well, I figured this way," said my father. "I'm not going to tell him I'd already had my lunch, like a dope, and let him go away. So I said, 'Mr. Ford, I'll take you to a very nice place for lunch.'

"Now I didn't say I'd had my lunch, and I didn't say I *hadn't* had my lunch," he pointed out. "I just said, 'I'll take you to a nice place for lunch,' and I did. In fact, we went to the same restaurant I'd just come from."

Once at a table, Mr. Ford promptly ordered lunch and got down to business. "He said, 'You know, Mr. Sack, I'd like to know how to furnish that inn.'

"I said, 'Mr. Ford, I love the Wayside Inn. I knew Mr. Lemon well, and he loved the inn, and he would have loved to furnish it with the kind of things the inn required because of the early periods involved. He was a poor man, and he couldn't afford to do it. Now that you own it, Mr. Ford, everybody knows you can afford to buy the best. If you give me the job, you shall have the best.' "

My father's proposal suited Mr. Ford perfectly, and since the man from Detroit was noted for his prompt decisions, the answer came within seconds. "Go ahead," instructed Ford.

"He didn't ask me what, where, or how much," my father said, years later. "In the navy they have a saying — they tell you — 'When, where and why, but not how.' That's up to *you*." Mr. Ford obviously operated on the same basic principle.

Mr. Ford left Mr. Campsall in residence at the Wayside Inn, and returned to Detroit. My father went to work and began to pick up various antiques to furnish the historic structure. In a matter of two weeks, the job was done, with furniture that was contemporary with the inn. "I'll say this for Mr. Campsall," said my father. "He never interfered or said a word, not one word. I sent Henry Ford a bill, and he sent me a check. And he didn't see the inn for a year after that check."

When it became known that Mr. Ford had, with my father's considerable assistance, completely restored the inn as a showplace, there was great relief in Massachusetts, and eventually an approving editorial in the staid *Boston Herald*.

From then on, the relationship between my father and Henry Ford thrived. "Antiques were plentiful then," he recalled, "and if I had something I thought Henry Ford could use, I'd ship it. He didn't give me an order — he never said a word. After the inn was done, it was a free-for-all. I'd send him a picture, or send him the actual piece, and I'd get an answer — 'Yes' or 'No.' There were no ifs and buts."

My father early on accurately assessed Ford's particular appetites. "It was the history that appealed to him," he said, years later. "The picture of the Wayside Inn, built in 1686, and Longfellow's *Tales* — it appealed to him, so he bought it. Before that, he'd never known anything much about American historical things, but now, there was American history, right in his lap. It was just as plain as day to me. He wanted the early American, with the history. He didn't have to study history, he came right into it."

My father knew his customer well. "If I got anything historical, such as the Longfellow collection, Mr. Ford would buy it. I bought the General Stark collection direct from the Stark house, I dealt with Mrs. Stark herself, and Henry Ford bought that. He liked antiques which had a story attached. You get a Longfellow collection, and you look at the bed, and you look at the desk where Longfellow worked, and you've got Longfellow in your home already. Mr. Ford wanted something with a background. . . .

"One time I sold him the Mary Ball Washington highboy. It was a William and Mary highboy that had belonged to Mary Ball Washington, George Washington's mother. When Mary Ball Washington died, she left debts, and her effects were sold at auction. That highboy was bought by a neighbor, and the initials *MBW* were scratched right on the surface. Well, I bought that highboy and sold it to Henry Ford. I figured he would like the idea of the history of the family, and that the highboy had been exhibited at the World Fair, in 1893, by the Colonial Dames of Virginia."

By that time, so close was the relationship between Ford and my father that it was the automaker's habit to stop by my father's shop immediately upon his arrival in Boston. One afternoon, the two men encountered each other on Beacon Street. "This is very fortunate, Mr. Ford!" my father exclaimed. "You're here just at the right time."

Whereupon he led Ford up to the newly rented Beacon Hill mansion which he had recently opened, and gave his client a tour of the premises. When they had completed viewing the rooms, Mr. Ford had picked out some $75,000 worth of fine Chippendale.

It was at that moment Mrs. Ford arrived on the scene. She walked in to survey the rooms.

Her reaction was one of immediate dismay.

As my father remembered it, Mrs. Ford told her husband, "I don't like these things at all. Don't buy them. I don't like the claw feet."

My father stood by, quietly.

Mr. Ford was silent for a moment, and then he finally said to Mrs. Ford's escort, "Bennett, do you remember that Mrs. Ford has an appointment at Stearns, the department store, at two? Hadn't you better take her over there?"

After his wife had left, Mr. Ford and my father concluded the arrangements.

"You take big men," remarked my father, years later. "They don't want anybody telling them not to do something — *after* they've done it. If Mrs. Ford had told him not to buy before he bought, he might have listened to her. But after he made up his mind, he didn't want to be told not to."

*   *   *

Ford had begun to collect on a grand scale, not only antiques, but the historic American buildings in which to house them. His master plan became to recreate what would be known as Greenfield Village, in Michigan, where there would be exhibits showing "life among ordinary Americans of the past." According to one of the contemporary newspaper commentators, ". . . Mr. Ford collects buildings as casually as he buys jugs and warming pans."

Set among the genuinely old structures, there would be one which was newly built, in true Colonial style. This huge building had a central portion modeled on Independence Hall, and it would become the Henry Ford Museum. Inside its rooms, Ford's master plan presented, chronologically, the development of everyday items used in the American home, in industry, and on the farm. Later on, Ford would transport, intact, to the Dearborn locale his great friend Thomas Alva Edison's laboratory and workshop from Menlo Park, New Jersey.

By 1929, the master plan had been fulfilled. When Ford opened the Edison Institute, he said, "We shall have reproduced American life as lived, and that, I think, is the best way of preserving at least a part of our history and our tradition."

My father was fond of recounting various facets of the automaker's personality. "I saw him in action," he said. "You see, Ford felt sympathy with the small people. He went to small dealers. He knew I could take care of myself. I matched the antiques I found to his personality, his taste, and I wasn't going to sell him anything that he could pick up in any one of fifteen antiques shops in the country. I left that to the country dealers, because I didn't handle those things."

My father would sometimes accompany Ford on those forays into the rural areas. "When he got out there and found a dealer," he remembered, "and he got to talking with him, and the man would bring out his wife and his children, and he had a batch of little stuff in stock, say, Ford would ask, 'How much stock have you got?' The man would say, maybe eight thousand dollars' worth. Ford would nod his head and then he'd ask, 'Would you like to sell me the lot?' "

The response was usually immediate, and affirmative. Mr. Ford would promptly write out a check, or have one sent, for the $8,000. The rural dealer would sweep out his store and go on to other pursuits, having achieved his own version of the American dream. The antiques would go off to Dearborn, but whether or not they were worth the price paid for them by Ford, the fact is, the automaker had gotten his money's worth in public relations.

Inevitably, the question of authentication arose. One day Mr. Ford brought my father in to view some antiques he had purchased from someone else, and politely asked for my father's opinion. Were they real, or could they perhaps be fake?

My father's response was immediate. "I said, 'Mr. Ford, I'm in the antiques business, and I don't think it's ethical for you to ask me to pass judgment on any of my competitors' furniture. You have a perfect right to take in any authority you want. You can bring in Luke Lockwood, or you can bring in Wallace Nutting. Bring in anybody you wish and show the pieces to them. But I'm not going to pass judgment on them.' "

The response did not satisfy Ford. He persisted. How was he supposed to find authentication for his purchases?

"I told him, 'Do what Mr. du Pont does, or Francis Garvan, or what the Metropolitan Museum does. They hire somebody who isn't in the business, and he gives it a postmortem, goes over it, checks it all out . . . but *not a dealer,' "* insisted my father. "I don't think it's fair for one dealer to go look over another dealer's furniture."

Eventually, Ford consulted Henry du Pont and Francis Garvan, two other leading collectors of the period, and an authoritative expert was recommended. Ford hired him, and the man began to sift through the vast collection of antiques assembled in Dearborn.

"I'll tell you what Mr. Ford told me," said my father, "and what was on his mind, because he said so. He said, 'Sack, I don't mind the money I spent on antiques, only I'm greatly disappointed in having been fooled.' "

As were so many of his contemporaries who were self-made tycoons, Ford was a benevolent despot, accustomed to constant and

unquestioning obedience on the part of his employees and associates. Around the Ford executive offices, on the factory assembly
lines, and then in the developing Dearborn museum, his word was
law, with no argument expected.

Inevitably, although there was considerable mutual respect between my father and Ford, there would come the time when the
two would lock horns, and my father, also the individualist, would,
no matter what the consequences, speak his mind.

It was at the time before the actual museum was begun, and Ford
was still housing his ever-growing collection of Americana in a huge
barn, some six hundred feet long. The automaker often amused
himself by seeing how fast he could run from one end of the structure to the other. In the cavernous building, he kept a crew of four
skilled cabinetmakers working full time on his acquisitions.

One day, Ford brought my father in to show him the work his
cabinetmakers were doing. Proudly he brought him to a gleaming
antique desk. "This is a wonderful job of repairing, isn't it?" he
asked. "My men have put sixteen coats of shellac on this piece."

After each coat, the experts had polished the piece, so when the
work was done, according to my father, that innocent early American desk resembled a modern-day Steinway piano.

Ford stood by, waiting for my father's approval, and his secretary,
Mr. Campsall, asked, "Isn't that a marvelous job?"

My father did not hesitate. He spoke his mind. "Yes it is," he told
Ford, "but if you're going to do that to the furniture I've been selling
you, you're going to ruin your antiques."

The gray-haired Ford's face froze, and he walked silently away,
obviously angry.

"Campsall was pulling me by the coat," my father recalled. "He
was upset. He said, 'You mustn't talk to Mr. Ford that way! He
comes pretty near always doing things the way he wants to do them.
Nobody can tell him anything.' "

My father was undeterred. "Mr. Campsall," he said, "you know
I'm not working for Mr. Ford, and he can't fire me. I thought it was
my duty to tell him what he's been doing."

My father understood Ford's personality well by then. Ford was
first and always a mechanic, with a mechanic's thirst for the *why* of

craftsmanship, and the principles of construction. Patina, the charm, the intrinsic glow given off by an old antique piece, did not interest him.

Not that my father felt any sense of elation at having locked horns with his most important customer. Far from it. As he recalled, years later, "I didn't go there to antagonize Mr. Ford, but when a man says something, he's in the same position as a man who jumps from a sixteen-story window. There's no turning back, once you jump. And once you've said something, you've said it."

Happily for both men, the contretemps had a positive outcome. A month or so later, my father was back in Detroit, where he often did considerable business with the Detroit Institute of Art, working closely with the curator in assembling a collection of early American furniture. As was his regular custom, he went from the institute out to visit Dearborn. This time, fortunately enough, he found Mr. Ford alone in his vast barn.

My father decided to venture once more into the lion's den. Gently, he said, "Mr. Ford, I want to explain to you what I meant about your antiques. You see that hard wood, with its patina? That took at least a hundred and fifty years of natural wear, people living with it, and using it every day, to get that beautiful patina. Now, if you take that finish and plane it, and scrape it, and make it look like that desk you had your cabinetmakers polish, believe me, neither you nor your children, nor your grandchildren, will live to see that patina grow back again."

There was silence, and then Mr. Ford nodded. He had accepted the lesson from his teacher. The cabinetmakers were called off and assigned to other duties. "He never touched one single piece after that," recalled my father. "He wouldn't let them go near the pieces—he wouldn't even let them dust things!"

What my father had finally succeeded in educating Ford to understand was the danger involved in even the simplest restoration of an antique finish from the original "in the rough." Far too many of my father's original Boston customers had persisted in refurbishing family heirlooms, with disastrous results.

"It was fortunate for him," commented my father. "He'd have gone on to ruin at least half a million dollars' worth of antiques if I hadn't stopped him. As a matter of fact, his men did a restoration to a very fine clock they had in Dearborn, and ruined the value of it."

Since Ford's interest in machinery lasted all his life, it was inevitable that he would be fascinated by the workings of clocks. He dearly loved them, in all shapes and sizes, and whenever he visited my father's Charles Street shop, and found one, he would open it up, either front or back, to study its design. If it were, say, a grandfather clock, he would practically edge himself inside the tall structure, in order to peer up at some Colonial artisan's machinery. When I was young, in the 1930s, I would stand there and watch as he did this, and I remember always being afraid Mr. Ford might get himself stuck inside one of those antique wooden pieces. It would have been an interesting sight; one of the world's greatest industrialists, wedged and trapped into a set of clockworks.

My father sold him dozens of clocks, of all shapes and makers. One time, he found a large watch in a collection, a beautiful old specimen, quite large, in a gold case. When the back was opened, it revealed the inscription "John Ford, London" as its pedigree.

My father promptly sent it off to Dearborn, on the assumption that perhaps the maker might be one of Ford's ancestors. "I was right," he said. "Mr. Ford was very pleased to get it. Way back in his ancestry somewhere, there must have been a watchmaker. There was a Ford family up in Ireland, and then London."

When my father purchased the General Stark collection, it contained, among many other items, such historic pieces as a Willard banjo clock, a Martha Washington chair, a McIntyre bed, and a rare cane, with a gold cap, bearing the inscription "Presented by Robert Moses to John Hancock, 1794." Historically, that cane was priceless, and in show of thoughtful gratitude to his Dearborn client, my father presented the cane to Mr. Ford as a gift.

Whether it was specifically in return for such a gracious gesture, or merely out of his own constant regard for his friend, Mr. Ford soon reciprocated.

One morning, as we were having breakfast in our house, the doorbell rang, and when my father opened the door, he found a polite man on the doorstep. The visitor held out a set of car keys.

"Mr. Sack," he announced, "Mr. Ford sent me out here to give you these — they're for that car."

Parked outside our house was a large, elegant Lincoln, a mammoth touring sedan, certainly the most expensive model produced in the Ford factory.

My father eyed the battleship-gray monster. "Good Lord," he said, finally. "I don't need such a big car. Thank Mr. Ford for me, but you'd better take it back, I can't use it."

"Oh, I could never do that, Mr. Sack," said Mr. Ford's messenger. "Mr. Ford says it's yours — so it's yours. Enjoy it."

With that, he tipped his hat and went down the steps, leaving the keys safely in my father's hand.

"What should I do with such a car?" sighed my father. "It's much too spendid for a simple man like me — it's so big — the only thing I could use it for is maybe to deliver furniture!"

Nevertheless, the oversized Lincoln remained in our family for years afterward.

It was, after all, a major improvement over that open touring car in which my father and I had jounced across back New England roads, years before.

When my father was asked, years later, his opinion of Ford as a collector, he said, "My overall impression of the Ford collection is that it is phenomenal. Like all great things, it needs perspective. All the great collections of American art will be appreciated a hundred times as much fifty or a hundred years from now."

Time has proved my father correct.

But there were stresses to their friendship. In the late 1920s, Henry Ford encountered loud and persistent accusations that he was anti-Semitic, because of the articles continually published in a paper which Ford had subsidized, William J. Cameron's *Dearborn Independent.*

Mr. Ford took those accusations as a personal insult, and an unjust interpretation of his personal feelings. Eventually, he made a public apology in 1927, which commanded a full page in most major newspapers around the country, and in that paid advertisement, he specifically mentioned his long and fruitful relationship with my father, citing him as a worthy and most reputable man of the Jewish faith, with whom he had dealt for many years.

Long after Ford had died, my father was asked about his feelings in that situation. He thought for a moment, and then he said, "I always looked up to Henry Ford as a genius, along with Thomas Edison. I never looked for flaws in Henry Ford. I looked at his greatness and overlooked everything else."

I myself first met Mr. Ford in 1934. He came into the store one day, and I vividly recall being enormously impressed by his phenomenal memory. He went around our place, asking the price on many pieces in rapid-fire fashion, everything from furniture to such minor items as andirons. I followed him around and could barely keep up with him, so quickly did he move from one item to another. When he had finished his tour of our inventory, he recalled each and every price, including the most insignificant items on which I'd quoted him.

Thereafter, whenever he'd come in, he always had a habit of feeling the bumps on my head, as if he could read my character from them, and then he would gaze into my eyes. Lifting an eyelid, he would examine the eye, and then say, "Good boy . . . I see you're leading a clean life."

How he arrived at that conclusion I will never know.

By that time I was a graduate of Dartmouth, but I'd picked up a copy of a book Mr. Ford had written, called *Today and Tomorrow,* in the library at Hanover. I'd read it and found it most interesting, and when I told him so, Mr. Ford became as excited and pleased as any author who encounters a true fan. He instructed his ever-present secretary, Mr. Campsall, to leave us alone, and not to interrupt us, and we spent a long time in conversation. I was impressed to be so involved with the inner thoughts of such a powerful figure, and to have such an intimate private audience with him.

Both my father and Mr. Ford are long gone now, but years later, there still arise curious connections between the Sack family and the great Detroit automaker.

One of them involves a fine antique highboy, one which has always been my particular favorite William and Mary piece. I saw it first in 1925.

It is known as the Holyoke highboy, and it was on display at the Park Square Loan Exhibit, in Boston, a very important assemblage of American decorative arts, furniture, silver, and paintings, loaned for the show by a distinguished group of New England families.

The highboy had originally belonged to Edward Holyoke, one of the early presidents of Harvard. Since my father had loaned some of his finest pieces to the Park Square show, he took me with him to see the display. I was inexperienced, but when I saw that Holyoke highboy, something inside me immediately responded. Broad, somewhat massive, almost monumental, that fine piece seemed to embody the greatness of the early part of the eighteenth century in our country — it dates from 1700–1720.* Perhaps it impressed me as a statement of the strength of our Founding Fathers. Whatever the reason, in my father's words, it spoke to me, and love found Harold Sack.

After that, however, the highboy passed from view, dropped out of sight, vanished completely. As the years passed, that Holyoke highboy became merely a mute illustration on the pages of the Park Square show catalogue, tucked away on the extensive research shelves of our firm's library, an impersonal number attached to its catalogue description.

Where had it gone? It would be half a century or so before it reentered my life.

About seven or eight years ago, Douglas Dillon, who had been Secretary of the Treasury and was then President of the Board of Trustees of the Metropolitan Museum, phoned and asked if I would be kind enough to go out to his father's house in Far Hills, New Jersey. "My father has a few American antiques," he said, "and he's

---

* The early highboys had cup-turned or trumpet-design legs, joined by horizontal flat cross-stretchers, and were accompanied by lowboys of similar design. (The highboy usually had six legs and the lowboy four, although there are a few examples of six-legged lowboys.) The top section had applied lower moldings which fit into overhanging lower case moldings. In the Queen Ann period, which followed, the moldings on the top section were eliminated and the lower case moldings did not overhang. Later on, the six-legged trumpet or cup-turned understructure was replaced by four cabriole legs, and the stretchers were eliminated. Thus a combination of both periods appears in the early, transitional Queen Anne highboys.

now thinking of possibly willing some of them to us, provided you thought they were worthy of the museum.''

I agreed to do the appraisal, and made an appointment to visit with his father. I drove out to Far Hills and arrived at a marvelous thousand-acre estate, to be greeted at the door of a beautiful Georgian mansion by Mr. Clarence Dillon himself. Mr. Dillon, a spry gentleman in his nineties, jauntily dressed in tweeds and knickers, was only too happy to have me as his guest for the day.

We had lunch in his spacious dining room.

"I do have a few American pieces, Mr. Sack," he told me, "but I really don't know too much about that particular field. So why don't you walk through and perhaps you'll find something that the Metropolitan might be interested in."

Mr. Dillon's collection filled room after room, mostly very choice English antiques, which he had purchased over the years with the constant assistance of his good friend Mr. Moss Harris, a London dealer. I observed quite a few pleasant things. At each point, Mr. Dillon stood beside me and watched as I made my notes and then added my valuations.

Then we entered his library, where I spotted a highboy.

But not just *a* highboy. A superb William and Mary period highboy. One which instantly reminded me of a highboy I'd seen, many years ago —

— no wonder it reminded me of that highboy.

It was.

I let out a yell. "There it is — in full bloom! the Holyoke highboy!"

Mr. Dillon was astonished.

"Yes, it is," he said. "But how did you know that?"

"Why, that's my favorite highboy," I told him. "I never dreamed I'd find it here!"

I told him of its history in the Park Square exhibition, back in 1925, of its place in the catalogue, and how for all these years it had totally dropped from sight.

Together, we went over it carefully, lovingly, and then I wrote down a meticulous description of the great piece, along with a whopping evaluation.

Holyoke William and Mary highboy or high chest, circa
1725–1740. The William and Mary highboy, dating in America from the first quarter of the eighteenth century, was
somewhat similar to its English cousin, but soon American
makers adopted the architectural details, proportion, and use
of wood to their own style. (Courtesy, The Metropolitan
Museum of Art, Gift of Clarence Dillion, 1975 [1975.132.1]

When I finished, Mr. Dillon was grinning mischievously.
"Would you like to know *how* I got this highboy?" he asked.
"I certainly would," I told him.
"Well," he said, "I really don't know anything about American

antiques, but some years back I was motoring up in Massachusetts, and there was a sign in some small town we came through which announced an auction sale of the possessions of the Little family. I happened to have my agent with me, and we stopped and went in to examine the show. I saw this lovely piece, and liked it, so I told him to bid on it and buy it, which he did.

"After the sale, while I was claiming my prize," said Mr. Dillon, "a lean, gray-haired middle-aged gentleman came over to me. He said, 'My name is Henry Ford, sir. I understand you're Mr. Dillon, and you purchased this highboy. I missed it. I didn't bid high enough. Perhaps you've heard that I bought the Wayside Inn?'

"I told him yes, I had heard that.

" 'Wouldn't you agree with me that this beautiful piece absolutely belongs in the Wayside Inn?' asked Mr. Ford.

" 'Oh yes, indeed, absolutely,' I agreed.

" 'Good,' said Mr. Ford. 'So you sell me this highboy, and I'll put it in the Wayside Inn.'

" 'Well, Mr. Ford,' I said, 'I'll tell you what I'll do. Since I agree completely with you that this highboy does belong in the Wayside Inn, *you* sell *me* the Wayside Inn — and I'll put the highboy there!' "

And now, whenever I see that beautiful Holyoke highboy on display at the Metropolitan Museum, I can't help feeling part of a link between Israel Sack, Henry Ford, old Mr. Dillon, and its own impressive history.

SIX

1929 and After
(Mr. Chippendale's Best)

THE year 1928 was next-to-closing of a tumultuous decade. To paraphrase the motto of M. Émile Coué, the contemporary French psychologist who was enjoying such a fad in those years, my father's motto might have been "Every day, in every way, the antiques business is getting better and better."

The rapid disposition of the Arthur Kelley collection was such a tonic to my father's spirits that he decided to tackle the sale of an even more impressive collection, and he bought the estate of Mr. George Palmer, in New London, Connecticut.

The late Mr. Palmer had been a wealthy wool dealer who had been one of the country's earliest and most important collectors. A cousin of my father's old and respected friend Eugene Bolles, Mr. Palmer had specialized in seeking out highly developed Chippendale forms. His collection encompassed superb examples of that style, not only of English origin, but comparable pieces from the great Colonial city centers, such as Boston and the Philadelphia workshops of the skilled William Savery.

My father not only bought Mr. Palmer's collection, but also his home, "Westomere," a beautiful copy of "Westover," a Georgian brick mansion in Virginia. So abundant was Mr. Palmer's assemblage of furniture, glassware, and china that even though he had

"Westomere," New London, Connecticut.

sold many of the choice examples of high-style Chippendale — sixty-six separate pieces in 1918 went to the newly established American Wing of the Metropolitan Museum for the then-astronomical price of $107,250 — there was still a vast and sumptuous display left at his death. There it remained, in New London, in beautifully paneled rooms, broad and spacious.

The grounds of "Westomere" consisted of over five acres of beautifully landscaped gardens, with a private beach front on the Thames River. In the main house was a full staff of servants, all housed on the third floor. Three full-time gardeners were needed to tend the grounds; they also lived on the property in a small cottage. The Palmer place was a remarkably opulent layout, typical of the affluent, solidly rich pre-Depression society we were enjoying under Silent Cal Coolidge and his successor, Mr. Herbert Hoover.

After my father bought it, he had an opulent brochure printed, replete with illustrations. "Mr. Sack," said his text, "wishes to draw attention to 'Westomere,' containing Mr. Palmer's well-known collection of Georgian furniture. Mr. Sack purchased 'Westomere' in his belief that it would interest collectors to inspect the Palmer collection in its original environment. These rare and important pieces of furniture, porcelain, pottery, paintings, and the like, comparable only to the best exhibitions in our national museums, will be sold direct from New London. Mr. Sack will reside in New London during the summer months to meet his clientele. Admission will be by special appointment only. Admission cards may be had by request."

It all began most auspiciously, with nowhere to go but up.

Or so we all thought.

By that time I was entered as a freshman at Dartmouth. Not, mind you, Harvard, which all good Boston Latin School students would customarily enter. That decision had been taken, on my behalf, in my senior year at Boston Latin. My father had been visiting his good friend Homer Eaton Keyes, the first editor and one of the founders of the prestigious *Antiques* magazine. When Dad told Mr. Keyes his son was headed toward Harvard, Mr. Keyes, a former Dartmouth professor, began to lobby for his own alma mater. Both he and Dad persuaded me to change plans, and I was accepted at Dartmouth, from which, four years later, I was to graduate in 1932.

But during those next two summers, I spent idyllic weeks working for my father in New London at "Westomere." The third floor of the Palmer mansion was huge, and I was permitted to invite my Dartmouth friends to spend time visiting me there. At times the place took on the aspect of an army barracks. Nor did we lack for female company. There were two beautiful young girls living in the gardeners' cottage, and up on the third floor, at the other end of the huge house, there were other maids in residence. As guardian of her son's and his friends' virtue, my dear mother had her hands full, day and night, and although she did her best as chaperone, to serve as buffer between us and a helpful staff, the job she did was good . . . but not good enough.

My daytime duties were relatively simple. I escorted the visitors who had been invited from the various fine New London hotels and inns, or from nearby Fishers Island, as prospective customers for the Palmer antiques, through the mansion. Needless to say, my "sell" was always very soft.

As were, alas, any sales.

Psychologically, the entire setup was a mistake. That opulent establishment, Mr. Palmer's mansion, set amid the lovely grounds, with his collection carefully displayed — all of it had been assembled by him with such loving care and good taste that somehow it put off anyone who might have bought. To most of the potential buyers I escorted through those rooms, it all must have seemed sacrosanct. To purchase some fine pieces, to break up Mr. Palmer's fine collection by taking that item out of its carefully chosen setting, obviously induced resistance.

The lesson was obvious: Mr. Palmer's collection should not have been displayed for sale in such beautiful settings. Each piece should have been allowed to shine on its own.

Perhaps it was also that I wasn't a very good salesman. Not yet, at least. Whatever the reason, very little was sold out of the Palmer house, although, in my own defense, I should add that even my father, who did his best, wasn't very successful, either.

But we all enjoyed two lovely summers.

Eventually, a few years later, the Palmer house was sold separately to a religious order, and the collection was auctioned off in a series of successful sales at the American Art Galleries, in New York.

By that time, my father had become a favorite of those New York auction houses. They kept on urging him to buy more such collections; his name on the items in their sales catalogues had become an endorsement of authenticity. So he continued his quest for larger and ever-larger collections. Why not? To locate a good one eliminated his running here and there, taking overnight train trips or arduous motor trips to dozens of different homes and shops in search of a single item for sale. With one completed sales contract, that major collection thus provided him not only with prestige, but with ample inventory for months to come.

Certainly, the market was thriving, and interest in fine early American antiques had never been so intense. In 1929, two historic events took place in New York which expanded public consciousness of early American treasures on two separate levels, the first commercial, the second aesthetic.

The first was the sale, at the American Art Galleries, of the Reifsnyder collection of Philadelphia Queen Anne and Chippendale furniture. Consisting of pieces which fully represented the American cabinetmakers of the richest and most luxurious Colonial city of the Revolutionary period, Reifsnyder's collection brought prices at this peak of the inflationary period which set new records. Collectors and dealers vied with each other to purchase rare items; the $600,000 total was astonishing. The highest single price was achieved by the elegant Van Pelt Philadelphia Chippendale highboy, which Mr. Henry du Pont purchased for $44,000, a true masterpiece which would become one of the prizes at Winterthur.

The second event was the legendary loan exhibition of American antiques, sponsored by the Girl Scouts of America, and also held at the American Art Galleries. According to the *New York Times,* it would provide "aid for those interested in the fine points of American antiques. Presenting only genuine examples of the work of master craftsmen in their various lines, the displays will furnish much material, it is hoped, to enable students to differentiate between the merely old and the true collector's piece."

Most of the pieces displayed were from such distinguished collectors as Francis Garvan, the Rockefellers (who were now busily purchasing for Williamsburg), Mrs. J. Insley Blair, Mrs. Amory Haskell, and Henry du Pont. Mr. du Pont took a very active part in physically arranging the Girl Scout show. It was reported by other members of the prestigious committee that he spent many hours at the galleries overseeing the actual placement of the assembled treasures. In his shirtsleeves, he personally moved furniture, hung pictures, and arranged most of the displays. It was obvious that Mr. du Pont's innate sense of decor and good taste were a valuable contribution to the ultimate results.

The show, held under the guidance of Louis Guerineau Myers, a leading collector of the New York cabinetmaker Duncan Phyfe furniture over the years, had been conceived originally by his wife as a fund-raiser for the Girl Scouts. It was truly a memorable display. Even the catalogue, which illustrated the contents of this rich and historic show, has over the years become a collector's item.

The displays of furniture, silver, and paintings were arranged in beautiful settings. Previously, American antique glassware had not received very much serious attention, but in this landmark show, there was a display of over five hundred pieces of fine antique glass from the collection of George McKearin. In years to come, especially during the Depression, collectors with thinner pocketbooks would turn away from expensive furniture to begin concentrating — at least for the time — on less expensive glassware.

The show ran from September 25 to October 9, 1929, and elicited from a writer on the old *New York Sun* the comment that it was "the finest display of early American furniture ever got together in one place at one time."

It was also, for some time to come, the last. A scant few days after the show closed, on October 24, the stock market, which had been soaring for years, went into an astonishing decline. Abruptly, there would be a violent crash, with disastrous shock waves running across the entire country, and then the world.

In the years immediately after that terrible event, there was still a good deal of activity in the antiques market. It's been my experience that financial crises do not cause unfavorable reactions in our business, at least not at first. It is the general business decline which follows, if it does, that has an effect. But after the financial crises have run their course, and an upturn seems imminent, people would be wise to invest their capital and buy antiques for the profits which inevitably follow.

Timing is, of course, essential.

In the years which followed October 1929, we were unfortunately not so prescient.

I remember being in my father's office in 1931 when we had a visitor, none other than Mr. Herbert Lawton of Boston, our good customer and a personal friend of our then President, Mr. Hoover. "Sack," he announced, "I have great news! I was down in Washington yesterday and had dinner with Hoover himself. He says the bottom has definitely been reached — things are turning around, the market's headed upward — the Depression is going to end, and now is the time to buy your head off!"

Such inside information, which in retrospect seems the ultimate product of the clouded crystal ball, could not be so easily ignored in those dark times.

Especially by my father, a congenital optimist.

To him, Lawton's bulletin was a psychological shot in the arm. Even though my father had a vast collection of his own merchandise sitting in warehouses and not moving, he decided to move promptly on Mr. Lawton's "inside tip."

My father's closest competitors and chief challengers in the antiques field had for a long time been Benjamin Flayderman and his father. The Flaydermans had sold, first in 1929, and then in 1930, at auction, an imposing collection of their early American pieces. At the 1930 sale, their wares had included a labeled John Seymour desk, for which Henry du Pont had paid $30,000, and a Goddard Newport open-talon-footed tea table (similar to the one we recently unearthed in Essex, Connecticut), with a bill of sale from John Goddard to Nathaniel Bowen, which went for $29,000. Even in the bleak year of 1930, the Flayderman sale totals reached an impressive $429,840.

The Flaydermans, father and son, had set about busily assembling yet another collection of fine early American pieces. Shrewdly — or so he reasoned — my father decided he could with one bold stroke do away with his major competition and make himself preeminent in the field. He went to visit Philip and Benjamin Flayderman and presented them with a bold offer. "How much do you want for your entire inventory?" he asked. "Lock, stock, and barrel?"

In those desperate times, my father must have seemed, to the Flaydermans, nothing so much as a fairy godfather with a golden wand. They were only too pleased to accommodate him. A deal was promptly settled, and their inventory was transferred to him for a price in the neighborhood of $400,000, which sum my father went out and borrowed, using the goods as security.

Now, clearly, my father was king of the hill. He was amply stocked with far more choice antiques than any other dealer, with which to face the oncoming wave of prosperity.

Unfortunately, prosperity remained somewhere else. Tantalizingly out of sight . . . around the corner.

By 1932, while I was a senior at Dartmouth, I noticed my allowance checks were being skipped at times, and although my father was doing his best to keep the bad news from me, it soon dawned on me that things were bad with him. Exactly how bad I was not to learn until later. When I came to realize the extent of his dire financial straits, it came as a shock.

In that same year, 1932, following his impulsive purchase of the Flaydermans' stock, my father had been forced to liquidate. Not only did he have to raise cash from selling what he'd bought from his rivals, but he also sold out his own merchandise. The catalogue of the final sale read "100 IMPORTANT PIECES," at the American Art Galleries. The results were disastrous. Choice pieces brought low prices, so low as to be unbelievable today. Eight Salem dining chairs, for example, two armchairs and six side chairs, were purchased by a fortunate buyer for $1,200 cash. Recently, we repurchased the same set of eight chairs from a lady who had inherited them, and paid her a hefty five-figure amount!

My father was far from the only person in trouble. Other large dealers, even such collectors as Francis Garvan, were liquidating inventory in order to raise cash.

After this frantic liquidation period, most of the major collections, which belonged to such wealthy buyers as Henry Ford, Henry du Pont, Miss Ima Hogg, the Rockefellers, were to become established in public museums, and thus removed from the marketplace.

Nowadays, we have, in place of such huge collections, hundreds of small but choice collections in the hands of a wealthy upper-middle class, whose fortunes have been amassed since World War II. And now, in the past few years, a new generation of wealthy young people in their thirties and forties have also become purchasers of the top-quality pieces. Hopefully, we will not ever again see such mass liquidation of fine antiques as we had back in the early 1930s, depressing the entire market to such incredibly low prices.

During the summer of 1932, after graduation, my boyhood friend Ben David, who was a senior at Yale, joined me in a brief business partnership. We assembled some pieces from the stock of Leon David, his father, and from what my father had left on Charles Street, and the two of us rented a small shop in Ipswich, Massachusetts. By the end of the summer, we had done very little business, certainly not enough to induce us to continue prospecting among those summer tourist buyers.

The fall and winter of 1932 were dismal. My father had made the acquaintance of two elderly ladies who belonged to the New York Social Register. Mrs. Hitchcock and Mrs. Walker resided in their own brownstone house at 23 East 73rd Street. The plan he devised involved the ladies' inviting in their friends for tea, and later interesting such guests in our wares, shown in two rooms on the second floor. There he could display some middle-class American antiques he'd brought down from Boston.

Not much evolved in the way of sales. Mrs. Walker's friends seemed far more interested in her pattern glass, in which she was an expert. The project shortly ended.

In the summer of 1933, with President Franklin Roosevelt in the White House, things began to pick up a bit. Using money borrowed from Leon David, my father was again able to purchase a collection, this one from the estate of a Mr. Davidson, in New London, Connecticut.

Mr. Davidson had left behind a vast, miscellaneous collection, numbering close to ten thousand lots of bric-a-brac, china, prints, antique fixtures, and furniture. All of this huge assortment was housed in a large Victorian mansion from which he had carried on his business. The interior of this vast place was filthy, littered in the same Collyer brothers storybook fashion one is accustomed to hearing about after the senile owner has passed away, with money and legendary treasure supposedly stuffed at random in out-of-the-way places.

My father sensed that amid this vast haystack were some valuable needles, and he was correct, although his optimism, still operating full time, was not totally justified. We found about six quality pieces there. One in particular was a flat-top paneled secretary, bearing on its inner door the label of its maker, the great Job Townsend, of Newport, Rhode Island. While the secretary was of a simple design, it had simple elegance and a fine quality of craftsmanship. There may be certainly greater secretaries known, but the fact that this one bore its maker's label gave it considerable importance.

In the ensuing years, the Townsend-Goddard school of cabinet-makers has come into its own, and today the work of those two craftsmen commands the highest prices of any early American furniture. But in 1933, my father sold that Townsend secretary to the Rhode Island School of Design for the sum of $1,200.

It's also ironic to note that the license to *reproduce* such Rhode Island forms was lately granted to a quality furniture maker who now sells the copies for prices starting at $5,000. Commercially manufactured reproductions now bring higher prices than the price my father was forced to sell an original for, in those bleak days!

The task of cleaning every item in Mr. Davidson's vast collection, dusting, labeling, and numbering, fell to Ben David and myself. A local auctioneer named Perkins was hired, and a huge tent was set up in a vacant New London lot. The ensuing auctions lasted nearly six weeks. They were a waste of time and effort. Later I found out that Mr. Perkins and his sons bought many of the items we'd offered for sale, and lived off that inventory for many years to come, long after the economic recovery induced by F.D.R.'s administration had begun to take effect. Such was my first lesson in merchandising antiques. The depressingly low prices we achieved under that canvas tent taught me that unless there was substantial demand, there was little hope of getting good prices from an uninterested public. To sell under pressure is the worst possible circumstance. When you're anxious to sell, people always seem to back away, wondering what is wrong with merchandise brought to them by solicitation. Conversely, buyers instantly snap into action once they're convinced that a lot of people besides themselves are interested.

Up in New London, we had an overabundance of goods, and a very limited local audience. All of which added up to a lot of work for Ben David and me, and very small profit for our fathers.

I prayed that someday I would be in a commanding position, where I had more customers than antiques.

Mr. David and my father then decided they would go into partnership in New York. My father had tried the city before, in the 383 Madison Avenue shop which specialized in brass hardware, and in a small way on East 57th Street, before the crash. But now he and Mr. David decided to try again. Mr. David, with his considerable cash and good credit, and my father, with his wonderful reputation, good contacts, and knowledge of the field, seemed to add up to a fine team.

On one of his trips to New York, my father had bumped into Douglas Robinson, a cousin of Theodore Roosevelt; he owned a four-story building at 422 Madison, between 48th and 49th streets. He had ample space for rent; the building was empty, and he was delighted to make a deal to bring in my father. In the space we rented from Mr. Robinson there was an elevator which served the upper floors, a platformed show window looking out on Madison Avenue, and what seemed to me to be an incredible vastness of empty floor space, to be filled with whatever stock we could locate.

A corporation was formed, with Ben David and myself as sole stockholders, and with Leon David's capital and my father's contacts. Ben and I were set up to go into business. For our initial stock, we had some of Mr. David's general run of antiques, and my father provided a few pieces he had left from the basement of 89 Charles Street, in Boston. Our plan was to solicit consignments from owners looking to sell, to run exhibits, and, in cooperation with a few cabinetmakers who had migrated down from Boston, to deal in reproductions, made to order.

No sooner had we gone into business than the banks were closed down under the emergency orders of President Roosevelt, who had cautioned us at his inaugural in March that the only thing we had to fear was fear itself.

As it turned out, our real fear was the lack of ready cash.

We managed to weather that immediate crisis, and were launched in business, as Israel Sack, Inc. There wasn't much in tangible assets behind that name; the truth is, my father was broke.

In the face of these hardest of times, he somehow remained resourceful and optimistic. A latter-day Wilkins Micawber, he never lost faith in the future. My mother had taken my younger sister down to Florida, where the doctors hoped the climate would help the asthma she had begun to suffer from; whatever my father could earn, and it was not much, came from various jobs he picked up liquidating estates around the country. That meant going to where the goods were, appraising them, putting them up for sale, and taking a commission for the owners or the heirs. It also meant that his life became nomadic. There was no more permanent home in Roxbury, and no longer a Charles Street store. But he kept on going, and somehow managed to stay afloat.

In New York, for salary, I was paid thirty-five dollars, and had my living quarters above the store. Our overhead was truly minuscule. Our rent was set at ten percent of any sales we might make, with no minimum guarantee. In our first year of business, we paid our landlord $3,300.

Our "staff" was certainly an interesting cast of characters. Leon David was a conservative and shrewd businessman who played his cards close to the chest. His interest in antique furniture was peripheral, but when it came to hooked rugs, he had an uncanny trading instinct and a real expertise. His son Ben, my close friend, was a devoted student of American antiques, had a flair for architecture and history, and being a tall and handsome Yale graduate, belonged in some luxurious showroom, dealing in sophisticated pieces — at least he gave off that aura. We also had with us Mrs. Catherine Howe, a tall and stately middle-aged lady, very shrewd, with a good knowledge of American country furniture. Before she joined us as a "sales hostess," she had been a collector and a part-time dealer in Manchester, New Hampshire.

People began to come in, and we took a few orders for reproductions, which turned out to be quite unprofitable, since the pieces we contracted to deliver were executed in such a high-quality fashion by the cabinet shops we used that their time costs and charges were usually underestimated.

One day, a very nice lady came in. Her name was Imogene Anderson, and she had a superb collection of dolls she wished to sell. We agreed to take it on consignment, to print a catalogue which she was to write, and to get as much publicity for a sale of her dolls as we could. We called the newspapers, held an opening party, entertained many visitors who enjoyed our refreshments, but as for sales, we did little, if any.

Of course, doll collecting was later to become a very active and lucrative field, and judging by the quality of Mrs. Anderson's dolls, the foresighted thing would have been for Leon David to buy her collection and hold it, to sell it later for large profits. But none of us was that prescient, and I learned another lesson: the big money made in any form of art or antiques collecting is usually taken in by those who buy when the items in question are unpopular, and hold on to them for a later surge in popularity.

One of the teachers who taught me this particular lesson — i.e., *buy when nobody else is buying* — was Joe Kindig, a tough-minded dealer from York, Pennsylvania. Joe was legendary throughout the business for his stock, which was always of high quality, and his prices, which more than matched the goods he sold. Joe was a bluff, hearty type, whose father had been a mule trader, and according to the story, had left $400,000 to Joe and the same sum to Joe's bachelor brother, John. When John died, he left his money to Joe. Joe thus had ample capital to invest in those grim years when few dealers had any cash at all. Already a dealer in guns and antique firearms, he began to make the Boston and New York rounds, or wherever he could find a dealer who needed to sell. Thus Joe bought many wonderful bargains, and was never in any hurry to dispose of them. In fact, his strategy was to place such high prices on his pieces that they remained out of reach to the buyer; Joe was convinced that time would always be on his side.

His vast inventory of fine antiques was housed in his store, and in a barnlike structure in York, with dirt floors.

Some years later, when Chamberlain had made his Munich Pact with Hitler in 1938, I had occasion to receive a lesson in psychology from Joe.

Everyone in his right mind knew that eventually there was going to be war in Europe. The U.S. government already had an M-Day plan — M being the abbreviation for Mobilization — by which it was claimed any future war could breed no future millionaires. By law, nobody was going to profit from the blood of American boys.

One day after that Munich Pact, Joe dropped by to find me in a very depressed state of mind. "Since this pact, I'm very despondent," I told him. "I just don't have the taste or strength to go through the war, or another depression."

Joe's philosophy was totally pragmatic. "Listen, Harold," he told me, "I don't buy the newspapers, I don't even listen to the radio. There's going to be a war, and regardless of what the government tells us, there will be millionaires made out of it. So I'm putting my money where my mouth is. I'm buying every good, genuine piece of early American furniture I can lay my hands on — and so should you."

He continued to do so, and Joe, with his inventory, thus became a multimillionaire. In years to come, after World War II, he grudgingly deigned to permit people to pay him ten times his cost for choice items, always provided they were polite to him. All through the hectic 1960s, while prices rose around him, Joe was still sitting tight on his huge inventory. People who went to York soon learned to say "I'll take it!" quickly when Joe mentioned his astronomic price, *if* he happened to feel like selling, because they'd discovered he might just as readily change his mind and take the item off the market. Or he might boost the price capriciously while the customer stood on his dirt floor, thinking it over.

During those dark gray years, two other New York dealers were amassing stock. Messrs. Ginsburg and Levy were well entrenched in their new building at 68th and Madison. They had purchased those premises during the late 1920s for a very reasonable price; at that time, being so far up Madison was to be on the outskirts of the action.

Mr. Ginsburg was the buyer for the firm, which had grown from a books and secondhand furniture outlet downtown to a major uptown dealership selling English furniture, porcelain, and a smattering of American antiques. Their prominence in American furniture did not become evident until their shrewd purchases in the depressed 1930s provided them with a comprehensive stock. I should add that a good deal of what they accumulated came from my father's sales, those dismal affairs at which he was forced to liquidate his Boston stock.

While Mr. Ginsburg picked up the bargains, Mr. Levy saw to it that the pieces were properly conditioned in their ample cabinet shops. When this was done, the pieces were brought into the store, where Mr. Levy made certain they were properly marked up, and at such prices each and every piece would thereafter remain, until Mr. or Mrs. Right Customer came along, no matter how much time it took.

Their trade speciality, however, was to the more modest home buyer, or to interior decorators, and since both men maintained such a tight ship, they could not be bullied by any collector who was accustomed to having his way with hungry dealers seeking to recoup their investments in stock.

While my father had always been a specialist, Messrs. Ginsburg and Levy were general merchants who dealt in a much wider variety. I admired their financial stability. In those uncertain early 1930s, they were unique, indeed. Although I didn't want to acquire their patterns of doing business, my dream was to top them, at all costs.

It would take me quite some time to do so.

Other prominent dealers of that period were Charles Woolsey Lyon, who with his two sons, Charles and Irving, kept a beautiful shop on 57th Street. They were wonderful promoters, good showmen, and had superb taste in American furniture. I remember walking into their shop one day and while talking to Mr. Lyon, senior, I spotted a glass paperweight with the then-incredible price of fifteen hundred dollars. I was staggered by that figure, but Mr. Lyon gave me another pointer which I've never forgotten. "Remember," he said, "to the person who has the wealth, that fifteen hundred dollars for the paperweight is no more hardship on his pocketbook than it is for you to buy a pack of cigarettes."

The one flaw in the Lyons' operation was that they took the liberty of embellishing, or changing some of their pieces to a point which they believed the items should have been originally. When Henry Ford had his antiques authenticated by a couple of experts, many of the Lyons' pieces did not check out, and they were returned, en masse, by an infuriated Mr. Ford.

The refunds they had to pay Ford forced the company into dire financial condition. I believe it was reorganized in bankruptcy under Chapter Eleven, an advantage which my father, who was unfortunately ill-advised, would never enjoy. In order to cancel leases and to pay off his debts, my father paid out large sums of his precious capital, leaving himself, and ultimately our new firm, Israel Sack, Inc., in a very precarious position.

Precarious was an understatement. In our Madison Avenue premises, cash flow continued to elude us.

Things were bleak. All over the city, unemployed men shivered on street corners behind piles of red apples they hopefully offered to passersby for a nickel apiece. Economically, the country had hit rock bottom — we hoped it was rock bottom — and we all prayed for our new leader, F.D.R., to lead us out of this darkness. But if there was a light at the end of this long tunnel, so far it hadn't flickered into view.

In a very short time, Mr. David and his son Ben became discouraged at the lack of trade, and they decided to pull out of Israel Sack, Inc. and to go their separate ways.

Our firm was now operating with precious little stock. What we did have did not belong to us, but had been mostly consigned for sale by other owners. A New Jersey banker who had been a collector of ironwork consigned his collection to us, as did a Mr. Kerfoot, who had written extensively on and collected antique American pewter. We were desperately trying to fill up that large selling space. Things were just as bad for our landlord, Mr. Robinson. He offered to sell us his entire building for seventy-five thousand dollars. No use. He might as well have asked us for four million — which is what those premises later brought.

My younger brother, Albert, who'd graduated from Andover, completed his first year at the University of Pennsylvania. Although his grades were high, he was discouraged with academic life, and he quit school. In 1934, he moved into the business with me, living upstairs in our quarters, and went on our payroll at a munificent twenty dollars a week. Since he had no inclination to run errands or to engage in the financial or administrative end of the business — what there was of it — he began to rummage in antique shops and to go to auctions, looking to pick up items for our stock. There was little, if any, money in customers' hands to purchase anything, and I had to make Albert's life miserable by turning down items he'd uncovered, usually general merchandise, which did us little good.

But Albert persevered, and kept on digging. Every so often he'd come up with a real find. We'd argue over whether it was feasible to acquire it. Usually it wasn't. It was all part of his early education. To this day he continues as our firm's buyer, an acknowledged expert.

My father, who only a few short years before had been so affluent and successful, was reduced to struggling for each day's survival. Traveling constantly, looking for pieces on consignment from cash-hungry collectors, or for an occasional estate he could settle for the executors, he never dwelt on the past. This day's struggle was more important than yesterday's triumphs. Ever the optimist, he continued to try his best, to sell the best. All he needed was buyers.

On one particularly grim day in the early 1930s began my relationship with the Chippendale mahogany Salem bureau — certainly one of the greatest masterpieces of its kind I've ever had the privilege of handling.

Into our quiet — far too quiet — establishment stamped a stooped old man who walked with a limp and supported himself with a cane. He wore a perpetually sour expression on his face. He was Mr. Willoughby Farr, an antiques dealer from New Jersey who had a clientele of a few important collectors. He resembled one of Charles Dickens's characters, and he had a reputation for parsimony and meanness which fitted perfectly with the sharp features of that lined face. But nobody ever questioned Willoughby Farr's appreciation and taste for the finest. In our trade, that was well known.

He had, unfortunately, not come to buy. "I have a choice piece to sell," he told me. "I bought it from your father in 1928, for sixty-five hundred dollars."

How much did he want for this piece?

"Exactly what I paid for it," he said, promptly, "sixty-five hundred dollars. It's worth every penny of it."

I didn't know Mr. Farr, but I certainly knew about the market for antiques. It seemed to me that he was asking, in essence, for his money back. Since he was a dealer, and since my father was not sharing in Mr. Farr's profits or losses (and his profits had to be considerably more at that time than my father's, of that I was certain), I thought it was presumptuous of him in these terrible times to demand sixty-five hundred dollars for a piece he had purchased at the height of the 1920s' inflation.

I proceeded to tell him so.

He became so annoyed at me that, for a moment, I thought he was going to strike me with his cane.

"This is a magnificent piece," he snapped. "Worth every penny of what I'm asking!"

To calm him down, and to make amends, I told him we could take it on consignment, and try to sell it for him at sixty-five hundred. "But you have to understand, Mr. Farr, I can't promise you anything. Things being what they are . . ."

"It's a beautiful chest!" he insisted. "Someone will buy it."

His optimism wasn't exactly contagious.

But several days later, a pair of moving men lugged in his chest, and when they put it down on the showroom floor, I stared at it, and I realized Willoughby Farr had been right. It was a magnificent piece. Certainly one of the most superb pieces I have ever seen.

That particular Chippendale mahogany bureau from Salem had gone a long way back with the Sacks. To document its travels since our early days, I checked its history. My father had purchased it in 1911, for a mere $150. He had sold it shortly afterward to Mr. Mollenhauer, the conductor of the Boston Handel and Haydn Society, for $350. The records showed my father had repurchased it some years later for $750, and then sold it to a Mrs. Waters for $1,000. By the 1920s, such fine antiques had become so collectible that Mrs. Waters had been persuaded by my father to take a handsome profit, and to sell the chest back to him at the very peak of the inflation for the handsome figure of $5,000. Then, in 1928, it had come to its present owner, Mr. Farr, for $6,500.

Mr. Farr's passion for the finest was obviously genuine, for he had kept this great Chippendale bureau in his private collection all this time. But now times were hard, even for him, and here was the chest, back in our hands, and again we were in charge of selling it.

But to whom?

At about the same time, a very nice elderly lady walked in and told me she was from New Jersey, and that she was a descendant of John Alden. "I'm the owner of a New England blockfront lowboy," she told me, "and I'd be interested in selling."

Could she tell me what it looked like? She promptly produced a

Chippendale serpentine carved chest of drawers, Salem, Massachusetts, 1783. This chest from the Cluett collection changed hands at least seven times since being acquired by Israel Sack in 1911. Originally thought to have been made by Cogswell of Boston, because of the related knee carving, the discovery of a signature on the bottom inscribed *T. N. 1783* (standing for Thomas Needham) has been accepted as a definite attribution. Needham worked in Salem and there are records that the Derby family ordered pieces from him in 1783.

snapshot of a magnificent blockfront lowboy similar to the one my father had sold to Mr. Henry du Pont in the late 1920s for $7,500. What price did she want for it? Her figure was far more realistic to the times. "Thirty-five hundred dollars seems fair to me," she said.

It was an impressive figure. But then, a tenth of that sum was impressive in those gloomy days.

I realized her piece was a jewel, and I told her we would be happy to take it and sell it. On consignment, of course.

She agreed. When her lowboy appeared, we put it out on the showroom floor, together with Mr. Farr's chest. What an ironic situation! We had two masterpieces, with not a nickel invested, and both priced extraordinarily high — at a time when customers were rarer than the furniture we had for sale.

I didn't dare to mark them up to earn our firm a profit, but I kept them there, on display, hoping and wondering when — or if — they'd ever sell.

Then it happened. A few weeks later, a middle-aged well-dressed gentleman of obvious importance walked in. He introduced himself as Mr. George Cluett. Immediately, I got the shakes. Mr. Cluett was a legend to me; I knew of his superb collection, and here he stood, in person, one of the prime antique collectors of the 1920s, a true giant in the field.

With his practiced eye, he spotted the chest and the lowboy and asked, "What are you asking for these?"

In retrospect, I wonder how he had decided to deal with me, a youth just out of college, rather than wait for my father to appear. But I must have seemed young and determined enough for him. I was. Times were very tough; I'd been cast into troubled waters, and I was trying single-handedly to keep a very insecure Israel Sack, Inc. on an even keel.

I stammered a bit. Then I figured the best thing to do was to tell the truth and place myself at Mr. Cluett's mercy. I explained the history of Mr. Farr's bureau, and that its price was $6,500, and that the lowboy had come down from the Alden family, and its price was $3,500.

He nodded, and then he said, "Well, since your cost is ten thousand dollars, why don't you accept that figure, and get your commission from the owners?"

Finally! A customer — and not for one, but for both at once! Remarkable — but then I tried not to allow myself to be carried away. I wasn't sure how to answer Mr. Cluett, but I did have sense enough to counter his proposal by suggesting that he agree to protect me. That should no commission be forthcoming on the sellers' end, I'd expect one to come from him. How much? One thousand dollars seemed fair to me.

He thought it over and then he agreed. We had a deal. He ordered me to have both pieces sent to his home in Williamstown, Massachusetts. "Prepare a bill, and I'll pay you after I've received the two pieces," he instructed. We shook hands, and he left.

I was ecstatic. I wasn't sure how much our commission would finally be, but it was such a huge sale to have accomplished that the very act itself was exhilarating.

*   *   *

My father had an old saying, which he often repeated, when he'd made some sale, and then in retrospect, had been chided, either by a friend or a competitor, that he could have gotten a higher price. "Sell and repent!" He'd sigh. "Sell and repent!"

In this particular case, although I didn't yet know it, my father's truism certainly applied.

I called Mr. Brown, of Brown's Warehouse, the expert packers to the antiques trade, and soon off went those pieces to Mr. Cluett's home in Williamstown. I was so excited, I hadn't even thought to ask for crating costs from Mr. Cluett. In my youthful innocence, I was completely certain all would go well.

In the meantime, Mr. Farr had been by several times, stamping in on his cane to check on the progress I'd made selling his Chippendale bureau. When he arrived the following week, he spotted its absence. "I've just sold it to Mr. Cluett, and would hope you'd at least pay me a commission for this deal," I said. He nodded vaguely, and left.

As for Mrs. Alden's lowboy, I felt I couldn't ask her for a commission since we had agreed on a net price, and it was up to me to turn a profit.

A few days later, Mr. Cluett called.

"Mr. Sack," he announced, "I have some very sad news."

My heart raced. I was certain he was canceling the deal, and I could already picture Willoughby Farr's rage.

No, it was worse than that. "The pieces arrived safely," he continued, "but one of the carved legs on the bureau was missing, leaving only three remaining."

A missing leg from a Chippendale masterpiece? Irreplaceable, after two centuries. This was worse than a cancellation!

I don't know how I survived. "You'd better call the packers, young man," suggested Mr. Cluett, ominously.

Minutes later, I did. Mr. Brown assured me there were four legs when he'd packed the bureau, but he urged me to call Mr. Cluett right back, as there was a strong possibility that the missing leg had worked loose and was still in its paper wrappings.

Still trembling, I got Mr. Cluett on the line, and he promised, somewhat dubiously, to check with the gatehouse of his estate and find out if that had happened. "I'll call you back," he promised.

I will never forget the tension of waiting for his return call.

I will also never forget what he said when the phone rang. "I've found it," he announced. "It was in the wrappings. Now I'll have to charge you seventy-five dollars for having it glued back by a competent cabinetmaker."

I was so overjoyed that I agreed. It wasn't until later that I began to consider going up to Williamstown and spitting in Mr. Cluett's eye for treating me with such arrant high-handedness.

But there was more anguish awaiting me.

His check arrived. $9,925. He'd deducted the $75! And I had to pay Mr. Brown for the crate.

I sent full payment to Mrs. Alden, and when Mr. Farr came in, I handed him his $6,500. So far, I was behind over $75 on this enormous sale.

But I was going to recoup, in spades, as soon as Mr. Farr paid me a commission. Could I have it now?

Mr. Farr shook his head. Absolutely not. "Mr. Cluett's a very rich man," he snapped. "I'm sure *he'll* pay it."

With that, he stamped out.

I sent a letter to Mr. Cluett, reminding him of our agreement regarding the commission, and respectfully suggesting he send me his check for the $1,000, in view of the fact that Mr. Farr had refused me, and he, Mr. Cluett, had agreed.

He sent me back an answer which said, in essence, that I was a young fellow who had indeed a lot to learn. Since it was common knowledge that no dealer collects a commission from both parties to a sale, and since Mr. Cluett had checked with Mr. Farr, and Mr. Farr had told him he had paid me a commission, he, Mr. Cluett, owed me nothing!

Of course, Mr. Farr had lied. But what could I do about it?

Right then and there, I could have broken down and wept, for having been so trusting and naïve.

It was a bitter lesson, again, to learn that so-called big men could stoop so low.

. . . *sell and repent.*

*   *   *

But it wasn't to be the end of my experiences with that beautiful Chippendale bureau. Despite its early unpleasantness, the story would come full circle with a traditional happy ending.

But not for almost thirty years.

In the early 1960s I received a call from Mr. Cluett's daughter, who now lived in Connecticut. Her father had long since passed away, and divided the bulk of his fine collection between his two daughters. Since I was familiar with so much of Mr. Cluett's collection, would I come up to Connecticut and appraise what she had inherited?

I went up and examined everything in her house. There they were again, that Alden blockfront, and that marvelous Massachusetts Chippendale bureau. Many times during the intervening years, I had wondered if I'd ever see them again. Now, here they were, in all their elegance.

For a fee, I appraised that bureau, for which Mr. Cluett had paid $6,500, for a present value of $50,000.

Then I went through the rest of the family possessions, carefully making notes. During lunch, Mr. Cluett's son-in-law asked me if I had finished the dining room. "What's your figure on the Sheraton side table in there?" he asked.

"I've omitted that table because I don't think it's absolutely right," I told him. That was a polite euphemism for my suspicion that it was not authentic.

"Show me why you're doubtful," he said.

I proceeded to show him certain points about the table that bothered me, including the artificial staining. "It's the kind of fake I might even be able to identify," I said. I mentioned a possible source from which Mr. Cluett might have obtained it. "Mind checking your list and finding out if I'm right?"

He checked the inventory, with its list of sources for each piece, and then he shook his head, astonished. I'd guessed correctly.

Then he confessed that Mr. Cluett had himself had doubts about that table. "I have to tell you we've had it stored in the attic," he confessed, "but when I knew you were coming, I brought it down so I could get an unbiased opinion.

If that table hadn't passed the test, at least I had.

Several years went by before I got another hurried call from Mr. Cluett's daughter. A reappraisal was needed; there had been a robbery in the neighborhood, and they felt, for insurance purposes, it would be prudent to place new values on their treasures.

Back I went to Connecticut, and since I had all my descriptions, the chore was simple. All I needed to do was to revise my prices — substantially upward.

But it was a pleasure to revisit that Chippendale bureau again.

While I was finishing my reappraisal, Mr. Cluett's son-in-law asked me if I'd done a Philadelphia Chippendale side chair in the living room. I had, and when I told him the price, he asked, "Would you be willing to purchase it?"

"Gladly," I told him. "But since you're willing to sell that chair, perhaps we could consider discussing another piece or two."

He thought that over, and then he nodded.

"Would you consider that Hepplewhite inlaid two-chair back settee in the den?" he asked.

Now we were off.

"No," I said. "I've always considered that piece to be of English origin, and you know that's not our stock in trade." I took a deep breath.

"How about chests?" I asked.

"Well," he replied, "I do have several chests of drawers, so I *might* consider selling."

He led me into the bedroom, where there stood two chests, one of which was the same Salem Massachusetts Chippendale my father had bought in 1911, and which I'd sold for Willoughby Farr.

My heart began to race.

He pointed to it, and now it was my turn to nod.

"Yes, I'd be interested," I told him.

He thought it over.

Then he said, "I don't know."

"Why not?" I asked.

"Well," he said, dubiously. "I'd need a replacement. Something that would hold my shirts."

"I have just the piece in my warehouse," I said quickly. We had a Hepplewhite bowfront chest that was large and genuine, but of no collectible importance.

I waited while he thought about that, and then he asked me the crucial question. "How much would you offer for the Chippendale side chair *and* the chest here?"

"Well," I said, "how about my giving you a check for both pieces, large enough to make a significant certificate of deposit to yield a considerable income?"

"How significant?" he asked.

We batted numbers back and forth for a few moments, and ended at one hundred thousand dollars.

"Agreed," he said. "On one condition. I must get my wife's approval, so I'll let you know by ten o'clock tomorrow morning."

I was so nervous about the possibility of regaining that magnificent Chippendale chest that I still can't imagine how I got back to New York in one piece.

When I told my brother Albert of the offer I'd made, he became as excited as I was. "No," he said, finally. "It can't be. Something is bound to jinx it."

"I don't think so," I told him. "There seems to be some sort of a higher force handling this."

But when the phone rang the next morning at ten, the son-in-law did not sound at all optimistic.

"We have a problem," he told me. My heart stopped.

Had Albert been right? The whole prospect of that chest being returned to us was too good to be true.

Dejected, I asked, "What's the problem?"

"My wife insists you furnish us with a replacement chair," he told me.

Once again, my heart began beating. "Why, I have just the chair in my warehouse!" I said. "It looks very much like yours, but it happens to be English."

"That will be fine," he said.

I heaved a great sigh. "All right," I said, and as much for Albert's benefit as for anything else, I repeated the terms. "I furnish you with a replacement chest and a chair, plus one hundred thousand dollars, and your chest and your side chair are ours?"

"Agreed," he said.

"I'll have a check and the truck at your house tomorrow," I told him. And I promptly hung up the phone, for fear I might say something untoward that could hex our deal.

I looked upward, and I thought I could see my father, smiling.

All those years of waiting, since Willoughby Farr had caused me such pain and anguish, since Mr. Cluett had hassled me over a supposed missing leg . . . they were finally over, and indeed the old expression — "everything comes to him who waits" — had been proved correct.

Where is the chest now?

I'm happy to say it now belongs to a knowledgeable Texas collector named Bill Kilroy. He was very happy to pay a record price at that time, and we were both proud to see it illustrated in the *In Praise of America* catalogue of the fiftieth anniversary of the famous 1929 Girl Scout Exhibition.

The Chippendale side chair that had also come from the Cluett collection? That went off to another perceptive collector, who was willing to pay $65,000 for it.

It had taken more than three decades for me to get what was coming to me, but it was worth waiting for. I'm only sorry old Willoughby Farr wasn't around to gnash his teeth and stamp his cane in frustration over his loss.

Sell and repent? Not this time.

SEVEN

Rock Bottom
(With My Friend C. K. Davis)

I SRAEL SACK, INC. struggled on through the 1930s.

We managed to pay our utility bills, and so there was heat and the electricity stayed on at 422 Madison. Somehow or other, we kept our fledgling business open, but customers were sporadic, and our cash flow a mere trickle. Between what we sold in the shop — usually on consignment for customers — and what my father occasionally brought in from his endless travels, we had enough cash, but barely enough, to keep us all solvent.

And then we came dangerously close to complete disaster.

One day Mrs. Francis Garvan, the wife of the famous collector, walked in and introduced herself. When she proceeded to buy several pieces from us for $3,700, I was very excited. I promptly had them delivered and sent her an invoice.

No money was forthcoming.

Since we were so desperate for cash, I telephoned her, but was unable to reach her. It took several more calls to get her to talk to me, and when I asked her when we could expect payment, her reply stunned me.

"I have no intention of paying this bill, Mr. Sack," she said. "Further, you have a nerve asking me for money!"

Why was that?

According to Mrs. Garvan, my father owed her a considerable amount of money.

How could that possibly be?

"For things he bought from our auction sale," she snapped. "Which we've been owed since 1931!"

I was stunned.

I had heard at the time that my father had tried very hard at that auction sale to support the market. These were bad times, and he had tried to keep prices up by "buying in" several items from the Garvan collection. In the ensuing years of the Depression, he had sold them, and although I am certain he intended to pay everyone he owed at some later time, when the economy recovered, evidently he still owed Mrs. Garvan.

And what was worse, that debt to her was only one item in the heap of obligations it seemed he'd incurred. Mrs. Garvan's complaint was the top of a very ominous iceberg.

It was indeed a dire situation. Especially since my father had for all these months never opened up to reveal his problems. If there had been anything negative or pessimistic in his life, he'd stubbornly kept it to himself.

When I tried to discuss his debts with him, he shrugged and walked away.

What could we do about Mrs. Garvan?

Going into bankruptcy and resorting to the relief of the courts, as so many others were doing in those dreadful times, was foreign to my father's thinking. In his own mind, he was certain he would square everything with all his creditors. He knew he owed debts, he acknowledged them, and he had every intention of paying. And since he had always been generous to other unfortunates in trouble, he deemed it only reasonable that he should now be treated in the same fashion. Had he not behaved in good faith, supporting his good customers the Garvans at their sale, by bidding up the prices? So now, for him it was time for them to show him good faith. And somehow, it would all work out.

Alas, it did not.

I began to realize my father's financial condition was abysmal, and that his silence was far from golden. The most frustrating part of it, over which I began to lose considerable sleep, was that I could not know from which direction the next hammer blow would fall.

It didn't take me long to find out.

One day my father sold a fine bandbox New York Sheraton table to Joe Kindig in Pennsylvania, for two hundred and fifty dollars. Proudly, he flashed Joe's check, and it promptly went into the bank.

At the same time, I'd reported to my father that he'd been getting telephone calls from Mrs. Louis Guerineau Myers, the widow of that famous collector who'd been so instrumental in arranging the Girl Scout Exhibition of 1929. But for some reason, again unexplained, he had not returned her calls.

While he was off on one of his many trips, Mrs. Myers called again, and this time she was quite abrupt. "Tell your father I want my bandbox Sheraton table back, as well as an accounting for all the other pieces which were consigned to him!" she snapped, and hung up.

I went into total shock. The table was hers? What other pieces?

When my father returned, I asked him about it. Was Mrs. Myers right? *Had* that been her table he'd sold to Joe?

"Yes, of course," he admitted. "But why are you so upset? If she wants it back, all you have to do is call Joe and buy it from him."

I kept on asking him for particulars, and he admitted that Mr. Myers had in fact consigned many pieces to my father during the past few years, at his 89 Charles Street shop. When we opened Israel Sack, Inc., in Manhattan, my father had sent them down, and they'd become part of our stock here.

But where are they now?

My father promised faithfully to try to itemize everything.

Frantically, I called Joe Kindig, hoping that he hadn't yet sold Mrs. Myers's table. No he had not, and if I wanted it back, I should bring down a check.

"Two hundred fifty dollars?" I asked.

"Oh, no," said Joe, pleasantly. "Nine hundred dollars."

I pleaded with him, but with no success at all. When it came to business, Joe Kindig was tough. After the deal had been transacted, he could be jovial and charming, but over commerce, his motto was simple à la Herbert Lawton — *ask no mercy, give no mercy.*

I don't know where I dug up the money, but ten days or so later I went down to him with it, retrieved the table, and then called Mrs. Myers.

"I have your table," I told her, "and we will be glad to return it to you."

"Along with the rest of the pieces we consigned to you," she told me.

I protested. It wasn't quite that easy. I needed time. Mrs. Myers became upset. "From now on, I'll only communicate with you through my lawyers!" she warned me, and hung up.

Now I was really confused. When my father came into the showroom, I took him aside and insisted we must confront this situation. Where were Mrs. Myers's pieces?

He shrugged. "Sold," he said.

To whom? He wasn't sure.

And for what prices?

He either couldn't, or wouldn't, discuss it.

I kept after him, but it was no use. If he hadn't kept books, if his memory was faulty — if items were missing and he couldn't remember what was and what wasn't our property or belonged to customers, so be it. The past several years, he had been too busy — scrambling to provide for my mother and my sister and to stay in business. "Who's had time to keep specific records?" he demanded, and walked away.

Perhaps he thought by ignoring this crisis it would simply vanish from sight. I knew better; I'd heard the anger in Mrs. Myers's voice, and with dread, I awaited the next development.

A few days later, I received a letter from a very prominent New York law firm, which was signed by a Mr. Gardner, representing Mrs. Myers. Attached to the letter was an inventory of the Myerses' property, consigned years before to my father, itemized, and with estimated prices.

The estimates were ironic, in view of the currently depressed prices. That bandbox table, for example, which I'd retrieved from

Joe Kindig for his outrageous price — it actually had been consigned to my father in the pre-crash era for the same nine hundred dollars! But I wasn't in the mood to enjoy the irony. Firmly, specifically, Mr. Gardner was demanding immediate return of everything on his inventory list, plus an accounting of sums earned.

Nobody had to explain to me that we were in very big trouble.

My firm, Israel Sack, Inc., organized in 1933, was a corporation, and after the Davids, father and son, had withdrawn, I was left the sole stockholder. Since we had no legal liability for my father's business dealings in the past, theoretically, any claimant such as Mrs. Myers — or Mrs. Garvan — would have to collect damages from my father. And should they decide to take legal action, Mrs. Myers's lawyers could certainly hit, not me, but my father, with a big judgment claim, possibly even a criminal one.

Obviously, despite my father's perennial optimism, this storm was not about to blow away. I was petrified.

Certainly I was not liable, legally. Emotionally, however, I could not separate myself from my father. There he went, each day, silently trudging off down the city streets, looking for some sort of business, anything that would enable him to support his family, never giving up. All right, so there was no malice intended, it had been sheer desperation, fine — but what sort of legal defense would that provide him? In the eyes of the law he was certainly liable, and what judge would rule that Israel Sack had not behaved with criminal intent?

I decided to meet this crisis head on. I called up Mr. Gardner. At the end of the phone I heard a pleasant voice, a man most appreciative of my call, who seemed eager to meet me. We made a date.

I arrived downtown in his office doing my best not to show my nervousness. Mr. Gardner turned out to be tall, thin, and quite young, obviously from one of the Ivy League schools.

I took a deep breath. "Mr. Gardner," I told him, "I'll put my cards on the table. My father is an honest man. He did sell Mrs. Myers's pieces, but I'm sure he expected to recover and to pay her for them. He's a victim of the times. He's financially demoralized. But he's done more for the field of American antiques than any man alive.

He helped the Myers collection, he helped the Garvan collection, he made the market, he's made a lot of money for all these people along the way, even those who are at his throat right now. Today, he's in a very bad position; as far as being able to pay the money, he's helpless, but what he did was not out of malice, or criminal intent. It was only his desperation — and these rotten times."

Mr. Gardner nodded, and continued to listen to my plea.

I plunged on. "Israel Sack, Inc. is a corporation," I said, "so I have no legal liability in this situation with Mrs. Myers, but I am my father's son, and I do feel I have to help him, even if it involves personal sacrifice on my part. So, if you could persuade Mrs. Myers to sell *me* the collection — including the pieces which have already been sold — then the corporation will buy it, and pay her over a three-year period. And I will accept the corporate responsibility for paying her."

Mr. Gardner stared at me for a long moment. Finally, he said, "Mr. Sack, let me see what I can do."

I went back to the shop and waited. With such a Damoclean sword hanging over our heads, it wasn't easy.

Mr. Gardner took my proposal to Mrs. Myers and served as my advocate. At first, she wouldn't agree, but finally he persuaded her to do so. Mr. Gardner drew up a series of notes, which were dated for the next thirty-six months, and I signed them. We all understood I was buying a nonexistent collection; everything had already been sold. But I signed those notes promptly, and gratefully, because by so doing, I had moved Mrs. Myers's property out of the consignment status, and thus saved my father from any criminal prosecution.

When we finished the signing, Mr. Gardner shook my hand and said, "Mr. Sack, I'd like to tell your father what a fine son he has. He doesn't know how lucky he is."

I'm certain my father did.

I brought back the signed agreement to our shop. My father was sitting in the office, waiting to go out on another estate liquidation, which would hopefully produce some fees. I showed him the agreement. He nodded.

He never commented on what had happened. He didn't have to. I understood how he felt. Circumstances had battered him unmercifully, and it had been a long ways down from his halcyon days in the 1920s, on Charles Street.

Now, all I had to do was to pay off those notes.

I was in the antiques business, and all I had as inventory was the name, Israel Sack, Inc., the goodwill, and of course, those debts.

All around us there were conflicting reports in the trade about this new shop we operated. Some dealers were openly remarking that we couldn't last another year.

They would never know how close we came to proving their ominous predictions correct.

My hardworking younger brother Albert, who continued doggedly canvassing dealers, attending country auctions, and taking phone calls from owners of pieces who wished only to sell and who could never be persuaded to buy, had me to contend with as well. Whenever something good showed up, and he brought me the news of our opportunity, I had to turn him down.

How could we buy? We had no cash.

I went to several banks for credit. If loans were available, they certainly would not be for antiques.

Dejectedly, I left one more bank, after having been turned down for the umpteenth time. I trudged down Madison Avenue, when I heard a voice calling my name. It was Dick Stern, a classmate and fraternity brother from Dartmouth, whom I hadn't seen in several years. We went off and had coffee.

He had moved to New York and was selling menswear and enjoying himself. How was I doing?

I told him my lugubrious story, the lawyers, the lack of cash flow, and the procession of reluctant bankers.

How much did I need?

I plucked a number out of the air. "I could use five thousand dollars," I said. The truth was, I could have used anything that was cash.

"Well, if that's your only problem," said Dick, "I'll be glad to lend it to you!"

I couldn't believe what he was telling me. But he assured me that he was serious. His father had recently died and left him a good inheritance. In fact, for the next year, he planned to go around the world, using some of the money he'd been left. Since he had such confidence in me, it would be to his advantage to have some of his assets at work. If I made anything of a profit with his five thousand dollars investment, then it would be up to me to determine what would be his fair share. And if I lost his investment, then that would be the gamble he was willing to take.

Did Dick want notes? Absolutely not. "This will be on a friendly basis, between the two of us," he insisted. "Let me have the five thousand sent up to you this afternoon. Agreed?"

We shook hands. In a complete daze, I left him and walked back to the store.

Reality intruded. While I'd been away, there had been no customers. Not even any phone calls.

I settled back to my customary depression.

But it ended after lunch, when Dick's check arrived, brought up by a messenger.

And in time for me to deposit it in the bank, where our account had almost reached bottom.

In a matter of hours, we'd gone from near-insolvency to being back in the antiques business — at least for a while.

Fred Fuessnich, a former wealthy collector who'd gone broke during the crash and decided to try his luck as a dealer, drove up to our Madison Avenue shop in a battered old station wagon. Fred had been having just as tough a time of it as we had, but he excitedly called me downstairs to see what he had brought in the back of his wagon.

There stood a magnificent Connecticut block and shell cherrywood desk, large and, as it turned out, remarkably heavy. Together, we tugged and heaved at it until we had it standing out on the sidewalk.

"Harold," he announced, after he'd regained his breath, "I begged, borrowed, and stole until I raised enough cash to buy this masterpiece from Mrs. Paige, up in Connecticut. I couldn't think of anyone else except you or your father to bring it to. Are you interested?"

"Yes, but how much do you want for it?" I asked.

"Give me sixteen hundred and fifty dollars, and I'll kiss you," sighed Fred.

"Sold," I told him. We'd acquired our first item. How could I resist it? It was choice — and also, it was far too heavy a piece to reload into Fred's ancient car. "Come on upstairs and I'll write you a check," I told him.

He was astonished. "Just like that?"

"Absolutely," I assured him.

The timing had been perfect, for both of us.

With some outside assistance, we got that beautiful Connecticut desk up the stairs and into the showroom.

At about the same time, Mr. Benjamin Flayderman, my father's old rival — and my early customer for Realsilk hosiery — had finally thrown in the sponge. He'd also moved to New York, and he too had found the market nonexistent. He had moved to Third Avenue and decided to auction off his inventory.

Albert returned from the viewing with a report that he'd spotted several fine items, especially a shell-carved corner cupboard, which had once belonged to my father.

I told Albert I didn't think we should invest the rest of our precious capital on a Flayderman auction, especially not after what had happened to my father when he'd bought out the Flaydermans, a few short years back.

On the day of the sale it was raining, but Albert decided to go up to the auction anyway, and to sit in. Why not? We rarely had customers who needed two of us to wait on them — if we had customers at all. As he left, I told him to check in with me about noon, for that cupboard would go up for sale at about one o'clock.

"Why should I call?" asked Albert, sadly. "We aren't about to buy it, you told me so yourself."

"Just for checking," I told him.

At about eleven o'clock, a tall, well-dressed man came in. He wore an expensive cashmere coat and carried a briefcase — obviously someone of substance. He said he came from Bridgeport, Connecticut, and wanted to look at grandfather clocks. He'd purchased some pine and maple pieces in the various antiques shops along Route 7, in Connecticut, and he'd bought the two volumes of Wallace

Nutting's *Furniture Treasury* and studied them carefully. Since he'd found my father's name attached to so many of the illustrated items in Nutting's definitive reference work, and they'd appealed to him so much, he'd decided to pay us a personal visit.

I showed him around, explained the quality of the pieces we had on display, and told him our family philosophy of collecting only the very best; we seemed to hit it off at once. His name was Charles K. Davis, and he told me he was president of the Remington Arms Company, in Bridgeport, as well as a director of several other national companies.

The more we talked, the more I became aware he was perhaps more interested in making an impression on me than I was on him. I also began to see the advantages of having the name Sack included in Nutting's two-volume work, as well as having this prominent Madison Avenue location, in order to build our business back to its former status.

Mr. Davis began to buy. Fred Fuessnich's beautiful Connecticut block and shell desk went to him for $3,200, and he also purchased a serpentine bureau, a blockfront bureau, and a Martha Washington chair. Total, $6,800! Not a bad day.

And I also sensed I had made myself a friend.

At a little after noon, Albert called, checking in with me as agreed upon.

"That cupboard is coming up in half an hour," he said, sadly. "Such a beauty. Damn — I certainly wish we could bid on it."

"All right, go ahead," I told him firmly. "Buy it — at any price!"

Now it was Albert's turn to go into shock.

"Are you kidding me?" he demanded. "What's happened?"

"You wouldn't believe this," I said, "but some sort of angel has just descended on us, and bought sixty-eight hundred dollars' worth of our stock. So let's go — buy the cupboard!"

Albert was delighted. He hung up and ran back to the auction. Within an hour he was the successful bidder on my father's beautiful cupboard, back from Mr. Flayderman, and now ours again for six hundred dollars.

And we were finally on the move.

*   *   *

Over the years I have had many good relationships with customers. Somehow, those who love and appreciate the arts seem to have a warm and friendly feeling toward those of us who are experts in the field. Often, I've come to recognize that collectors tend to place us on a pedestal, and there are many times when people seem flattered to have me in their homes as a celebrity. So be it, but I've also learned to differentiate between such temporary relationships and true friendship.

With C. K. Davis, my relationship became, in short order, authentic. We developed a natural affinity for each other, and over the years shared many wonderful experiences.

For me, a young dealer just getting started in a business which my father had dominated for so long, C.K.'s trust was a wonderful asset. As so many major collectors had trusted my father's judgment, so did C.K. trust mine — implicitly. I did his entire collection of early American furniture for him, and it became one of the purest in the entire country.

We became so close that when my first son was born, we assumed that the K. in C.K.'s name stood for Kenneth, and we named our child in his honor. Later, to my dismay, I found out that the K. actually stood for Krum. I'm sure Kenneth, however, has never regretted my mistake.

C.K. had a lively interest in old pewter, so I introduced him to a young man who was then in the circulation department of the old *Herald-Tribune*. The young man was Charles Montgomery, and he was buying and selling pewter on the side. Charles had a real feel for metal, and went on to deal in antique silver. Years later, when C.K. was elected to the board of directors of Winterthur Museum, he was instrumental in endorsing Charles Montgomery's appointment there as chief curator.

C.K. was a strange mixture of connoisseur and successful businessman. He was a quick learner; his taste was excellent. And he was also a born production genius, as skilled in handling assembly lines and production workers as he was in picking out what was the best in one-of-a-kind early American. In years to come, I had ample proof, as did the rest of the country, of what a truly great production

C. K. Davis, president of Remington Arms.

executive C.K. was. During World War II, when the British forces
lost all their ammunition in the debacle at Dunkirk, he was called
upon, as head of Remington Arms, to try to fill the gap. He went to
work, organized an emergency program in his factories, and in
those of other arms manufacturers, and performed a small miracle
in small arms ammunition production. Within weeks, ships loaded
with precious tons of ammunition were convoyed across the Atlantic to the desperately beleaguered British. The eighty-eight thousand
assembled employees C.K. personally supervised resupplied
Churchill's troops in time to head off any potential Nazi invasion of
Britain.

Years after C.K. became well known in the field, chiefly through
an article which I wrote for *Antiques* magazine about his collection,
he was to become besieged by dealers and owners of furniture offering him all sorts of "treasures."

On one occasion, he called and said he'd been offered a collection
in Connecticut, and since he was a bit nervous about buying on his
own, he asked if I would accompany him.

We wound up in the Connecticut countryside, at a very attractive Colonial-type mansion. We were escorted inside by our host, and the moment I stepped in, I was on guard. The first piece I saw was a Queen Anne veneered highboy, which, at least to my eye, had been reveneered and had new legs. The further we explored, the more I was convinced everything in that house was doctored, and in some cases, miserably faked.

I let C.K. stroll about, and after we were somewhat out of earshot, I suggested we exit gracefully from this obviously salted gold-mine.

Which we promptly did.

Whether or not C.K. would have spotted those spurious pieces is a moot question. True, he had a good eye for line, form, and quality, but it's one thing to be an appreciative viewer in a safe shop, or at a museum collection, and something else entirely to be able to judge an antique piece cold turkey.

C.K. knew that the astute collector always brings along somebody who has done his homework. My father had a stricture which also pertains. "Remember, for every piece of fake antiques," he cautioned, "there's some buyer looking to pick up a bargain."

It was during those depressed mid-1930s that my father had become friendly with a collector named Mitchell Taradash, a man who, despite the difficult times, was making money as an appraiser for estates.

With my father's assistance, Taradash put together a very fine collection. The combination of my father's expertise, plus Taradash's ready cash, at a time when nobody else had money, proved very successful. Much of what he bought from my father was at rock-bottom prices, but the sales were more than welcome. In fact, they were vital, since he invariably paid us promptly, with checks that went directly into our depleted accounts.

There were days when I watched with dismay as some of our finest newly acquired pieces disappeared into Taradash's collection, at prices I knew were far below their worth. But many years after, in 1974, his widow would pay us back handsomely. By then, she and my brother Albert had become close friends, and despite the attempts of other dealers to secure prizes from the collection she'd inherited from her husband, Mrs. Taradash gave us first consideration. The pieces we regained, and later resold, brought huge prices.

In the Taradash collection were a matching Queen Anne curly walnut highboy and lowboy, with the signature of Benjamin Frothingham in chalk, as maker for Nathaniel Richards, and having the original brass hardware, stamped I. Gold.

They were truly a superb pair, examples of that Charlestown, Massachusetts, maker's finest work. They'd originally been acquired by my father for Mr. Taradash, in a sale of the Motley estate, for fifteen hundred dollars. As agent for Taradash, my father had received his ten-percent commission, one hundred fifty dollars. And in those times, he was happy to get it.

I was quite surprised one day in 1935 when Mr. Taradash came into the shop to inform me he didn't want this superb pair any longer. "I want to turn them into cash," he said.

How much did he want for them? We were, as usual, desperately short of ready capital. "You don't have to buy," he said. "I'll consign them for three thousand dollars the pair."

Which meant that whatever profit was forthcoming could be ours to keep.

When the highboy and lowboy arrived and took their place upstairs on our showroom floor, I stared at these two beauties, and the more I looked, the less I could understand why he'd wish to sell them. Since he had his own warehouse, I knew it could not be a space problem. Taradash had such a fine collection, and they properly belonged in it. So be it. Now it was my job to find them a home with someone who would truly appreciate them.

A week or so later, C. K. Davis walked in. Whenever he came to New York for one of his many board of directors meetings, he would leave the corporate world behind and head across town to our shop, where he could enjoy himself among antiques. Always jocular, he liked teasing me, often making me work hard for a sale. On this day he asked, "Well, Harold, what have you got that's choice for me today?"

"You're very lucky you came in," I told him. "Come upstairs and let me show you two of the most beautiful antique pieces you've ever seen."

That was a sweeping statement, and I could tell he was skeptical. He followed me upstairs, and when he'd examined the matching lowboy and highboy, he promptly became as impressed as I was. I told him in great detail about Benjamin Frothingham, and his place in American antiques history. And what was I asking for these beauties?

I told him $4,500 for the pair.

C.K. whistled. "That's a lot of money," he observed. "Do you realize I could go to General Motors and have them custom-craft me a Cadillac on special order, practically hand-made, for that same price?"

"You certainly could, C.K.," I agreed, "and not only you, but anybody with forty-five hundred dollars has the same privilege. But there's only one man in this country who's going to own this pair of masterpieces, one man who has the understanding and the good taste to appreciate and to love them."

"You're too good a salesman for me," he smiled. "You son of a gun — I'll take them."

When the sale was completed, C.K. brought up something he had never before asked me. "Harold, how much do you think these two pieces will be worth, say, twenty to thirty years from now?"

Who could answer such a question? In those survival-of-the-fittest days in our Madison Avenue shop, I was too busy worrying about next week's bills to project past the first of next month, let alone two decades hence. But I thought for a bit, and then I said, "Possibly twelve thousand dollars for the pair."

"As much as *that?*" he asked me.

"Well, then, let's be conservative," I said. "Safely — ten thousand dollars."

I simply could not stretch my mind beyond that sum.

How could I possibly have foreseen a future in which those two pieces would be sold, after my friend's death, to the Winterthur Museum, and that today, were they to appear on the open market, their sales price could conceivably be half a million, or more?

Another day, while I was up in Fairfield, doing business with C.K. in his home, I noticed a beautiful New York antique silver flattop tankard, and I asked him, "Where did you get this marvelous piece?"

Davis Queen Anne matching highboy and lowboy, Charleston, Massachusetts, circa 1750–1760. This curly walnut pair numbers among the Massachusetts greats. The Queen Anne highboy as a form in America achieved great excellence and was so successful that its life as a form extended from the 1740s through the 1790s, never having been supplanted in the Federal period after the Revolution. (Courtesy, The Henry Francis du Pont Winterthur Museum)

He told me he'd acquired it from Charles Montgomery, that same young man I'd sent him to for pewter, and who now, it seemed, had branched out into antique silver. I realized that C.K. might occasionally want to buy more silver, as well as pewter and furniture.

A fortuitous piece of information, considering what was to take place shortly thereafter.

The story of the John Burt candlesticks, with snuffer and tray, is indicative of the depths of gloom and pessimism which permeated our society in the mid-1930s.

I've come to believe we talk ourselves into many of our economic difficulties, and our attitudes many times are misread by our enemies. They do not understand that we Americans tend to accentuate our weaknesses, and likewise to gloss over our own strengths.

It was still 1935, and I happened to be in Boston. I had a couple of hours to kill before the next train left South Station for New York; I decided it would be a good idea to visit the Museum of Fine Arts and look around. I'd been there and seen the furniture often enough, so this time I concentrated on the antique American silverware. As I was looking through the glass showcases, I spotted a beautiful pair of silver candlesticks and a snuffer and tray, loaned by Mr. Herman Clarke. I got very excited; early American candlesticks are the rarest things one can find, and this set, the only one known to be made by John Burt, with the snuffer and tray to match, had to be unique.

Herman Clarke, who had loaned them to the museum, was a Bostonian with a fine collection of silver and furniture, much of which he had bought from father. He had also written a book on American silver. I knew that lately he had also sold back to my father a couple of pieces of fine furniture.

I don't know what impelled me to do so, for I was not, at least in those days, aggressive, but I found myself in a phone booth, and after looking up Mr. Clarke's number, I called him. When he answered, I said, "Mr. Clarke, this is Harold Sack. I believe you know my father, Israel Sack."

His answer was gruff. "Yep," was all he said.

Somewhat timidly, I said, "I just wanted to call you before I take the train, to tell you I was in the Boston museum, and I wanted to congratulate you on those John Burt candlesticks you loaned. They looked so fantastic to me, I wanted you to know how much I appreciated being able to see them."

His next words staggered me.

"Can you sell them?" he asked sharply

I almost dropped the phone. Then I managed to stammer something to the effect that I thought perhaps I could.

"Where are you?" he asked.

When I told him South Station, he said, "Get in a cab and come to the house." Then he gave me instructions, and hung up. I did as I was told.

John Burt candlesticks, snuffer, and tray, Boston, Massachusetts. John Burt (1691–1745), one of Boston's early silversmiths, fashioned this set. One of the prizes of early American silver are pairs of candlesticks; to have retained the original matching snuffer and tray is unusual, if not unique. (Courtesy, The Henry Francis du Pont Winterthur Museum)

As the cab took me to his house, all sorts of thoughts went through my mind, and I also recall I was quite frightened, although of what, I couldn't explain.

I arrived at Mr. Clarke's house, went up the steps to the front door, and rang the bell. The screen door was eventually opened; Mr. Clarke didn't even invite me in, but popped his head out the door to hand me a photograph. "Here," he said, brusquely. "I want three thousand dollars net."

Then the door closed, and I was left on the doorstep.

I didn't know whether to be insulted, or angry, or what. Actually,

I was too surprised to entertain any emotions. I went down the steps, got back into my cab, and returned to South Station.

All the way down from Boston on the New Haven train, I sat and considered what to do with these masterpieces of antique silver. I must have dozed off, but I was awakened when I heard the conductor calling "Bridgeport!"

Then a thought struck me — C. K. Davis, whose factory was here, and whose home was in Fairfield — perhaps he would be able to take advantage of this bonanza. He was one of the very few people I knew who had any cash. His income, plus his bonuses from Remington, gave him a surplus of between twenty and twenty-five thousand dollars a year with which to buy antiques. In those days, that was a huge amount of money.

I got off the train, and called him from the station. He was still, luckily, at his plant. "I've got something for you that's unbelievable," I promised.

He told me to meet him at his house. There, I quickly told him what had just happened to me in Boston, and then I produced the photograph.

C.K. examined Mr. Clarke's photo, and his eyebrows went up — he was as astonished as I. Even in a photograph, John Burt's masterful craftsmanship was apparent.

"How much does Mr. Clarke want for these?"

I suddenly realized I hadn't even thought of what to ask. "C.K., all I know is he wants three thousand net. He slammed the door in my face and left me with this photograph."

"What would you say to forty-five hundred?" he asked, after a moment.

I was staggered. "I would be more than delighted," I told him, which was certainly true. It was still such an unreal situation, I was totally confounded by the rapid turn of events. "I'll go to work and get the silver for you right away," I promised, ". . . if there are no hitches."

I promptly called Mr. Clarke and told him I'd found a customer, and I'd be coming to get the silver from him.

There were no hitches, and this time, he seemed far less gruff than he had on my first call.

When I arrived at his house, he was sad and subdued, and willing to talk to me. I explained to whom I would be selling his superb John Burt set, and then he began to explain to me why he had decided to sell. He had no confidence in America's future. All he could foresee was deep trouble ahead, and with our national debt of some thirty-five billions, there was little economic hope. Better, he'd reasoned, to dispose of his treasures while there was still a market in which he could realize cold, hard cash.

When my friend C. K. Davis died, he bequeathed those beautiful candlesticks, the snuffer, and the tray to Winterthur.

What would *they* be worth today?

The word *priceless* certainly applies. But since I was asked by his family to take on the job of appraising certain major items from C.K.'s estate, I had to attest to the value of that silver set, and I placed it at fifty thousand dollars.

Setting such values was difficult indeed. How could I put a price on the friendship that went along with all the items I'd sold to C.K.?

Alas, C. K. Davis's later years were dreadful. After World War II, when he turned sixty-five, the mandatory retirement policies of Remington Arms forced him to relinquish his top-level position. From that point on, everything deteriorated. Even though he had his outside interests, he began to lapse into sporadic periods of depression. The abrupt deprivation of the daily job and its duties, at which he'd been so efficient all those years, was too much for him to deal with. C.K. became more and more of a hermit, locking himself into an upstairs bedroom in his Fairfield home, taking his meals on a tray when they were brought up to him.

Downstairs were all his treasures, so carefully and selectively chosen; but the salt had lost its savor, and they no longer interested him. We continued to talk, now by phone, but the calls were less and less often. He truly lost his desire to live. Mandatory retirement for such a dynamic personality as C.K. can eventually be fatal. How else can one explain his abrupt end?

Ours was a strange relationship, almost symbiotic: he, the bluff corporate executive, trained in the rough-and-tumble of the factory production lines, but for some deep-rooted reason, responsive to the beauty of native American arts; and I, the struggling young dealer, fighting my daily battle to pay off family debts and to stay in business. When we came together, and he began to believe in me and my expertise, we both benefited. But I more than he, because he was a principal factor in our survival.

Customers come and go every day through our doors. They may buy a piece, or they may not. Most of them disappear. Rarely do most of them get close to me as friends, on a one-to-one basis. Not so C.K. His was a powerful loss, but when he died, I could at least fall back on the knowledge that my life had been enriched by our years of give-and-take.

And his faith in young Harold Sack.

EIGHT

Mid-1930s
(Duncan Phyfe Card Tables
and Mr. Henry du Pont)

B Y 1936, the economy seemed to be definitely on a welcome upswing, and so were the fortunes of Israel Sack, Inc. Our landlord, Mr. Robinson, quite reasonably began to feel he should have more return on his investment. He offered to sell us the entire building we were in, but finally we decided we couldn't possibly afford to buy it.

Eventually, with the help of an enterprising young real estate agent, Robert Zuckerman, we located premises at 61 East 57th Street, a superb set of showrooms which had previously housed Charles Woolsey Lyon's imposing antiques establishment. There, behind a beautiful Colonial-style doorway, was very ample and impressive space, vacant since Mr. Lyon had gone out of business.

The real estate market was so depressed that Zuckerman was able to negotiate a deal by which we could actually afford the rental for such a dream location, and uptown we moved. To be in such lavish quarters was quite exhilarating, and it was a good move psychologically for our firm. Other dealers in the antiques trade perked up their ears, and rumors began to fly through the business that Sack must have hit some mysterious jackpot. We began to get attention from the best outlying picker-dealers in Connecticut and New Jersey, sharp-eyed antiquers who knew where the truly great pieces were hidden away.

We hadn't yet sold that great shell corner cupboard which my brother had purchased at the Benjamin Flayderman final sale, so uptown it went, along with a few other choice pieces we had in our inventory. Installed in our new surroundings, everything looked beautiful, and the appropriate settings we'd found gave us new confidence.

Soon, it was justified.

One day, a very pleasant-looking lady in her thirties walked in, quietly well turned out in obvious high style. She looked around and began to ask the price of a few pieces. I noticed her eye fell on only our top items — our shell corner cupboard, a Queen Anne desk on frame, and a beautiful Simon Willard banjo clock, among others. She obviously knew quality when she saw it, and we took our time discussing each piece, its history, and its origin. When we were done, she asked me to make a note of her selections, and to put down their prices. When I handed her the list, she glanced at it, then she smiled and said, "They're very nice, but your prices are exorbitant."

Exorbitant? No. I'd already learned from my father, who'd always strictly adhered to the policy *sell the best, to the best, at the best price.* Perhaps that rule meant losing a sale, but more often than not it didn't. What I'd shown this obviously affluent lady was absolutely first quality, and not to be challenged. Besides, had it not been here in Charles Woolsey Lyon's own premises, years before, that he'd told me — in reference to a fifteen-hundred-dollar paperweight — "Remember, to the person who has the wealth, that fifteen hundred dollars is no more hardship than it is for you to buy a pack of cigarettes"?

I shook my head. "They're only high because you've picked out the very best," I told the lady, politely. "Anyone who can afford the best is very foolish to consider anything but. Could I have your name, please, for this memo?"

"Of course," she said, with a faint smile. "It's Mrs. Paul Mellon."

Then she left.

I had no idea whether or not I'd said the wrong thing. Should I have used more diplomacy? Certainly, these were not the times to alienate such an affluent potential customer. These days, they weren't exactly growing on trees.

Shortly afterward, we got a note from Mrs. Mellon saying she'd decided to take all the pieces, except one. And at exactly the prices I'd quoted.

As a teacher, my father had proved his point.

Nancy McClelland, the famous decorator who specialized in Regency decor and wallpapers to match, was preparing a book on Duncan Phyfe, the famous New York–based cabinetmaker, and the Regency era. Phyfe, of Scottish ancestry, lived and worked in New York after the Revolution, when the burgeoning population and the accumulation of wealth among the upper classes attracted fine craftsmen to that city.

He, and Charles Honoré Lannuier of France, left behind a body of superb work; their creations are eagerly sought after and command very high prices from both collectors and museums. Phyfe's styles over a period of years varied from Sheraton forms to the classic, with French Empire influence.

Nancy had consulted quite often with us, and used photographs from our files to illustrate her book. Not long after its publication, she called to say she had a pair of Duncan Phyfe card tables of very high quality in her showroom which I might enjoy seeing.

When I walked into her shop, I was confronted by two of the most magnificent tables imaginable. Instantly, I knew they had to be ours. They had come from an estate in Irvington, New Jersey, and the executors wanted fifteen hundred dollars for the pair. The price seemed high — at the time, at least — but not impossible. In a burst of enthusiasm, I took the plunge. I offered to purchase them if she'd give me sixty or ninety days in which to pay. Miss McClelland was certain that would be fine with the executors, and I told her to prepare a bill, and to add five hundred dollars to it for herself. She declined, but I insisted. Even though I wasn't sure how I would finance this deal, I reasoned that time was on my side. And besides, these two tables were so great, I was certain they'd sell.

My father agreed with me; when the tables arrived, he was delighted to see such beautiful pieces of Phyfe's work. He promptly called his friend and good customer Mitchell Taradash. Mr. Taradash came to look, nodded, smiled, and then informed us he'd been

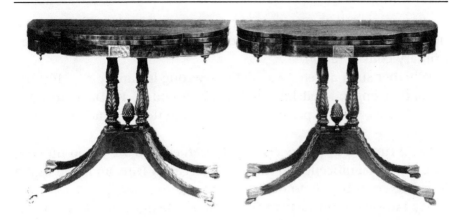

Pair of Duncan Phyfe card tables, New York, circa 1810. Although
the late Edward Jones classified these tables to be attributed to
Charles Honoré Lannuier rather than Duncan Phyfe, their magnificence is not at all diminished. These tables, with the added importance of being a pair, have the distinctive design of the pineapple
(symbol of hospitality) as well as the acanthus carving on the pedestal. Few examples have the brass casters of acanthus design as
well. Scholars believe that most brass fittings of this period were
originally gilded.

previously offered the tables. He'd already declined, and now he
declined again. My father was dismayed. He'd wanted his best customer to affirm his son's own judgment, and Taradash had let him
down.

I promptly called C. K. Davis, who came down to look and was
truly impressed with the two tables. After he had taken their mea-
surements, I began to have a premonition that the news from his
end would be bad. I was right. C.K. told me he had a problem up in
his Fairfield home with the proper space. "Such magnificent tables
simply won't fit in," he explained.

How could I argue with him? I'd encountered a new phenomenon among collectors — the need for a proper setting for their prize
pieces.

There was one thing to be said of the pioneer collectors, Eugene
Bolles, Francis Garvan, Louis Guerineau Myers, et al. For them,
acquiring the piece always came first. Where to house it, or to show

it, was unimportant. But now they were gone, and we'd come to a new era with this new breed, to whom display had become the primary consideration.

Whether such a trend was right or wrong is hard to say. But the attitude it engendered had caused my friend C. K. Davis to deny himself two superb pieces. Later, he regretted it, and often told me so.

We'd run out of prospects, and it seemed as if we'd end up with those two magnificent and expensive pieces by Duncan Phyfe sitting in stock, contributing to our already large overhead.

My father got in touch with his friend Maxim Karolik, who was beginning to amass a collection for the Museum of Fine Arts in Boston. Karolik came down, examined the tables, approved of them, and was interested in buying. But not the pair.

Not the pair? Only one.

"A museum would only need one such superb piece," he remarked, and asked us for the price for one.

I dug in my heels and refused his offer. The tables could *not* be separated. Karolik shrugged and left, and that was that.

My father was annoyed, but since I had acquired them, he agreed I had a good deal to say about the disposition of those two great tables.

We were desperate.

Then, I thought of Mrs. Paul Mellon. She understood quality.

I sent photos of the tables to her Virginia address. I waited. Silence. No phone call, no letter. Nothing.

Two weeks later, I received a cable from Switzerland, where my mail to her had been forwarded; she wished to know our best price for the tables!

I quoted her five thousand dollars. And waited for her reply.

This time, there was no haggling whatsoever. Mrs. Mellon paid the price, and acquired two superb Duncan Phyfe tables.

They were crated, and shipped off to her newly built Virginia home. I was not to see Mrs. Mellon again. Subsequently, I heard this lovely lady had died at a very early age.

Her husband remarried, but since he had no interest in American antiques, we never had an occasion to meet. I often wondered

In the early 1900s collections were eclectic — pieces with no regional identification. Early collectors couldn't differentiate between American and English, let alone among the different Colonies from which pieces came; they cared little for decor and used their homes merely as storehouses.

what had become of those two great tables, and the Queen Anne desk on frame, the beautiful Simon Willard banjo clock, and my father's favorite shell corner cupboard which she'd bought from me that day on 57th Street, but there was no gracious way of finding out.

Then, remarkably, about fifteen years ago, I received a call from John Walton, a very aggressive dealer who'd gone into the business in the 1950s and had rapidly made quite a name for himself in the trade.

He wanted to know if we'd seen the pair of Duncan Phyfe card tables that were listed in a forthcoming sale of miscellaneous furniture up at Parke-Bernet. "I think they're very good, and they look

The emphasis after the Great Depression and World War II was on decor. Pieces were collected for home use and had to have a definite arrangement; this opened up a new market. I opted to show how choice pieces could be used, and this inspired *Antiques* magazine to publish "Antiques in Domestic Settings." Likewise, the use of period rooms in the American Wing of the Metropolitan Museum did much to encourage such a movement.

fine to me," he said. "But they're catalogued as reproductions."

I went up to look. Sure enough, there they were, the two Duncan Phyfe card tables I'd sold to Mrs. Paul Mellon! Big as life — we checked them both out carefully. There was no doubt about their authenticity. They even had the same blemishes on the apron which I'd remembered from all those years ago!

How could the "expert" at Parke-Bernet have made such a mistake?

Later, I found out that the second Mrs. Mellon had redecorated their Chicago apartment, and her decorators had gotten rid of everything as they saw fit, according to her directions. Since the Mellons fancied English antiques, out went the two Duncan Phyfe tables, which had been sent to auction with not a line of provenance or history. And the current cataloguer at Parke-Bernet had muffed them totally.

A considerable error on his part.

At auction they were bought for four hundred dollars the pair. But since keen-eyed Mr. Ginsburg, of Ginsburg and Levy, had also spotted them, we made a prior three-way partnership with him and Mr. Walton, and the two tables were knocked down to us as a buying group.

We don't customarily buy in such a fashion; we don't make partnerships, but since we hadn't been the only ones who'd spotted the tables, and John Walton had been decent enough to tell us about them, we decided that the circumstances warranted our forming a temporary troika.

But it was a temporary one. Once the tables were bought, we embarked on a long and complex negotiation, which ended by our buying out Messrs. Walton and Ginsburg with liberal sums for their interests. When the dust had settled, once again Israel Sack, Inc. owned those Duncan Phyfe tables at a cost of four thousand dollars, a very reasonable price, even for those times.

Although Phyfe and the post-Revolutionary Federal period of furniture have not enjoyed the price rises shown by pieces of the pre-Revolutionary era in the Colonies, the superb quality of this pair of tables places them in the masterpiece category. Their grace and beauty defy popular trends.

Since then, they've passed through three owners, with steadily escalating prices. Today, they repose in a Virginia home, two jewels in a marvelous collection. I can only hope they remain in those loving hands for many years to come.

I often speculate — what if those Chicago interior decorators had not sent these two tables off to New York, consigned to auction, as they did — and what if that cataloguer had realized they were Duncan Phyfe — as he did not — and what if John Walton had *not* wandered by Parke-Bernet and spotted them for the masterpieces they are?

Chances are they'd have been sold off as "in the style of" reproductions, to some unwitting owner who'd have taken the two tables home and put them in one of his rooms. And there they'd be still, perhaps even today. Unnoticed, unappraised — useful for plants, or lamps, certainly — but as far as history is concerned, lost.

And I don't like to speculate on what the odds would be *against* their being part of a Remarkable Discovery.

From the time I first began to spend my Saturdays at my father's Charles Street store, until our move to New York, I met many wealthy collectors, but Henry du Pont's meticulous attention to the accumulation of only the finest early on earned him the title of "Mr. Big" in the trade. He remained so, undisputedly, throughout his life.

But Henry du Pont was more, far more than a tasteful collector. He was the dominant force in that trend I've already mentioned, the placing of fine American antiques in their proper settings.

To arrange great pieces in rooms surrounded by paintings, mirrors, wallpaper, glassware, porcelains, with fine carpeting and the like of the same period, thus restoring everything into one harmonious whole — that was the total thrust of du Pont's wish. So determined was he that arrangement and decor be preeminent that he was once quoted as saying, "It's one of my first principles that if you go into a room and right away see something, then you must realize that *that* shouldn't be in the room."

During those depressed 1930s, every dealer who acquired an important piece would automatically offer it first to Mr. du Pont. Everyone knew how well he had outbid everyone for the Van Pelt highboy, a magnificent Philadelphia piece from pre-Revolutionary times, for forty-four thousand dollars at the Reifsnyder sale in 1929, and how he had picked off two other prizes at the 1930 Benjamin Flayderman sale, a Rhode Island tea table and a John Seymour secretary from Boston.

In response, Mr. du Pont always paid strict attention to such dealers' offerings. His reaction was prompt, and he was absolutely reliable. If he called to make an appointment at two o'clock on such and such a day to visit us, I learned we could set our watches by his arrival.

Once he'd arrived, Mr. du Pont, tall and brusque, was completely businesslike. No time for small talk, nor would he chuckle at any of my father's store of cheerful jokes. No matter how many anecdotes my father tried to tell him, Mr. du Pont would not be diverted from the business at hand. All that concerned him was whether or not he wished to acquire the item for that great collection down in Delaware, which would become the basis for Winterthur.

And the decision to buy or not was always strictly his own. Years before, he'd relied on such dealers as Mr. and Mrs. Collings, or the famous Boston decorator Henry Sleeper, for guidance. But later on, he developed total confidence in his own judgment and taste, and rarely relied on the advice of any subordinate.

In fact, Henry du Pont's own taste was so impeccable that one has only to tour the magnificent rooms at Winterthur, the museum he created at his home in Delaware, to sense how brilliantly he functioned as a collector.

I remember well the time I made my first Remarkable Discovery, one which ended up in Winterthur, but not without an argument.

It was during the 1930s when my father was away on a selling trip — he traveled so much that his reputation was "Sack has slept in more houses than Washington!" — that I had a call from an industrious Connecticut picker-dealer named Willy Richmond. Up in Riverside, Willy wholesaled huge quantities of late period pieces from his large frame house, mostly to dealers in outlying areas. Because he was in a strategic location to receive calls from affluent — or once-affluent — Connecticut families who had pieces to sell, in this depressed market, Willy was carefully watched by other dealers.

So when he informed me that he'd gotten in a piece on consignment which puzzled him, I lost no time in hurrying up to Riverside.

When I arrived, he led me into a separate small cluttered room in the back, where amid all his collected odds and ends, I suddenly found myself gazing at a wonderful piece.

I knew I was looking at one of the top prizes of early American furniture, a Queen Anne marble top tea table, from New York, circa 1740–1750.

Queen Anne marble-topped tea table, New York, circa
1740–1750. This tea table is unique in having a scooped-out
marble top rather than the customary mahogany tray top, usually with notched corners. Tea tables of this form are seldom
found with the pull-out candleslides, adding to its otherwise
superior form and quality; there is probably no other tea table
extant with so many unique and rare aspects.

In all the Colonies except Pennsylvania, the usual tea table is
rectangular in form; in Philadelphia, the customary tea table is circular, or piecrust, carved with a birdcage support for tilting and
turning on a circular column, supported by a tripod cabriole-shaped
pedestal, often with carved ball-and-claw feet.

Willy's table had C-scrolled cabriole legs, *and* candleslides, and
also every other possible embellishment. It also had a unique scooped
and mottled marble top, a feature I'd never seen before.

"This looks foreign to me," said Willy. "The woman who brought
it in only wants five hundred dollars, and that's why I'm afraid it
really isn't anything much."

I couldn't control my excitement. Such a superb piece — and
right here in front of us! In my youthful exuberance, I promptly
blurted out that indeed it *was* something — "It's Queen Anne, it's
American, and that marble top is absolutely unique!" I babbled.

"You go buy it from that lady, and as soon as you do, we'll buy it from you!"

Willy cheerfully agreed. I hurried back to New York, bursting with excitement. To acquire such a masterpiece for our firm would truly be a delicious prospect.

In my naïveté, I hadn't considered the possibility of any sort of double-cross.

When my father returned, I blurted out the wonderful news of Willy's find, and he promptly called Willy.

But Willy's response was noncommittal. Yes, he had bought the table for five hundred dollars, but now that he knew he had himself a rarity, he had no intention of selling for a while. "Maybe I'll hang on to it and see what happens," he told my father.

For once, my customarily jovial and gentle father lost his temper. He took the next train to Riverside and went storming into Willy's shop. He might have been an Old Testament prophet, invoking all sorts of divine wrath on Willy — and he argued Willy into keeping his word.

When the dust had settled — and in Willy's crowded establishment there was always an oversupply of dust — my father had bought that marvelous Queen Anne table for four thousand dollars.

Once it had arrived safely in New York, my father called up Henry du Pont, and offered it to him.

"Sorry," said Mr. du Pont, "but I have no money to buy with at this time, Mr. Sack, and I've deferred all purchases for a while."

Again, my father would not accept no for an answer, not even from Henry du Pont. He persisted. Such a great piece must be placed in loving hands, and become part of a great collection. "Let us bring it down and show it to you," he suggested.

Of course, once that table arrived at Mr. du Pont's house in Delaware, it never returned. Mr. du Pont managed to find the funds with which to acquire it, and today it remains one of the great treasures of the Winterthur collection.

And it is a measure of my father's love for that great table that he was willing not only to find it a good home, but to take a mere five hundred dollars as our profit in the deal.

*　　*　　*

In 1980, on the occasion of the hundredth anniversary of Henry du Pont's birth, I was honored by an invitation to address the trustees of the Winterthur museum. I gladly accepted the offer, but afterward, I began to have doubts. What was I to say about Mr. du Pont? That he was a great collector, with a superb, innate sense of decor? Certainly, his collection, all those magnificent rooms at Winterthur, spoke for the man better than mere words.

Then I began to wonder — what exactly was the nature of his relationship with my father over the years? Had it always been so businesslike, so cut and dried, or had they ever had their differences?

So I drove down to Winterthur and went to the archivist at Mr. du Pont's museum, and asked her if there might be an existing correspondence filed away between the two men, which might shed some light on their attitudes toward each other. Had it always been harmonious?

No, indeed, it had not, and herewith a few revealing letters, dating back to 1933, which reveal the diplomatic give-and-take between two men of taste.

Aug. 1933

DEAR MR. SACK:

I enjoyed very much seeing you here the other day.

Did you tell me that the red painted highboy I saw in Boston, which is similar to my maple one, came from Stratham, N.H., and also would it be possible to have one small drawer of that highboy sent here, as I want to see if it matches my other reds in color. If it is very carefully boxed I don't think it will come to any harm, and I will re-pack it and send it back equally careful[ly]. . . .

YOURS VERY TRULY,

H. F. DU PONT

My father obligingly sent off the red painted drawer, since he well understood Mr. du Pont's passion for harmonious decor. Then he waited. Soon he got an answer.

Aug 20, 1933

DEAR MR. SACK:

Having failed to match anything in Southampton, I brought the red drawer down here to see if it would go with the things I have in Delaware. I am sorry to say that it does not seem to match anything I have, so I am returning it and must give up the idea of purchasing the highboy . . .

YOURS VERY TRULY,

H. F. DU PONT

Obviously, it was a disappointment to my father, and his reply rather diplomatically explained why he firmly disagreed with Mr. du Pont's thesis.

DEAR MR. DU PONT:

I am sorry that you find yourself unable to use the highboy, although in antiques colors do not have to match. I personally believe they look much better if they do not. The highboy is of such fine quality that I know it would lend a lot of charm to your collection. However, I would not expect you to purchase the piece unless you were of the same opinion. . . .

YOURS VERY TRULY,

ISRAEL SACK

And here is another diplomatic exchange, this time on the subject of whether or not an antique piece's history is of importance to the collector.

DEAR MR. SACK:

I recall seeing in your advertisement in Antiques *magazine several years ago, statements you made concerning the histories of antiques. Specifically, that a genuine piece did not need a history, and those which were not genuine were not helped by it. Have you revised your opinion?*

YOURS VERY TRULY,

H. F. DU PONT

To which my father replied:

DEAR MR. DU PONT:

I went to see the Gladding blockfront chest on chest. Although Mr. Karolik claims that Goddard could not have made it, it has the same Goddard signature on it as any piece of furniture that he has made— if he ever made any. I never was as greatly interested in the name of the man who made a piece of furniture as much as the results the man achieved. A Stradivarius violin would play as fine a tune if the maker's name was other than Stradivarius. In my opinion, the blockfront chest on chest with the nine shells is one of the rarest and most unique pieces of furniture in the Rhode Island school of craftsmanship.

YOURS,

ISRAEL SACK

Mr. du Pont's reply is a most revealing statement of his collecting philosophy. Decor was always his primary motivating force.

DEAR MR. SACK:

Many thanks for your letter of August 28th.
I agree with you that whether the chest-on-chest is Goddard or not does not make the slightest difference if it is a beautiful piece. Please don't think I am turning it down because of what Mr. Karolik may have said about it. I am simply turning it down because the two little rooms in which I have my Goddard furniture are too small to take such a big piece; and as I am trying to confine all my Goddard furniture to those two little rooms, a large piece is out. . . .

YOURS VERY TRULY,

H. F. DU PONT

Fortunately for all of us, in this particular case, Mr. du Pont relented, and eventually bought the magnificent Goddard chest on chest. Today it is one of the finest exhibits at Winterthur.

Collectors, even the most gentlemanly and restrained types, can become quite emotional when the hunt is on.

Consider one of my own later experiences with Mr. du Pont — one which involved a very rare chair, possibly one of the rarest we'd ever encountered — and Miss Ima Hogg, another great collector, from Texas.

Though Miss Ima was far removed from the Eastern seaboard, she was an ardent collector of early American, and enjoyed snatching up great pieces, especially when it meant she'd outdone any of her fellow collectors.

Early in the 1960s, my brothers and I had heard rumors there would be an auction coming up around the New Haven, Connecticut area, but we could not discover where it would be held. Usually, small dealers or local pickers will call us in advance, to tell us what items are to be included, hoping to have us retain them to represent us on a commission basis at the auction. But since we heard from no one where the auction would be held, our interest was piqued. None of the New Haven papers seemed to carry any announcements, and this made us even more curious. What could be for sale which would induce such secrecy?

Actually, as we later discovered, this particular auction was held by a firm which specialized in selling off farm animals, and which had no idea of how to get the word about the sale around to the proper buyers.

Somehow, the day before the auction, we did receive a mimeographed sheet from those auctioneers, in East Haven, briefly listing some American antiques coming up for sale at nine o'clock the following morning, and describing the items in the most general terms.

How had such a collection of antiques ended up in an East Haven home? I never found out. But by now my brother Albert and I were hooked; at least we'd learned the whereabouts of this sale. We decided to meet at the site, whose address was on the mimeographed sheet, at eight the next morning, to give ourselves an opportunity to inspect the items for sale.

We arrived in an inexpensive suburban area, then went down a narrow dirt road which passed by modest little houses, and finally came to the site of the auction, a ramshackle old place. A few cars were parked in front of the house, and a tent had been set up alongside. We went up to the door of the house and knocked. A voice inside called out, "Nobody's allowed in until the sale!"

"We want to look at the pieces!" I called.

"We had an exhibit for two weeks," answered a gruff voice. "You want to see something, wait till it comes up."

I lost my cool and began to bang on the door. "Listen!" I shouted. "If you don't open that door, I'm going home! I'm the biggest buyer of American antiques in the world — if you don't open this damned door, it's going to cost you a pretty penny!"

It worked. They opened the door and let us in.

We walked through the ramshackle house, looking over the items which were to be sold. Amazingly enough, there were quite a few quality pieces, which seemed genuine to our eye. Evidently, the owners had little experience in selling antiques; why else had they retained an auctioneer of farm animals?

While we were speculating on this odd set of circumstances, lo and behold, we found, sitting quietly in one of the small back rooms, the chair.

Not simply a chair. One of the greatest chairs Albert or I had ever seen.

It had the cabriole legs, the cabriole arm supports, a horseshoe-shaped seat, and all the characteristic carving motifs which made it unmistakably a New York chair, done for the Van Rensselaer family of Albany. We know of such side chairs, designed and made for that family; but this particular chair, sitting here in a rundown house in East Haven, Connecticut, was a *corner* chair, and that alone made it incredibly rare.

We examined it carefully, hoping not to attract anyone's attention. A poker face is absolutely necessary in this business; over the years, we've all developed one as standard equipment. Even when you're as excited as we were, while checking out this beauty, which wasn't easy.

However, we found two defects. The first was an iron brace, about an inch in size, a home repair job done when somebody, years back, had perhaps pushed one of the legs, and then had it reinforced. The second was a crack on the rear arm support.

Considering the magnificence of this chair, those flaws were rel-

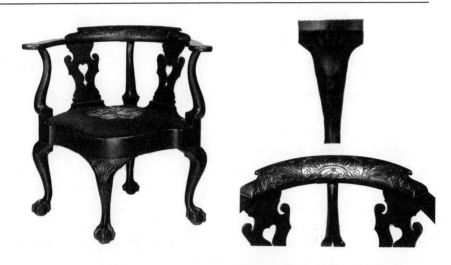

Hogg Chippendale mahogany corner chair, New York, circa
1760. While pre-Revolutionary furniture of the Chippendale
period in New York is not to be compared to its Philadelphia or
New England counterparts, a few examples defy this generaliza-
tion. Most corner chairs have developed cabriole front legs and
straight-turned side and rear legs. When the arm supports are
also cabriole shaped rather than straight turned, we have the
highest development of this form. The Hogg chair has likewise a
carved crest rail very similar in design to the crests of the large
Chippendale chair set made for the Van Rensselaer family. This
feature also identifies this chair to be of New York origin. This
corner chair vies in importance with the great Goddard corner
chair, which descended in the Herreshoff family of Newport,
later sold by Israel Sack, Inc. to Lansdell Christie and now in
the Wunsch Collection in New York City.

atively minor. I took Albert aside and told him to buy it, and I would
go back to New York and get whatever cash was needed. "But if
nothing else, get that chair."

I wasn't too worried about competition, out here in this remote
East Haven area.

I was wrong.

Albert called at two o'clock to report good news. "We bought the
chair," he said.

"Good, how much?" I asked.

The price had been $5,200!

"Good Lord, who was bidding?" I asked.

"I don't know," said Albert. "They seemed to come out of the woodwork!"

Under the circumstances, it wasn't a low price, but since that chair was such a rarity, it certainly wasn't excessive.

We got our new prize down to the store, and of course, we were very excited about it. We set it up in a small room on the side where it could be seen, still in its unrestored condition.

Then we began hearing rumors. A day or so later, in came Mrs. Katherine Prentiss Murphy, a good friend, a collector of early Pilgrim furniture, and also very close to Miss Ima Hogg. "Boys," she said, "you know I love your father dearly, and I've heard what happened to you, and I'm sorry."

"Sorry?" I asked her. "For what?"

"Well, I've heard all over how you got taken with some old restored corner chair," said Mrs. Murphy. "A wreck."

Obviously, the word had gone out among our rivals, and in the trade a story was spreading that we'd made a dreadful error up in East Haven.

"Come take a look at the chair," I suggested.

She came into the room where it was standing, stared at it, and then she turned and smiled. "I don't have to worry any longer about you boys," she said. "This is fine."

But the rumors persisted, and they reached Miss Ima Hogg, who was spending a few weeks motoring through New England in search of items for her collection. One day soon afterward, she wandered casually into our shop, accompanied by her longtime companion and secretary, Jane Zivley. "Harold," she said in her Texas drawl, "I'm sick and tired of hearing about it. Every dealer I go to, that's all I hear about, that old corner chair you got taken on. Let me see it."

I showed it to her.

"Now what are the problems?" she asked.

I described them to her, and showed them. An iron brace, a slight crack, and some replacements needed, little kneeblocks which should really be scrolled.

"And what else?" she asked.

"Miss Ima," I said, "I swear to you, this is it."

"Okay, Harold," she said, "I know what you paid. Everybody else does, too. What's the best you can do for a poor old lady?"

"Well, we have not really determined a price yet," I said, "but twelve thousand dollars might do it."

She nodded. "Ten thousand, and you've got yourself a deal."

Remarkable. Here was a lady who'd heard all the bad-mouthing, and the rumors, and on the basis of our judgment — and her own — she'd put her money where her mouth was. And a not insubstantial sum of money, by anyone's standards.

"You've got a deal," I told her.

We shook hands, and she left, obviously delighted at having acquired such a rare masterpiece for her home in Texas.

A few days later, in came my old friend, the tall, rangy Charles Montgomery, who was now the director of Winterthur. He looked around in a seemingly casual manner, poking here and there, in our various rooms. But I'd known Charles for many years now, ever since he'd begun dealing in pewter, years ago, and I knew he was here for a purpose. Was there something special he wanted to see?

"All right," he grinned. "Where is it, Harold?"

"Where's what?" I asked.

"The corner chair!" he said. "I have to see it."

"For heaven's sake, why didn't you say so?" I said. "It's been sold and shipped, but I have a picture here I can show you."

When I showed Charles the picture, he became quite upset.

"Oh Lord," he sighed. "The boss is going to be furious. I was supposed to get in here last week, but I missed the boat."

Absolutely true.

The very next morning, in marched his boss, Mr. Henry du Pont, and promptly inquired about the same chair. In our business, news travels rapidly on a form of jungle telegraph.

I told Mr. du Pont that the chair had been sold to Miss Ima, and had gone to Texas, but he refused to accept that as fact. Angrily, he said, "After all the millions of dollars I've spent with you and your father, when you get a rare piece in, you don't even *call* me?"

I tried to soothe his ruffled feelings, and it took quite a bit of doing. After he finally left, I called Miss Ima in Texas, to tell her of Mr. du Pont's irate reaction.

She squealed with delight. "He got one away from me a few months ago!" she said. "And now I'm even!"

Mr. du Pont's pique at having been outdone by Miss Ima eventually subsided, and we went on doing business with him until his death in 1969. I treasure the accolade he paid my father. He wrote us and said, "I wish I had begun buying from your father when I was in college. There is no telling how much better a collection I might have had, if I had started with you at that time."

NINE

Maxim Karolik, the Passionate Native

O<small>UR</small> business had gathered momentum, when suddenly, in 1937, without warning, we found ourselves again in the midst of a depression. Overnight, dire times descended on us. Every antique piece we sold, or thought we had sold, remained frozen in inventory. All those customers we'd counted on for payment were calling to cancel their orders.

However, I've found that in every recession period, there usually appears, most fortunately, some individual, or group, who runs counter to the trends. Like my friend C. K. Davis, these collectors are not concerned with any current crisis. Such hardy and determined souls pursue the great examples of fine furniture with vigor, and are willing to back their judgment with cash.

When everyone else is pulling in his horns, such contrarians are out busily buying.

Thank heaven — and the Czar Nicholas — we had another one of those.

He was one of the most colorful personalities I've ever encountered, and his name was Maxim Karolik.

If ever two men were made for each other, a Damon and Pythias bound together by their love of American antiques, they were Israel Sack and Maxim Karolik.

Karolik was a White Russian who had migrated to America after World War I, and, as he was fond of telling us, promptly "went native."

Certainly, in his earlier years, the same had also been true of Israel Sack.

Karolik was a dashing figure, a true connoisseur who seemed to have sprung, full-blown, from an earlier, more elaborate era. Very tall and stately, with high cheekbones and flowing hair streaked with gray, into our establishment he would stride, always in his fur-collared overcoat, the epitome of majestic style. Gesticulating with his hands for emphasis as he delivered himself of his opinions — which he did constantly — he was totally opposite from the usual quiet, re-served, and uncertain collector. His warm eyes flashing from beneath his bushy eyebrows, Maxim would approach a piece of fine furniture as if he were in the presence of some ravishing female. "Magnifi-cent!" he would exclaim. "See how the creator has mastered her line, her form, the integration of her detail. Ah — truly thrilling!"

He trusted my father implicitly. They did not always agree, but Maxim's respect for my father's taste was unbounded. To me and my brother Albert, he paid little if any attention at all. Nothing we could do or say would change his Old World attitude toward us. Father was the master, we were always his apprentices.

I realize now that in a sense, Karolik was correct in treating us as students, although at the time, I certainly didn't appreciate his at-titude. Years later, I've come to realize how much I was learning from my father all through those years, and to be grateful for the education I got from him — and from Maxim.

Their discussions were long and friendly. They loved to swap anecdotes, his stories of grand opera backstage intrigues and Boston upper-class society, in return for my father's Talmudic wisdom and philosophic anecdotes. They shared a wry sense of humor. One of Karolik's favorite sayings was, "If you want to feel better, get a good steak dinner. But if you want to *be* better, go to a museum!"

He not only obeyed his own instructions, he ended up creating a magnificent museum collection.

For both him and my father, transplanted Russians, one from an impoverished Lithuanian shtetl, the other from an elegant bourgeois family, the pursuit of the finest in American decorative arts in their adopted homeland would become a shared passion.

Karolik — he referred to himself as Maximum Karolik of the Minimum Prices — was an opera singer. The offspring of a patrician family, he had been sent to Italy before World War I to study voice. After the outbreak of the Russian Revolution, he stayed in Italy and pursued his career in opera. Eventually he came to America and settled here.

Then he became involved in a remarkable romance.

Among the bluest of the Bostonian Brahmin blue-blooded families were the Codmans. In Boston, whether the Codmans look down on the Lowells or the Cabots, or vice versa, has for many years been an arguable point. One of the Codmans, Miss Martha, a maiden lady many years Karolik's senior, met and fell madly in love with the dashing middle-aged Russian opera singer. In a very short time, they were married.

Mrs. Martha Codman Karolik was no stranger to American antiques. She had been raised and lived for years surrounded by the Codman, Derby, and Landers family treasures, handed down from Massachusetts generation to generation. And she had already been enormously generous to the Boston Museum of Fine Arts. She had presented that institution with several examples of the finest family heirlooms. They were Codman-Derby pieces, embellished by the wood carvings of the great Samuel McIntire, the renowned Boston architect-carver.

Probably among the most famous of American craftsmen, McIntire was a builder, architect, and master carver. He was commissioned in 1800 to build "Oak Hill" at Peabody, Massachusetts, for Elias Hasket Derby, one of Martha Codman Karolik's ancestors, who had been a wealthy ship owner and merchant. Several rooms from "Oak Hill" are in the Boston Museum of Fine Arts, where they are filled with furniture and carvings that are also McIntire's work.

Spurred on by her new husband's all-consuming love for early American, Mrs. Karolik joined him to announce that they would present to the Boston museum a definitive collection of American decorative arts — the M. and M. Karolik Collection of Eighteenth Century American Arts.

An admirable gift, indeed.

But there was one small problem, in 1936. No such collection as yet existed. It would have to be assembled.

Which is how my father became so intimately involved with Maxim. The curator of the Boston museum was a venerable gentleman named Edwin Hipkiss, a dignified Bostonian, who for years dealt with my father. He, Karolik, and my father would promptly become an informal troika, working together to assemble the new collection. There was rarely any problem with funding; Mrs. Karolik's financial resources were sufficient to back up the taste and judgment of the talented three.

Consider their accomplishment. The completed collection comprises three hundred and fifty separate items — furniture, silverware, paintings, drawings, and mirrors, of the finest quality. The majority of these items were studied and amassed within a period of six short years!

Karolik would readily admit that his success as a collector was based on his partnership with and respect for dealers. But he was also a collector who had his own most definite ideas. Up to that time, most American collectors generally preferred to keep their choice pieces absolutely untouched, with the old decrepit finishes left strictly as they'd been when found. In the trade, the expression for such an original state was "in the rough."

It was generally felt that to keep the finish of a piece as is was not only a protection, but also a guarantee of its authenticity. Therefore, in contrast to England, where affluent families had a profusion of servants at their beck and call, who would spend daily hours waxing and polishing, American pieces were generally dull and unattractive. The beautiful grains and various woods beneath, used by their original craftsmen-makers, would thus, over the years, have become disguised, almost obliterated.

Thus, many collectors shied away from American pieces for their homes. "In the rough" was synonymous with shabby.

Not for Karolik. Through those keen Russian eyes, he had a vision of the great beauty hidden beneath years of accumulated crud. Beneath the dirt and buildup lay elegance. He was determined to bring it forth.

He kept on constant call a little Russian cabinetmaker named Braverman. "Ah, Braverman will do it," he would promise when confronted with a fine old table, its finish dull and worn. "I'm going to have Braverman take this, and when he gets through with it, it will be beautiful! This table is like a little child in the gutter, who's been mistreated, but underneath, I promise you, there is a beautiful angel!"

In Maxim's own remarks, at the end of the M. and M. Karolik Collection catalogue, he expounds on the technique.

> *The collector, the connoisseur and the experienced dealer will notice that we do not use the English method of treating the furniture. We do not rub and wax it, as the English often do, to such an extent that the wood appears like a shiny glass.*
>
> *From the beginning, we have decided not to touch the natural colour of the wood; to leave alone the old patina and the mellowness which only age can give. We removed only the dirt and decayed varnish and gave the proper "food" to the wood. Without that "food" it dries up like the paint on a picture, and loses the life of its original colour.*
>
> *On some of the furniture pieces were chipped off here and there. We restored them with pieces of wood of the same colour and age. Some pieces, when acquired, were rickety, owing to the glue having dried up. We reglued them. Some pieces had been only neglected and looked dirty. We simply carefully cleaned them. All these slight repairs are considered by experts correct and legitimate. If the furniture in this collection looks "new" it is only because we used the ancient motto of the good housekeeper: "Keep things clean and in good order, and they will show up handsomely." They do, I think.*

Old-timers resented his approach. How dare this parvenu Russian singer restore our native American? Against all sorts of criticism, Karolik persisted. "Never mind them!" he'd insist. "Off with the scum!"

Perhaps his contemporaries thought he'd gone too far. But as time went on, and they'd see the beautiful woods and veneers beneath gleaming again, centuries after they'd first been designed and carved, most came to agree with him. Little Isidore Braverman's caring hands and magic potions continued to work their miracles. "Polish the brasses, everything, show it all!" Karolik insisted, a pioneer in his newly adopted homeland.

During the 1930s, as Maximum Karolik with the Minimum Prices, he bought principally the Queen Anne– and Chippendale-style furniture of the great city centers (Boston, Philadelphia, New York, and Newport, Rhode Island), which at that time was very reasonably priced. Federal, Hepplewhite, and Sheraton pieces were not only more popular then, but were of a much higher relative price level, one which was inherited from the inflated 1920s. Often, in lectures, I have displayed early bills from our firm which show how, in 1926, one of the Lehmans bought from my father a Hepplewhite sideboard for seventy-five hundred dollars, and on the same bill I can refer to a New England blockfront kneehole desk for which they'd paid a mere twelve hundred dollars. Such are the vagaries of the marketplace that today, half a century or more later, that Hepplewhite sideboard has not appreciated very much from its original cost then. That same blockfront? Today it would bring easily fifty times that price.

Karolik took keen delight in extracting masterpieces from the ancestral families of Boston and its environs. He'd become convinced that these owners did not respect or appreciate their heritage. "They don't *deserve* to own them!" he'd insist. With the fervor of the convert, he, a Russian, was going to show these smug New Englanders what they had forgotten about their treasures. With what secret weapon? "All it takes with these Yankees is enough money," he'd confide.

One of the greatest pieces in the Karolik collection is a chest on chest made by William Lemon, of Salem, and then carved by Samuel McIntire. That piece was originally owned by the two Curtis sisters, who inherited it along with their family home in Magnolia, Massachusetts. When Karolik found out about the piece and went to examine it, he discovered that the two ladies were using it to ripen their pears in its drawers. "They *especially* do not deserve such beauty!" he would declare, and his pleasure in getting it away from them was intense.

Since Maxim was primarily interested in the beauty of antiques, it was a thrill to show him a great piece. I would watch him examining an example of fine American craftsmanship as if it were a great painting, or a piece of sculpture. You would never see Karolik open drawers to examine the age of the wood lining inside, nor would he ever turn a piece upside down to verify its age or the authenticity of the woods used in its inner frame. For that sort of expertise, he relied on my father, or other experts. What Maxim was interested in, first, last, and always, was the aesthetic beauty of a table or a highboy or a beautiful Goddard-Townsend chest of drawers. He would stand away from the piece, eye it lovingly, and then he'd murmur, "Oh, what a curve!" It was, for him, almost sexual. To him, furniture was always female — to be admired, to be pursued, to be acquired, to be displayed — and to be loved and appreciated.

And his collection amply reflects his personal taste. Limited in quantity, it has no Connecticut pieces whatsoever, no primitive, nothing from New Hampshire. But overall, as a tribute to Karolik's persistence and taste, it is memorable.

Perhaps one of the highest points of his assemblage is a true masterpiece, a marble-top Philadelphia console table, a Chippendale piece made in 1760 or so, with a serpentine front, carved ball-and-claw feet, carved knees, and with its original marble top intact.

Believe it or not, this great piece had been found years before in a farmer's chicken coop, carelessly stored there by its undiscerning owner, and was now in the hands of a sharp-eyed Philadelphia dealer named Arthur Sussel. Sussel was a short dynamo of a man, a really tough operator down in his own bailiwick. He had gotten in touch with Karolik about this magnificent piece, and Karolik hurried to see it.

It was love at first sight. The table appealed to him as if it were a magnificent woman; he had to have it. But the consummation was, as in most love stories, difficult. The owner, Arthur Sussel, characterized by Karolik as "a greedy dealer," wanted $10,000. In the late 1930s, that was an unheard-of price.

Karolik refused, but he was determined to rescue that imprisoned beauty. He would come into our shop, raging like an angry Russian bull. "That son of a bitch!" he'd declaim. "He's a robber! *Ten thou-*

Karolik console table, Philadelphia, circa 1760–1770. Now in the Museum of Fine Arts, Boston.

sand dollars — I will die first! I will never give him such a price for that piece — why he got it for absolutely nothing — he is a *bandit!*"

Back and forth they would rage, and Karolik's passion for the beauty remained unrequited, for little Mr. Sussel was just as tough as Maximum Karolik with the Minimum Prices, and he knew well how rare and valuable this magnificent table was. For a long, long time, the two of them dueled for the maiden.

Finally, and luckily for the Boston Museum of Fine Arts, one day both must have tired of the hostilities. Negotiations resumed. Sussel yielded a tiny bit, and came down in price. Karolik came up a bit. They continued to argue and shout back and forth, but this time both had decided to bring the affair to a conclusion. For a price of about seventy-five hundred dollars, Maxim finally acquired the great table, and off it went to Boston.

Still a very high price in those days, true. But were you to try and acquire an equivalent rare Chippendale piece today, I'd suggest you ask some friendly banker to finance you to the sum of . . . say, $750,000.

Arms waving, eyes flashing, Maxim first acquired the finest collection of furniture he could find, and then he promptly went on to make another collection of early American paintings, then beautiful needlework, drawings and prints, and also fine antique silver, by the great Myer Myers, John Burt, and William Swan. As he accumulated these treasures, he was adamant about having each piece professionally photographed, in the most artistic manner possible. "They are great works of art!" he'd insist. "They must be treated as such!"

These photographs went into the elaborate catalogue of the completed M. and M. Karolik Collection, which was published in 1941, and which I unhesitatingly recommend as a truly comprehensive and erudite work. Everything in Karolik's collection is photographed, and with the assistance of Edwin Hipkiss, carefully described.

At the conclusion of the book, Maxim took pains to express himself most eloquently on his own philosophy of history, and on such subjects as Benjamin Randolph, the Philadelphia cabinetmaker, John Seymour of Boston, Samuel McIntire, and his own foresighted opinion that the Rhode Island school of cabinetmaking, namely the Goddards and the Townsends, were the finest in the Colonies.

For anyone who wishes to immerse himself in antiques collecting, the book is indispensable.

After Mrs. Martha Codman Karolik died, the aging Maxim became somewhat of a lonely and forlorn figure. In Boston, he stayed close to the Ritz-Carlton Hotel, where he held court in the downstairs bar, with a variety of daily guests.

Somehow, once the Karolik Collection had been completed, Maxim seemed to have lost most of his purpose in life. Whatever had created his need to express his love for early American, it had been satisfied; there seemed little else left.

He came down to New York often, and would browse through our latest acquisitions, but the collecting passion seemed to have abated. Now that his great and good friend, our father, was also gone, he would deign to treat us as mature grown-ups. "Have you listened to my records?" he'd ask. I would always assure him that I'd done so, for in fact I'd acquired them, and discovered that as a singer, Maxim had been quite tolerable. "Good, good," he'd say, pat me paternally, and continue to browse through our shop.

He was still in demand socially, for museum openings and other Boston social functions, and since all his life his sharp eyes would

light up when feminine attractions came into view, Maxim continued to flirt with any lady who caught his appreciative attentions. He
loved to tell us about one lady who came up to him after he had
given a talk on antiques and said, "Oh, Mr. Karolik, do give me the
chance to look you over, do you mind?"

"Madame," he replied, ever the Russian rake, "I don't mind at
all. I'd rather you look me over than *over*look me!"

He continued to come down from Boston, and whoever might be
in our shop when he dropped by would find himself engaged in
long discussion with Maxim Karolik on various aspects of collecting. "It's all in my book!" he'd insist. "Get the book. Turn to page
thirty-four. Read what I say there. Twenty years from now, they'll
understand what I meant!"

It's much longer than that since Maxim wrote his opinions, and
some of them bear repeating.

> *Thinking over our Museum plan from many angles [he wrote,*
> *back in 1941], my wife and I came to the conclusion that the only*
> *thing we actually lose is the feeling of possession. Yes, I admit it is a*
> *very strong feeling. But when we think of the thousands of people*
> *(Mr. and Mrs. Karolik among them) who will enjoy our treasures in*
> *the Museum, the reward is enormous, and very comforting.*
>
> *We are anxious to realize our plan very soon, while we are alive*
> *and in good health. We believe in the ancient Hebrew saying: ''What*
> *we give in health has the value of gold; what we give in sickness has*
> *the value of silver; what we give after death has the value of lead.''*
> *We prefer the value of gold, even though [sic] we are off the gold*
> *standard.*
>
> *I would like to impress you, the Trustees, and the People of Boston*
> *with the feeling that the gift is coming to the Museum not as a*
> *generous gesture of rich persons, who can afford to be generous, or a*
> *noble act of a standardized ''Patron of the Art'' — ''NO!'' — but as*
> *a feeling, which comes from within.*
>
> AS ALWAYS,
>
> MAXIM KAROLIK

A trip through the M. and M. Karolik Collection is proof positive
of the achievements of a remarkable White Russian emigré, my

father's good friend, who joined him in loving the style, the grace, and the inherent beauty of the treasures of their adopted country, in which they'd both "gone native."

Just last year, writing in the *New York Times*, critic John Russell said, ". . . that he was an obsessional collector, a great benefactor of the Boston Museum and a man of the liveliest social conscience is beyond question. This country made him. He had much to give in return, and he gave it. What better epitaph can a man have?"

Maxim would certainly have agreed.

World War II and Beyond
(Israel Sack's Final Years)

Tʜᴀᴛ sharp but brief depression of 1937–38 diminished. A year later, in 1939, I married my wife, Lauretta. By then, Israel Sack, Inc. had moved from those palatial quarters at 61 East 57th Street to a second-floor showroom at 5 East 57th.

I'd concluded that our business was such that our customers would seek us out wherever we were, and ground-floor traffic from casual passersby was just a time waster. The lower overhead at our new location, over the next few tumultuous years, would certainly prove to be a godsend. Besides, I've never felt we needed an imposing façade, nor a chic address, with which to sell our choice wares. Too many potential customers, myself included, are put off by opulent establishments with their doormen and cadres of dignified sales personnel.

And it's difficult to locate buried treasure amid such settings.

Such as the time my father and I unearthed a very rare piece, twenty-four blocks south of fashionable 57th Street, amid a mass of other items. It was when the legendary William Randolph Hearst arranged to liquidate his massive collection in, of all places, Gimbel's department store.

Mr. Hearst's eclectic assemblage had been put together in a highly haphazard manner. The Lord of San Simeon would receive catalogues from dealers all over the world who knew how avidly he bought. Legend has it Hearst would lie on his massive canopied bed in San Simeon, the castle he had built on the California coast, peruse the various catalogues, decide at random which items he wished to acquire, be it armor, old master paintings, tapestries, china, silver, or furniture, and then call up and instruct his representatives to buy, buy, buy.

Mr. Hearst had all the resources, and every opportunity to build up a great collection rivaling Ford, Henry du Pont, Miss Ima Hogg, or any of his contemporaries, but as a collector he failed dismally. Why? Because he never asked for advice. He never requested any dealer to try to educate his taste, nor would he listen to museum curators. He never saw the pieces he'd so capriciously decided to buy, never studied them, never really cared for them. Hearst was merely a driven accumulator, on the grandest of scales. Today, years later, his name means nothing as a collector of Americana.

In the late 1930s, the Hearst lawyers decided they needed to raise cash, and he thereupon ordered liquidation of some of the real estate and vast art holdings he'd collected.

Many pieces of Hearst's collection, including French, English, German, and some early American antiquities, were stored in an enormous Bronx warehouse. Mr. Hearst, it seemed, had also run up a huge bill at French & Co., the dealers, with his large purchases of tapestries and other assorted items, and by now he owed that firm a large sum.

Naturally, the customary advice was to sell on that most elegant center of fine arts and furniture dealers, our own 57th Street. So Hearst's people began consigning items from the Bronx warehouse to the dealers on 57th Street.

Very little, if anything, was sold.

Then Armand and Victor Hammer, two gentlemen who were innovative merchants and traders, and who'd had great success in creating trade deals with the Russian government, in swapping American goods for Russian antique icons, came up with a shrewd merchandising idea and presented it to Mr. Hearst and his lawyers. They proposed to be the agents for a deal with Gimbel's department store, where great quantities of the Hearst collection could be offered to the public on consignment.

On the face of it, their proposal seemed a ridiculous gamble for all concerned. Gimbel's, on 33rd Street, was a big department store with no prior history in art dealing. Merchandising "art" on a mass basis was something completely untried. But Bernard Gimbel was willing to gamble. He agreed to turn over an entire floor of his store to the Hearst people, and since they had been unable to sell much beforehand, what did they have to lose?

The deal was made. Full-page ads heralded the sale; they were clever. No fancy hyperbole, merely the news that good old-fashioned Gimbel's, which had always been noted for its reliable good-value-for-your-money merchandise, would now be offering its customers a chance to acquire hundreds of different historical antiques — at rock-bottom, reasonable prices!

The results were remarkable. Hordes of ordinary buyers from all over the East descended on that vast sales floor, to go through hundreds of pieces of armor, antique arms, tapestries, medieval furniture, Italian Renaissance paintings, English, Spanish, and German antiquities — all gathered together in a random assembly. Scattered here and there were some early American pieces, but one had to hunt for them.

Everything was displayed with brief descriptions attached, and carefully tagged with a Gimbel's no-nonsense price. It was very clever marketing. The combination of Hearst's name, plus Gimbel's reputation for honesty and good value, induced a sense of security in potential customers who'd probably never before indulged themselves in anything vaguely "antique." That vast sales floor was literally swept clean of Mr. Hearst's acquisitions.

My father and I went downtown to Gimbel's, to check out Mr. Hearst's purchases of early Americana. We took our own advice; each of us brought along an expert to seek out the possible values. He brought me; I brought him. Eureka! — amid the jostling crowds, we located two William and Mary–style highboys, very early American pieces, each tagged and priced at a very reasonable $600.

We examined both of them carefully. One piece had a completely new understructure, a restoration. The other — believe it or not — was completely original, centuries old, and perfect.

If Macy's wouldn't tell Gimbel's, neither would we. We bought the perfect highboy, and it promptly left 33rd Street and made its way up to our showroom on 57th Street, where it belonged.

*   *   *

When Pearl Harbor came, my wife and I had already had our first child, Kenneth. My two brothers, Albert and Robert, enlisted, but since I had an infant son, I waited to be drafted.

I already knew from government announcements that antique dealers were among the list of occupations deemed unessential, so I decided to learn a trade, something essential for the war effort, such as drafting. I'd seen ads for the Mondell Institute, and I realized a knowledge of blueprints would probably be useful to the military, so I enrolled in their course. After I completed my night classes, I waited for a call from a prospective employer in an essential industry.

It wasn't long in coming. One day, a new customer named Richard Loeb walked in and purchased a lovely eighteenth-century silver sugar bowl. He asked me to deliver it to his place of business in New Brunswick, New Jersey. When I arrived, I found myself at the door of Universal Plastics Corporation. In his plant, employees were busily engaged in compression and injection molding of plastics for industry.

The subject of my future came up, and I explained I'd taken drafting training. Loeb promptly asked if I'd be willing to go to work for him. He desperately needed draftsmen, and his foreman could train me. Before I left his plant, I'd been hired.

My father stayed on, running the shop on 57th Street by himself, without his sons to help him. Fortunately, he was still vigorous enough to do so.

By the time my draft call came a year later, Universal Plastics was inundated with military jobs, most of them top secret, and I was on a very essential status. In a matter of months, I'd become involved in the production of such war material as the M1 fuse, the frangible bullet for pilot training programs, and the nonmagnetic land mine housing, which presumably defied land mine detectors. From drafting, I went up to the estimating department, and from that job I became the overall troubleshooter for the entire plant. For the rest of the war years, and for a long time to come afterward, I was no longer a dapper 57th Street antiques dealer, dealing in one of a kind pieces and creations two centuries old, but a blue-collar worker superintending busy production lines which stamped out vitally needed plastics by the hundreds each hour.

Chippendale masterpieces and frangible plastic bullets may be light-years apart in their aesthetics, and their costs, but the lessons I learned at Universal Plastics, during the war and in peacetime, in manufacturing, distribution, and sales promotion were never forgotten. It would be some time before I returned to the antiques business, but I have always referred to those principles, ever since. While the products, antiques — or plastics — differ wildly in the separate marketplaces, certain fundamentals apply to both. The laws of economics are immutable.

After the war, I continued with the plastics manufacturing. Those years were filled with commercial success, both at Universal Plastics, and later in various partnerships that produced all sorts of products, ranging from radio cabinets to poker chips and plastic containers for food packaging. Aesthetically, none of our output ever "spoke to me" — if they had, it would only have been to reveal columns of welcome black ink.

The years passed rapidly while I enjoyed earning profits with our plastics business. But over on East 57th Street, the firm of Israel Sack, Inc. was foundering badly. At times I was glad I was able to help my father financially. But all sorts of family problems were crowding in. My brother Albert had moved to Cincinnati to try his own hand at the antiques business, but the venture had not prospered. Customers for whatever pieces were left in inventory in our 57th Street shop were scarce. Even when Albert returned, to wrestle with the problem of selling what was on hand, he had constant frustration with customers who were unable to see the fine points of the pieces we dealt in and were reluctant to pay the difference which the extra quality warranted.

Albert wrote an article for *Antiques* magazine called "Good, Better, Best," comparing the artistic merit of one type of piece with its superior counterparts, pointing out the subtle design reasons for the differences. Expanded, that article would become the basis for his book, *Fine Points in Furniture*, which is even now a primary source for collectors.

As for my father, his health was beginning to fail. He had reached his old age with a legendary reputation, but alas, with no financial means other than what I was able to supply. He had lost none of his enthusiasm, nor his knowledgeable eye for the best, but all around him, over the past years, the competition had grown very keen, and my father was finding it difficult to keep up with the newer, more aggressive dealers. Whenever I'd ask him about his financial situation, he would optimistically assure me the future was rosy. "Remember, there are always customers for the really good things!" he'd insist.

Unfortunately, as I found out, those same tasteful buyers were usually slow in paying. One in particular, a Mr. Moore, had owed my father money for years. One day my father proudly announced he'd just sold Mr. Moore a very fine expensive blockfront. When I protested that Mr. Moore already owed the firm a considerable amount of money, my father said, "But he's good for it!"

"He may be good for it, but he never pays!" I said.

By that time, my father was living alone in a room in the back of the showroom, in reduced personal circumstances. In his early seventies now, somewhat stooped and visibly aging, he ate out of cans, cooked on a hotplate, and yet he never complained. He was always willing to spend long hours in the front, chatting with prospective customers, educating them to the fine points of whatever furniture we had left in stock, and doing his best to keep what there was of the business going.

One day, a young Navy sailor dropped in to wander around, eyeing the various pieces on display. The following week he returned. After several visits, he had obviously fastened his attention on an antique screen, a folding piece of great beauty. One day he said to my father, "How I'd love to buy that. . . . It's so beautiful."

My father, who'd now grown used to the young sailor's regular visits, warmed to his enthusiasm. Yes, indeed, it was a lovely screen, and he loved it, too, and he proceeded to supply its history and demonstrate its fine points.

"But I could never afford it," sighed the young man.

"It's only six hundred dollars," said my father. "Very reasonable."

True enough. In that period, such a price was certainly rock bottom.

"I could pay you fifty dollars a month until it was paid for," suggested the sailor. "But that's all I could possibly handle."

"Fine," said my father. "You love it so much — take it."

He had found a kindred spirit who appreciated beauty as much as he did, and who was equally short of capital.

The astonished young sailor took his prize away, and dutifully paid the monthly installments until it belonged to him.

My father had come a long way down from his halcyon days as "Crazy" Sack on Charles Street.

But he still operated the same way. On trust.

Albert was trying to do his best to keep the firm afloat. It wasn't easy. My father, who had once been such a gambler, possessed of a gambler's iron nerve, had lost that instinct. The other antiques dealers in Manhattan were circling warily, waiting for the ultimate disaster.

One day, I stopped by the store to find two strangers taking inventory of what was left of the stock. Who were they? Representatives of Parke-Bernet, the successors to the American Art Galleries, where my father had over the years spent countless thousands buying items at auction. Now the pattern was reversed. What were they here for? "A liquidation sale," said one of the men. Hadn't I heard? My father had decided such a drastic move was the only way out of his desperate financial problems.

I made a decision on the spot. I hurried back to my office and informed my partners in the plastics business that I was planning to return to Israel Sack, Inc. full time. Nobody was happy about the move — except me. We arranged a future buy-out of my interests.

I went back uptown to 57th Street, and we called off the proposed liquidation sale at Parke-Bernet. I wasn't about to let our family business, which represented almost half a century of proud history, disappear in one or two ignominious sales sessions under an impersonal auctioneer's hammer.

My father welcomed my intention to return. He was feeling quite weak now, and had reached old age with his reputation intact, but with no financial means. Most of the firm's buying was from one of the country's great pickers, Harry Arons, of Ansonia, Connecticut, a legend in the antiques business. Harry would leave with his truck on Monday, and scour the countryside, calling on all his agents, small local dealers, or socially connected people delighted to make a finder's fee for turning up some valuable family heirloom. An astute and quick buyer, Harry had a keen instinct for authenticity and quality. Friday he was back in Ansonia, and over the weekend he would be on the phone to dealers waiting to snap up Harry's latest finds. Shrewd though he was in spotting fine pieces, Harry had another virtue. He was the only dealer who would "carry" his customers; he would cheerfully accept another dealer's trade note, and then bring it to his bank in Ansonia for financing. Thanks to Harry's help, my father had managed to keep the business afloat, but obviously, his health would not allow him to continue.

One of my good friends and customers before the war had been Ralph Blum, a prominent talent agent out in California. There was, and still is, little interest on the West Coast in American antiques of the top quality, but Ralph's vigorous and constant collecting was very exciting. He was married to one of the great stars of the silent-film era, Carmel Myers, who later became a leading tastemaker and decorator in Beverly Hills. I was Ralph's unofficial agent, and many nights we spent hours on long-distance, discussing various items coming up the next day at New York auctions, which I would then buy for him.

Trying to guide a customer some three thousand miles away was no easy task. On one occasion, Ralph had been offered a bombé Massachusetts secretary out on the West Coast for twenty-five hundred dollars, a sizable sum of money then. To attempt to authenticate it over a telephone was even more difficult than bidding for him, but I did. Ralph stood by the secretary, answering my questions about its feet, the interior of its drawers, what sort of decoration it bore, the finish, and so on, and when it was over, I said, "Buy." He did, and Ralph had acquired one of the country's great masterpieces — with the help of A.T.&T. and me.

In 1942, when I'd told him I was leaving the antiques business to go into plastics, Ralph wrote me a letter which I've kept for years.

He said, "I hope . . . of course, that someday you will come back to your old business. It would be a great loss . . . if a man of your integrity and of your experience and knowledge in that field were to abandon it for all time." Then Ralph went on to add a prediction. "Furthermore," he wrote, "I think your business is about to come into its own. It is the history of collectors' items that, following depressions like that which has existed for the past ten or more years, such articles go up to new heights, and that the demand for them becomes increasingly great. Your old business should, therefore, come into its own."

(Even he, prescient as he was, could not have possibly imagined where the values, and the prices, would go.)

It was time to prove that Ralph's prophecy was correct.

My younger brother, Robert, had finished four years of college, but so far could not find any meaningful employment. Albert and I brought Robert in with us.

Things were in a very sorry state in our shop. The inventory was down to a bare minimum, and most of what we had left to sell turned out to be the property of other customers, or joint ventures, with dealers, on consignment. Our firm had no bank credit, we owed money, our two cabinet shops on which we relied for repairs had let us know that, unless our outstanding bills were paid, they would not take on any more work, and even *Antiques* magazine let us know there would be no more advertising until our bills with them were settled.

It was the 1930s all over again. We were on the brink of another failure.

One morning, a member of a leading Massachusetts family walked in, to offer us a rare bombe Massachusetts secretary, a family heirloom. My brother Albert took a gamble, and bought it.

This time, he was determined that this prize not be frittered away at a small profit for a quick sale, which had been happening to us lately with monotonous regularity. Together with my brother Robert, he drove the piece down to Winterthur, to show it personally to Henry du Pont, and to offer it to him at the then unheard-of price of fifty thousand dollars.

An even bolder gamble, yes, but we were only following one of my father's earliest precepts, to sell the finest to the finest people.

The gamble paid off. Through his director, Charles Montgomery, Mr. du Pont made a substantial counteroffer, and purchased the secretary. The profit was an enormous help, but we still had a long way to go.

When my father's health began to fail seriously, we found a pleasant nursing home for him, in Massachusetts, where he'd begun his career so many years ago. By a stroke of extreme irony, the home was in Wellesley, and the view from my father's bedroom window looked out on the backyard of the home which had belonged to Helen Temple Cook, the headmistress of the Dana Hall girls' school. In that same home Mrs. Cook had kept her collection of fine antiques, the very same collection my father had bought from her in the 1920s and then sold to Henry du Pont.

Whenever I went to visit him, we'd sit and reminisce about all the experiences we'd shared together. Even though his memory was failing somewhat, certain times never left him, and he would constantly refer to them. He was especially fond of reliving that afternoon, many years ago, when he'd brought me into that New England lady's home, and suggested we both estimate the value of her antiques. "Do you remember — you came up with seventy-eight hundred dollars, and mine was seventy-five hundred dollars?" he would ask. "Wasn't that amazing — you were only a boy of fifteen, and already you had such a sharp eye!" And he would hold my hand tightly, as if we were back again in those days when he led me in and out of farmhouses.

I remember one afternoon I came to visit him, and I found him standing, in the midst of selling a Martha Washington chair, to his "customer," a psychologist from the nursing home staff.

There was no chair in sight.

It existed, however, vividly, in my father's mind, and the young man he'd selected as his customer was perfectly willing to let himself be educated on the invisible chair's fine points.

My father nodded to me, waved a hand to let me know he had a customer, and then went on describing that very fine Martha Washington chair.

Over all his years, I dare say he had accumulated a magnificent collection in his mind.

I spent months and months with my brothers trying to sort out what was left of our inventory. We recalled many of the pieces that had been consigned to other dealers. When business is slow, only the great examples sell, and that is the time when dealers check their stock, dust it, and lose patience with those pieces that haven't sold. They can be of good quality, but in the dealer's mind they have become stale. He forgets that the first time he saw them, they raised a healthy enthusiasm on his part.

Conversely, I had long since noticed that patience, with a capital P, as practiced by such experts as Joe Kindig or Messrs. Ginsburg and Levy, is the name of the game by which dealers make big profits. Some of those pieces we recalled were marked up and promptly sold. Some of those expensive pieces we held on consignment were reevaluated by us. I then called all the owners to tell them we were discontinuing consignment. If they wanted to reduce their asking prices and sell them to us, on a long-term pay-out basis, we would renegotiate. They all agreed. Now we had some good pieces which were ours, and they all sold in short order. There is always a different feeling on the dealer's part when he owns something; people respond to the inner enthusiasms which ownership generates.

Long before, I'd decided it was useless to try to emulate my father and his remarkable sales techniques. He had his patterns, I had mine. I knew that years ago, when he'd send me out to a New England home to try to buy a bureau from some fierce old Yankee lady. Where with me she would snap, "What? Can't be bothered, come back some other time!" and slam the door in my face, with my father it was another story indeed. Smiling cheerfully, he'd disarm her by a multitude of ploys. "May I come in and ask you one question, madam?" he'd ask. Half an hour later, he'd be sitting in her parlor, in her best chair, sipping her tea, and telling her jokes or a Talmudic parable. He'd also end up with the bureau . . . and perhaps the parlor chair.

The more implacable or obdurate the buyer, or hostile the seller, the more my father worked at winning him over. He relished the challenge; with him it was a lifelong game.

I couldn't rely on biblical stories or sly anecdotes designed to illustrate a buyer's stupidity in passing up some masterpiece. But by now I understood I could be as effective if left to my own devices. If I knew my subject, and did my homework, then the proper presentation of whatever item I might be selling should attract intelligent customers.

That, plus the lessons on presentation borrowed from our friend Maxim Karolik. Our brasses were polished till they shone, the rare woods and veneers gleamed with a lovely glow. Each of our masterpieces put its best ball-and-claw or hair-paw foot forward.

But on one principle of my father's, however, I could remain implacable.

One day, years back, a customer had stopped in to buy a prize piece from him, and remarked, "I'd like to be on your preferred list, Mr. Sack, but I'd also like a better price on this piece."

"Fine, fine," said my father jovially. "I'll give you a better price. But you won't go on my preferred list. The people I have on that list don't ever ask me for better prices."

Since, over the past decade in the plastics business, my training had been on the financial and business level, the looseness of our operation appalled me. I went to consult with my old friend C. K. Davis, who'd just retired from his position as head of Remington Arms and wasn't enjoying his new status on the shelf at the early age of sixty-five. When I asked him for financial advice, he offered it. "Get yourself connected with a bank, not a small one but a big one," he said, "and develop a sound credit line."

C.K. was now on the board of directors of the newly established Winterthur Museum. He suggested that I become a co-curator there, along with Charles Montgomery, whom he had recommended for the job. I was grateful for his suggestion, but I was also certain that if I took on such a position there would be a conflict of interest between our firm, the museum, and me. I also didn't want that sort of a job; the business side of the antiques business was as important to me as the academic expertise. I was now of the opinion that to be successful, to top our ever-growing competition, we needed both.

I thanked C.K. for his advice and encouragement, and went back to secure a line of credit with a bank.

We had one other major asset. The name of Israel Sack, now a legend. Nobody could take that away from us.

Shortly afterward, we celebrated the fiftieth anniversary of the firm, and my brother Albert solicited letters from major collectors and customers of the previous era. Their personal warmth and gratitude were overwhelming.

Now we had the next fifty years to contend with, and nowhere to go but up.

Which we were determined to do.

ELEVEN

Miss Ima Hogg
of Texas

Miss Ima Hogg, of Bayou Bend, Texas, was known to her friends and acquaintances as the First Lady of Texas. She was known to us for many years as a good friend of my father's, and later of my brothers Albert and Robert, and myself.

The daughter of the late Texas governor James Hogg, she was a keen-minded, outspoken spinster whose more than half a century of collecting resulted in generous gifts to her fellow Texans. In the early 1900s, she bought Picassos and Chagalls, long before they were fashionable. Later, she remarked, "They are so old hat now that even people who don't like modern art like them!" Her extensive collection of modern art went to the Museum of Fine Arts in Houston, in 1939. Five years later, she donated another collection, this one of Zuni and Hopi American Indian jewelry and art, to the same museum.

The Hogg fortune was built on the proceeds of the 1919 oil strike in the West Columbia fields, and from then on, years before any of her fellow Texans were interested in early American antiques, Miss Ima began accumulating fine examples. In those early days, prices were modest, and knowledgeable buyers few and far between. Miss Ima constantly did her homework. She studied, took notes, and kept meticulous records of her findings.

Miss Ima Hogg.

I remember once I sent her a photograph of a fine eighteenth-century Baltimore secretary for her consideration. She wrote back almost immediately, and in her letter she asked, "Why is the satinwood of the plinth a different color from the wood on the frieze?"

I promptly went back to study the actual secretary, and Miss Ima was absolutely right. It *was* a different color — and nobody in our shop had noticed it at all!

She spent many years furnishing her lovely twenty-two-room mansion Bayou Bend, at River Oaks, Texas, with fine early American pieces. Her collection in that graceful white mansion, with its imposing pillared portico, is now the Decorative Arts Wing of the Museum of Fine Arts, and everything in it mirrors Miss Ima's good taste and shrewd judgment.

We had many adventures together, usually involving such prizes as the corner chair from East Haven, Connecticut, which she snatched away from Henry du Pont. Miss Ima's regal manner masked a shrewd mind and a native Texas toughness. When a rare piece came into our showroom, she could almost smell it. Somewhere inside her, she had a radar screen, and that antique would cause it to blip, blip, blip.

Once she'd spotted it, her subsequent dealings were sharp. She could and would tilt with anyone, rival collectors or dealers, and the most remarkable part of her success as a collector was that she was in constant competition with such giants as Henry Ford, Francis Garvan, Henry du Pont, and all those other titans of the 1920s and 1930s.

Bear in mind, they not only had wealth, but they were much closer to the mainstream, here in New York and Boston. Since Miss Ima, because of an ear condition, could not fly, she had to rely, down in Texas, on dealers' photos and catalogues of forthcoming auctions. Thus she soon developed the capacity to coax metropolitan dealers into holding pieces until she could find a way to see them personally, or even to ask for the item to be sent down to Texas, on approval.

Her rivalry with Henry du Pont had very early origins. During the 1920s, he kept a standing order at Collings and Collings in New York to notify him when anything truly rare came on the market. In 1927, they acquired something quite special — eight perfectly matched mahogany Chippendale chairs, and a matching chairback settee. They dated back to 1760–1790, and had belonged to the Forbes family, of Worcester, Massachusetts. The Collingses had bought them from their present owner, and on the day the set of chairs and the settee were delivered to their showroom, Miss Ima, on one of her trips to New York, wandered into their premises. No one had had time to stow the valuable set away until Henry du Pont could examine it.

Miss Ima spotted them. Blip, blip, blip, went her radar. Years later, she said, "I went in there one day and saw them and said, 'I want that,' and I bought them right on the spot. I thought I had paid the most horrible price, but it is nothing. Mr. du Pont came in a little later, and he was furious!"

She was also exceedingly patient. When she began to collect, she went to visit and to study the collection formed by Luke Vincent Lockwood, whose *Colonial Furniture in America* had long been a standard work on American antiques. Although Lockwood did not wish to sell anything from his home in Riverside, Connecticut, Miss

Ima willingly waited some three decades to buy what she had always wanted, at auction, after Lockwood's death.

Some of her other prizes bear fascinating histories. One was a fine old Chippendale mahogany lowboy, circa 1770, from Philadelphia. It had stood, undiscovered, for many years in the basement of the First Congregational Church in Seattle, where the Ladies Aid Society attached a metal towel rack to one side, for use as a washstand. It was discovered, quite by accident — another Remarkable Discovery — in 1946, by a lawyer, who found it listed in one of his clients' wills, as "The old wash stand in the basement of the Congregational Church." The towel rack was removed, off came the washbasin and water pitcher, and the precious Philadelphia lowboy was sent East to a dealer, who sold it to Miss Ima.

Another one of Miss Ima's prizes at Bayou Bend is one of the best Philadelphia marble-top console tables in America. There is one other similar to it in the Rhode Island School of Design collection, which has been there since 1900, when it was donated by the early collector James Pendleton.

Miss Ima's table came first to us in the early 1960s through a New Jersey man who was in the steel business. Although he'd bought it for a reasonable sum years before, he offered it to us at a healthy five-figure price, high even for those times. We held a family conference and decided that if we could raise the price of such a masterpiece to a new high, say to forty-five thousand, then we could afford to buy it.

We later found out that the owner had acquired it at a New, Jersey auction for a mere twelve hundred dollars, so it was obviously he who had the nerve to put it up to such an unreachable price, not us.

We took the gamble and bought the table, and put our newly acquired prize in our front entrance hall. The price, forty-five thousand dollars, was based on our theory that it was a masterpiece. If we couldn't resist it, then some knowledgeable collector would be unable to as well.

But it was indeed a gamble, since the cash involved had severely depleted our corporate treasury.

All hell broke loose. Everyone in the business complained bitterly

Hogg Chippendale mahogany marble-topped console table, Philadelphia, circa 1760. The marble-topped console tables of Philadelphia are among the prizes of American Chippendale furniture. This table has the added beauty of a serpentine-shaped front and apron, which departs from the rectangular form of most other examples. The carving is organic to the piece and best illustrates the difference between embellishment on English forms, which is part of its design, and the American examples, which emphasize form and proportion rather than embellishment per se.

at our effrontery in asking such an inflated price. We had many visitors and browsers to see the table, but no buyers.

One day, in walked John Graham, curator of Williamsburg, whose many buying coups on behalf of that institution were legendary. He examined the table, and offered us ten thousand dollars. We turned him down. "Since you're so rich, I can see how you can afford to be so independent and unpliable," he remarked. When he left, he had warned us not to be so foolish, and to accept his offer.

A few days later, in came Miss Ima. When she saw the marble-top console, she was obviously quite impressed, but when she heard our price, she complained bitterly. "Why, it's 1929 all over again!" she said, and left.

I was sorry the price had irritated her, and I hoped her reaction was based merely on her customary outspokenness.

A few weeks later, she called and invited me to visit her at Bayou

Bend, where she wanted me to spend the weekend. "You know, my collection is going public," she said, "and I thought perhaps you might like to cull it for me, editing out the pieces which aren't top drawer."

I thought about this for a while, and although I'd quickly accepted her invitation, I was certain that Miss Ima's fine collection had previously been edited. Why did she need me for that? Then the thought crossed my mind: perhaps she wanted to negotiate on the marble-top console. Devious, perhaps, but typical of Miss Ima.

When I arrived, Miss Ima received me in her sitting room. "I do hope you'll be comfortable down here," she drawled. "Tell me, Harold, do you keep kosher?"

I was surprised at her question, and I confessed that indeed I had thought about diet on the plane coming down, and I wondered what to do if she served seafood, which I do not eat. "In essence, I do," I told her.

"Well," she told me, "my father, Governor Hogg, was strictly kosher, since his hobby was hygiene, and he long ago concluded that the Jewish dietary laws were the surest and the safest."

Next morning, at breakfast, Miss Ima asked if I'd slept comfortably. "Well, it is a lovely Salem bedroom, and I recognized some of the pieces in there — old friends which made me feel very much at home," I told her. "But I didn't sleep a wink."

"Why, wasn't the bed comfortable?" she asked, chagrined.

"Oh, no, a marvelous bed," I assured her.

"Then what was the trouble?" she asked.

"Well, Miss Ima," I said, "you know the best swindle is always the truth. I was up all night thinking of ways to sell you that Philadelphia marble-top console table."

She laughed heartily. "And what did you come up with?" she asked.

"Two things," I told her. "First, I surveyed your great entrance hall and noted that you had a superb Philadelphia lowboy, a choice Philadelphia chest on chest, and those superb Philadelphia Chippendale chairs. I believe that our great console table should be in such great company."

"But what about that marble-top Philadelphia console table that I already have there?" she demanded.

"That's the second thing," I told her. "Early this morning I got up and came downstairs, and I examined that table very carefully."

"What did you discover, Harold?"

"Well, Miss Hogg, I'm not a 'maven' on marble," I said, "but in my opinion, that is a new marble top, and if so, when your collection goes public and this is a museum, that table is not worthy of being part of it."

Miss Ima smiled across the breakfast table, a slow, enigmatic smile. "Harold," she said finally, "I have a confession. That table did originally have its proper old marble top, but one day the eagle ornament from the mirror above the table fell off, and it hit the marble at precisely the right spot, just at the nerve juncture, and caused it to shatter. I had the Vermont marble works make a reproduction, but I must admit, you're the first to recognize it. I'm truly surprised you picked it up."

"Well, I did," I said. "Now. What about *our* table?"

"All right, Harold," she said. "Let's us do business."

After we'd batted it back and forth, she agreed to purchase the table, provided we included a tall clock which she had fancied very much.

We agreed. I returned to New York with special instructions for delivering that precious table and protecting its original marble top. My brother Robert accepted the challenge, and the table was personally delivered to Miss Ima at Bayou Bend.

But before it left, John Graham reappeared in our shop, and asked to see it once more. I showed it to him. This was its farewell appearance before its departure for Texas.

Once again, John made his pitch. He asked what was the absolute lowest price I'd accept for the table. "Academic, John," I said. "It's been sold."

He left the shop, obviously irritated. His gamble had failed.

But Miss Ima would return quite often, and whenever she did, she'd always say, "Oh, Harold, I'm so glad you made me buy that table! Your father would have done exactly the same thing!"

In 1970, on her ninetieth birthday, there was a huge party honoring Miss Ima, to which I was fortunate enough to be invited. The lavish festivities were held at Winedale, Texas, a native German farm community dating from 1830, upon which Miss Ima had spent a great deal of time and effort in restoring the several antebellum homes and buildings to their original state, with appropriate decor and furniture.

The list of three hundred guests was impressive, for Miss Ima's constant contributions to the University of Texas and to the Houston Symphony, which she founded, and to the museum were legendary.

I rented a car at Houston, and with the aid of my road map, managed to guide myself over dirt roads until finally I arrived at Winedale, and the festivities. There I found my hostess, wearing a high-necked dress of yards of pink chiffon, tirelessly circulating amidst her guests. By that time she had been forced by illness to use a wheelchair. She gave me a profuse welcome, and embraced me. "Harold," she said, "I've got a marvelous piece here I want you to see. It's a must. We'll go together afterward."

I promised to do so, and the party went on until very late. Miss Ima told her guests, "I hope you all live as long as I do and enjoy life as much as I have."

I ran into my good friend Clement Conger, curator of the White House and State Department collections, and promised him a ride home after the festivities. About nine o'clock in the evening, the guests began to leave. I thought perhaps Miss Ima would be too tired, or would forget about whatever it was she wanted to show me, but not Miss Ima. She never forgot anything. Before I could leave, she'd waved me back. "Harold, I want you to come with me now!" she insisted.

Sotto voce, I told Clem we'd both better wait.

In a short while, she was lifted in her wheelchair into a station wagon, and we all drove through the dark Texas night to a nearby house which she was restoring and furnishing. Miss Ima was carried out. The house had high front steps, and there were no lights yet, and we had to lift her up the steps, across the porch, and into the darkened house.

We followed the shadows down the hallway and into another room. "Here it is!" announced Miss Ima. Suddenly, a large flashlight lit up what appeared to be a monstrous bed, one of the biggest I've ever seen. Massive, a four-poster made of oak, nineteenth-century German in style, heavy, and covered with elaborate carvings of wings and cherubs, it was awe-inspiring.

"Well, Harold," asked Miss Ima, "how do you like it?"

It took me a moment or so to answer. "Miss Ima," I said, finally, "I've never in all my experience seen anything like it."

To which she promptly replied, with great satisfaction, "And you never will again, either!"

She died in London, while on a trip, at the age of ninety-three.

I think my fondest memory of Miss Ima is of the day I called on her in Texas when she'd already turned her home at Bayou Bend over to the museum and had moved into an apartment, where she still had a few fine early American pieces.

We were chatting, and then she said, "Harold, I've got something here to show you."

We went into another room where she had a recently acquired piece, a sofa by John Henry Belter, circa 1850. It was part of a new nineteenth-century collection she was assembling. In Bayou Bend, there is now a room, the Belter Parlor, dedicated to the creations of that nineteenth-century craftsman.

"Well, Harold," she asked, "what do you think of my Belter piece?"

That nineteenth-century style had never been my cup of tea, and while I was polite about her sofa, I must have made it quite clear to Miss Ima I was unimpressed.

In her most colloquial fashion, she shook her head sadly, and said, "Harold, there's the future. You'd better get with it!"

And, as she had so often been during her long life, Miss Ima's good judgment and taste, her nerve and her independence would again be absolutely right.

Washington
Shopped Here

E ARLY in 1959, several members of the National Society of Interior Design called on us with a project they wished to present
to us, the redecoration of the White House.

"Its furnishings are a public disgrace," said one of our visitors.
"We've formed a committee to raise funds for a complete face-lift.
For a start, we'd like to do the Oval diplomatic reception room, on
the ground-floor level."

A fine idea, long overdue. As we all knew, the furnishings and
decor of the White House had in past administrations always been
executed at the taste and direction of whichever President and his
lady were in residence. The results over the years had been, to put
it diplomatically, a hodgepodge.

We heartily agreed. And what sort of furnishings were to be used?

"We're planning to use the best examples we can find of early
English and American," he told us.

We could not believe what we'd been told.

To furnish the White House, one of our most historic structures,
with *English* pieces?

For such a notion, inappropriate was hardly the proper word. Not
only were we so strongly chauvinistic because we Sacks have been
dealing exclusively in American works for all these years, but also

because we felt the White House, of all possible showplaces available, should represent the finest of our *own* heritage.

We responded, diplomatically of course, that such a mix of English cum American was of no interest to us. However, if this committee would consider their project an exclusively American undertaking, we would start the ball rolling by donating a choice Hepplewhite sofa, of New York origin.

They agreed. Our contribution sparked Mr. Scalamandré to donate the fabric for its reupholstering, and Mr. Field to weave a beautiful rug on which it would stand.

When it arrived in its new home in the White House, photographs were taken of President Eisenhower standing by the mantel, near the newly acquired sofa. Ironically enough, on that mantel behind him stood a gilded French clock, made for the American market, topped by a figure of George Washington. Most of these clocks were made in France by Debuc with beautiful enameled dials, and were shipped from France to the port of Baltimore.

We had no quarrel with a French antique clock. They had, after all, been our allies in the war against the British crown.

A year or so later, after President John F. Kennedy was elected, his first lady, Jacqueline, decided to further that project for redecorating the White House, and wisely formed a Fine Arts Committee, to be headed by Henry du Pont. A young Winterthur Museum graduate, Lorraine Pearce, had written her thesis on the early Classical period of American decorative arts, a subject which appealed to Mrs. Kennedy's tastes. Ms. Pearce became Mrs. Kennedy's personal curator.

In those Camelot years, the restoration of the White House induced a great surge of response from collectors everywhere. Everyone agreed that such a recognition of our American heritage was long overdue; the job was accomplished without taxpayers' funds, but solely through private donations.

At first, some of the collectors with whom we discussed such gifts were hesitant. They did not wish to have any treasures disbursed, sold, or given away by some future incumbent President whose first lady's tastes did not agree with Mrs. Kennedy's. That problem was solved by an Act of Congress, which when passed, forbade the disposal of such gifts and made it a law that once an item was removed from the White House, it would go to the Smithsonian.

Mrs. Kennedy came into our shop several times, and once spent time admiring a colored antique engraving of the Battle of New Orleans. I offered it to her with our compliments. She was delighted. "I'll give it to the President for his birthday," she said. Then she studied it a few moments more. "Can I ask you," she said, "just whom were we fighting then?"

After a little thought on my part, I remembered. "The British," I told her. "But although peace had been declared, the news hadn't yet reached New Orleans."

She nodded, and then she commented laughingly, "We fought so many different people, I have never been able to keep track of them!" Her candor and humility touched me.

One day I was out in Muttontown on Long Island, having lunch with my friend Lansdell Christie, when I received an urgent call from the White House. It was a small crisis. It seemed that the Kennedys were on their way to Vienna, where they would meet with the Soviet premier, but no one had remembered to provide a suitable gift for Mrs. Kennedy to present to Mrs. Khrushchev. Time was very short. Could we help?

I rushed back to 57th Street and looked around our shop. Then I received another call from the White House. The gift would have to be picked up by five o'clock that afternoon and flown immediately to Vienna. To help me solve the problem, somebody in the White House had suggested possibly an antique sewing table. Not possible. We had none with a properly restored embroidery bag, and such a gift didn't seem too appropriate for the occasion.

I noticed a fine porcelain antique pitcher, on which was the decoration of an American eagle, carrying a banner on which was emblazoned *Peace, Plenty,* and *Independence.* I called the White House and suggested the pitcher. The response was affirmative. Sold, for $350, and would I please wrap it up?

I was doing so when I noticed, at the rear of the pitcher, an old poem, whose first lines were:

> *Let the Wealthy and Great*
> *Roll in Splendor and State . . .*

I stopped wrapping. Were such thoughts by an anonymous early American poet appropriate for a gift to Mrs. Khrushchev? It didn't seem too likely. I called the White House again. When I read them the poem, the answer came back, Absolutely negative!

What now?

I suggested a piece of Sandwich glass, that beautiful early American glassware, made in an early Cape Cod factory. Since Sandwich was so near to the Kennedy family compound in Hyannisport, would this not provide a personal quality to the gift?

The answer was once more affirmative. But now there arose another problem. We did not carry any such Sandwich glassware, and time was really running out.

I hurried up Madison Avenue to Louis Lyons's shop on 68th Street, and there I unearthed a beautiful crystal clear covered sugar bowl, with an impressed eagle. It had been illustrated in George McKearin's definitive book on Sandwich glass. Truly a piece worthy of presentation to the heads of the Russian state.

Mr. Lyons wanted $500. I told him to hold the piece for fifteen minutes while I checked with my buyers. I dashed across Madison to the Westbury Hotel, called the White House from a pay phone, and proposed the Sandwich glass bowl. "Perfect!" said the harried White House aide. "Buy it, and we'll send the courier to pick it up!"

I ran back across the street, and told Mr. Lyons to bill me and that I'd explain later. Carrying that precious sugar bowl with care, I found a taxi, and got it safely back to our place. I finished packing it minutes before the courier arrived, and off it went to Vienna. Mission accomplished.

I never did find out how Mrs. Khrushchev liked her present.

But I sent the White House a bill.

Several months of silence ensued. Then, one day my secretary came in holding a check which had arrived that morning. It was for $500, there was no bill attached, and the check was signed by a Mr. Joseph P. Kennedy. She wasn't able to match it with any of our invoices. Did I have any notion for what this check was payment?

Suddenly it became clear to me. The President's father had taken it upon himself to endow Mrs. Khrushchev's sugar bowl.

More than two decades later, since both Mr. and Mrs. Khrushchev have passed on, one is forced to speculate, where in the vast USSR can that historic piece of early American sandwich glass be today?

The impetus of the official government recognition of the early American crafts spilled over into other projects. The new State Department headquarters building was completed. Its interior decor was indifferent, similar to that of any modern corporate headquarters. Up on the seventh floor were the Secretary of State's offices, and on the eighth were the diplomatic reception rooms and a great banquet hall. Up there, huge windows gave the rooms the appearance of a department store main floor, and the furnishings truly fortified that impression.

When Christian Herter became Secretary of State, his wife surveyed this new set of official rooms and decided something drastic needed to be done to rescue them from the aggressively mundane bureaucratic decor.

Little did Mrs. Herter realize that in selecting Clement Conger, then the Assistant Chief of Protocol for the State Department, to assist her in redecorating that eighth floor, the end result, under Conger's keen direction, would be a collection of Americana the equal of any great wing of our most illustrious public museums.

Clem, as I have learned to call him, has a most patrician bearing, acquired, no doubt, from his maternal ancestor, the first Lord Mayor of Alexandria, Virginia. He can mix with anyone, and like most great personalities I've met, he possesses a certain humility. But not out of whimsy is Clem known as the Grand Acquisitor. Over the years, he has proceeded to beg, borrow, and steal the hearts of patriotic Americans, and to pry loose from them their choicest pieces, either by gift or by outright purchase. His lectures throughout the country, with the fees going to the State Department, captivated many collectors, and family-owned treasures were forthcoming in surprising quantity. I am proud to say that I have served as Clem's unofficial adviser over the years as he bent to the task of accumulating his remarkable collection. His industriousness is remarkable.

He has visited every known collector, attended every important auction, and browsed through the stock of every major antiques dealer. A few dealers loaned him their best pieces, and eventually, true to his word, he obtained the funds for the future purchases. All this activity as well as hosting the various State Department functions and dinners given for major donors!

Serving on Clem's Arts Commission was an honor not to be lightly treated. His devotion to his task was so intense that very few have ever defied his will.

On one occasion, a choice Newport block and shell carved kneehole desk came on the market at Christie's. I'd received a call from a Detroit customer who asked me to bid on it for him. I was reluctant to do so, for we were interested in that fine piece for our own collection, but I finally acceded to his wishes. We agreed we were to go up to about $150,000, which at that time would have been a record price.

The sale was to take place on a Saturday at two o'clock. Midmorning of that day, I received a call from Washington; Clem Conger was on the other end. He had raised some pledges of money, and he wanted that same kneehole desk for the State Department rooms. "Harold, will you bid it in for us?" he asked.

When I explained I was already committed to another buyer, I thought that would end the subject. But I didn't reckon on Clem's persistence. For whom was I bidding? I told him that was confidential.

"Mm," said Clem. "Tell me, is the party in question on my Arts Commission?"

I had to admit that he was.

"Fine," said Clem. "You bid for the State Department, and I'll handle the rest of it. Agreed?"

I had no way to inform my Detroit customer of the new situation.

I went to the auction and did Clem's bidding. When that desk came up, I bid it in for $140,000, plus the ten-percent buyer's commission. For $154,000, the State Department had acquired that superb piece.

When I told my Detroit client who had secured the desk, he was far from pleased. In fact, he literally hit the ceiling.

"Please don't complain to *me*," I told him. "This is a matter between you and Clem Conger. But one thing I'm sure of — if you want to stay on his Arts Commission, I'd suggest you start thinking of yourself as a highly patriotic underbidder."

The gentleman from Detroit was not ordinarily one to knuckle under, but Mr. Conger prevailed. After all, he had the United States government squarely behind him. One does not tread on the American flag, nor on Clem's wishes, lightly.

I was to find that out for myself, sometime later.

Six magnificent Queen Anne Philadelphia walnut chairs, made between 1740 and 1750, by any stretch of the imagination one of the finest such sets ever to turn up in the marketplace, were announced at an auction in Detroit. I knew those chairs well. They were part of a choice collection formed by a Detroit couple who'd been very good customers. They'd originally bought the chairs from Joe Kindig, in Pennsylvania, and if the owners had not been divorced, the chairs would probably still be in their collection.

One of my good friends, the collector Martin Wunsch, had preceded me to Detroit. This time, Clem was operating on a strictly undercover basis. He'd given Martin instructions to acquire those chairs for the State Department collection. I wasn't privy to those plans, so when the bidding began, I went to work. So did Martin. When the bidding finally ended, I'd been beaten out by Martin, all the way up to an unheard-of one hundred thousand dollars. I can assure you that had I been aware of the nature of my competition, I'd have bowed out at a much lower figure.

Next day, I had an urgent call from Clem. "Harold," he said, "this is a terrible situation. We need your help. As much as we want them, we don't have any such sum available to pay that price for those chairs. Could you possibly get us out of this situation?"

Well, it could be argued that I'd had some responsibility in the matter. So it became my patriotic duty to help him out.

"Let me see what I can do," I said.

The very next day I had a call from another collector, the lovely wife of a Cleveland man. They'd been away and had missed that Detroit sale, and now that they'd returned, she wanted to know how everything had gone, and for what prices.

"The chairs were the opportunity of a lifetime," I told her. "Magnificent specimens."

"Oh, I'm so sorry we missed them," she sighed.

"Don't be sorry," I told her. "There's a chance you might just be able to get them."

"*How?*" she asked.

I explained about the new turn in events with the buyer.

The following day she called back to say she and her husband definitely wanted them — but what to do about that whopping price?

Eventually we put our heads together and worked out an arrangement. The six chairs would be split within her family, three for her and her husband, three for her brother-in-law, another collector. Thus they'd be kept together, and treasured.

Triumphantly, I called Washington. "Clem," I announced, "you are off the hook. The chairs are resold, and now you don't need to come up with all that money to pay for them."

"Harold, I was just about to call *you*," he said. "This morning I managed to find someone who was willing to donate the cost of the chairs to the State Department, so we're going to keep them here after all. Isn't that fine?"

. . . Yes, but what about *my* customers?

"I suppose you'll simply have to *un*sell them, Harold," said Clem.

Not easy. How?

"Appeal to their patriotism," suggested Clem.

"I've already *done* that," I told him, sadly.

. . . It was one of the very few times I've ever had to persuade a customer to forgo a purchase. Which, considering the enthusiasm I'd whipped up, not only in myself but in my Cleveland customers, was far from easy.

The six Queen Anne chairs look marvelous in the elegant State Department rooms. Visiting dignitaries and heads of state from all over the world have been impressed, whenever they've been entertained there, by the genius of native-born American craftsmen.

The rooms are a proper tribute to our ancestors, and also to Clem Conger's single-mindedness and good taste.

And persistence.

*   *   *

My dealings with official Washington, and its minions, have not always been so serene and rewarding. Take, for example, the battle I found myself embroiled in a few years back, over a magnificent early Newport highboy which stands today on exhibit at the Metropolitan Museum in New York. It had its proud origins in the Goddard-Townsend workshops of Newport, Rhode Island, that Colony in which our ancestors fought so many battles to secure their eventual freedom from England.

Those struggles were two centuries ago, and they were waged against King George III and his implacable tax collectors. Ironically enough, this superb ancestral masterpiece of the Colonies would become the focal point of another battle, two centuries later, again over taxes. The tax collector this time was a representative of our own Internal Revenue Service.

I've always felt this superb Goddard-Townsend piece is one of the most beautiful single items which has ever passed through our hands.

Speaking of John Goddard and the Townsends, Maxim Karolik said it all when he wrote,

> *Their work, it seems, was only of Chippendale's period, not of his style. Not only the design is their own, but even the features, so to speak, have their own characteristics; for instance, the agee feet, with the "curlicue" coming down; and the claw and ball, with the light showing through; and the typical shell, of course. All these things bear their own individual stamp. Even if they were adapted, let us say, from another source, they certainly recreated them.*
>
> *This is the reason why I think that these men stand alone; they were creators. And as is known, those who create must have the spark of genius in them. Goddard and the Townsends, I believe, had that Divine Spark.*

The highboy first came to light back in 1952, when it was brought to my father by a pair of very sharp-eyed New Jersey dealers. Where had they bought it? We never found out. It remains to this day a trade secret. But it was unmistakably authentic, and in prime condition. What had they paid for it? Immaterial. What mattered was the choiceness of this highboy, and how, as my father always said, it "spoke to him."

Queen Anne plum pudding mahogany bonnet-top highboy, attributed to John Goddard, Newport, Rhode Island, circa 1750–1775. The Colonies developed the highboy form to its maximum, achieving grace and proportion to a much greater extent than England, where the chest on chest survived but not the highboy. Newport highboys are among the stars of New England, combining all the best qualities of form and select choice of wood, whether walnut, maple, or mahogany. The bonnets of these Rhode Island highboys usually had paneled scrollboards and had either slipper or ball-and-claw feet, with cabriole-shaped legs, sometimes carved with leafage and cameo motifs. The ball-and-claw foot seldom had the open talons of this example.

My father bought it from the dealers for what was then a huge price, twenty thousand dollars. Since they'd obviously paid far less for it, they were satisfied with their profit. My father sold it, shortly afterward, to Admiral and Mrs. E. P. Moore, of Washington, D.C.; his price of twenty-two thousand earned him far less.

When this beautiful piece arrived at Admiral Moore's Washington home, he opened one of the drawers, and a card dropped out. Inscribed by my father, it read, "Dear Admiral and Mrs. Moore. Hope you enjoy this great Newport piece. Just be sure it will go up a thousand dollars a year in value."

No one ever accused Israel Sack of understatement, but in the case of this highboy, time has proved him remarkably guilty.

In 1965, the Rhode Island Historical Society mounted an impressive show in Providence, the John Brown House Loan Exhibition of

Rhode Island Furniture. Prepared and catalogued by Darby Ott, it was a notable assemblage of the choicest furniture, porcelains, and portraits of that Colony. The catalogue of that show extols the Moore highboy as being "of the limited number of Rhode Island highboys with carving on the knees and open claws, this is the only example known with four such feet. The rich plum pudding mahogany case and fine open brasses create an arresting appearance."

The Metropolitan Museum had long been interested in acquiring this prize piece for its Early American Wing. When Admiral Moore died, his widow decided to present the highboy to the museum as a gift, a most generous act. She got in touch with me and asked if I would take care of the appraisal, for gift tax purposes. As the dealers who had sold it to her, we were the proper auspices for such a knowledgeable appraisal, and I was glad to do so.

I carefully set down its pedigree, attempting to reduce its great beauty and style to mere words.

Should you ask me how many such pieces survive today, I would estimate that the number of highboys from those Goddard-Townsend workshops cannot be more than two dozen. And since it is the only one known with knee carvings on all four legs, plus the open talons on all claw feet, I placed a value on it, back in 1980, of $235,000, more than ten times what Admiral and Mrs. Moore had paid for it, thirty years previously, true; but in my educated opinion, based on the highboy's quality and scarcity, a very fair price.

Two years passed, and one day I received a letter from Mrs. Moore's attorneys in New York, to the effect that my appraisal of her gift to the Metropolitan had been disallowed by the Manhattan district office of the I.R.S. What was their decision? That the high-boy was appraised at $40,000, and it was their absolute ceiling.

"Are you willing to discuss this with the man from the I.R.S.?" asked the lawyer.

It was my legal obligation to do so, and I agreed immediately. But before the meeting downtown, I had a week or so to think about this turn of events, and to prepare my case. After a bit of research through auction records, it began to dawn on me that the $40,000 figure on which the I.R.S. was insisting was not arbitrary, but had been arrived at by someone who had researched through the same Sotheby's auction records for prices of similar types of highboys. In fact, I well remembered one that had come up at auction a few years before which had brought $40,000. However, while it was indeed a fine piece, that highboy had major problems; certain restoration work had been done to it over the years. Certainly that would have reduced its value to dealers and collectors.

In going through other sales catalogues, I found several similar Newport highboys, with illustrations and references to previous sales within the past five or six years. Again, I found most of the descriptions of those pieces also did *not* note the various degrees of restoration, which again is crucial to value. Nor did they discuss the quality of the pieces. In providing provenance, the sellers had somehow always omitted such important matters.

I called the cataloguer at Sotheby's and discussed this with him. I told him I was locked in controversy over valuation with the I.R.S. which could possibly end up in litigation, and that I was certain their experts had consulted Sotheby's catalogues. "Several of your descriptions do not note the restorations, but we both know they were serious. Could you send me photostats of those highboys, with *your* descriptions, and your own determination of the restorations that had been done, in your own handwriting? I know they exist, because I was there at the sales."

He promptly agreed to do so.

"You know the Moore highboy that's now in the Metropolitan?" I asked.

Of course he did. Its acquisition had caused quite a stir among collectors and dealers.

"Without discussing any figure with me, would you put your neck out and estimate its value, on the Sotheby letterhead?" I asked. He agreed to supply that, as well.

I then called the people at Christie's, and asked them for a similar appraisal of the Moore highboy.

A few days later, both estimates arrived. The figure from Sotheby's was an estimate of $250,000–$300,000.

As was the estimate from Christie's!

Armed with this unimpeachable information and facts, I accompanied Mrs. Moore's lawyers downtown, to a meeting in the lion's den.

We were shown into a small conference room furnished strictly in late American utilitarian. There we sat down with the examiner from the I.R.S. who had challenged my appraisal. (I'll call him "Smith," since I have no desire to have my annual return examined in perpetuity.)

Mr. Smith was brisk, very polite, but in the tradition of all tax collectors since the days of George III, implacable.

We faced each other across the conference table. Had I anything I wished to bring up in this matter?

I had. "I understand that any and all appraisals of art works, including furniture, over and above the value of twenty-thousand dollars must be forwarded to a review panel in Washington, D.C.," I said.

"No," said Mr. Smith. "You're staying right here." He opened a book of documents, and cited a regulation from it, which he read aloud.

"Now," he said, with a certain amount of obvious hostility in his voice, "let *me* talk." He proceeded to lay out his reasons for estimating the piece at $40,000. He *had* consulted Sotheby's auction catalogues — I'd been correct in my assumption — and that was that. He had also consulted an appraiser of his own choice.

Might I ask who this gentlemen had been? No I could not.

"May I ask his qualifications?"

"Yes, you may," said Mr. Smith. "He does prints, paintings, glass, china, furniture, everything, in fact." He added, a bit defiantly, "He's very good at his job."

I knew better than to antagonize Mr. Smith, but I couldn't allow him to close this case so simply, so I raised the question of restorations to the pieces sold at Sotheby's. Hadn't those restorations devalued them?

Obviously, according to Mr. Smith, they had not.

I passed on to the question of quality. I handed over a copy of the catalogue of the John Brown House show, and its photograph and description of the Moore highboy. "This description proves the piece is head and shoulders above all the others you've cited," I said. "It's unique."

"So unique that there were no others made like that one," Mr. Smith countered, quickly. "Because this one obviously wasn't accepted as a form."

"Not at all!" I said. "Now you're talking about a 'maverick' piece, offbeat and strange, which this certainly is not. It's an absolute masterpiece, and far more valuable than any others which have ever appeared on the market."

Mr. Smith pulled out a set of photos of other highboys which had previously been sold at auction — exactly the ones I'd expected him to use. "You see?" he asked, triumphantly. "Nothing here over forty thousand dollars."

I had brought photographs of my own, and it was my turn to produce them. Two similar highboys sold by our own firm. One, a Chippendale mahogany highboy attributed to Goddard-Townsend, had gone to a private individual in 1969 for $95,000, and the second one, which we sold in 1981, a Queen Anne Massachusetts bonnet-type, had gone for $265,000.

"I also brought two appraisals with me," I said, and I produced the two letters from Sotheby's and Christie's. "I believe these will substantiate what I quoted as my appraisal."

Anyone could see that Mr. Smith was becoming more hostile with each item of documentation, but I was determined not to let his feelings prejudice the case. "Understand me," I said. "Mrs. Moore is not looking to rob the United States government, or any such thing. It was only out of the goodness of her heart that she so generously gave up this wonderful piece. Besides, in my estimation, I'd certainly pay her two hundred thirty-five thousand for it myself."

Mr. Smith was not impressed. He glared at me. "What qualifications do you have?" he demanded.

"Well," I told him, "knowing I was coming here today, I thought I'd get some qualifications together for your inspection, and I think I should show you this letter."

I handed him a letter on White House stationery, signed by Mr. Clement Conger, the Chief Curator.

Part of Mr. Conger's description of me read, "The firm of which he is the president has been in business longer than any other firm dealing in American antiques. The firm is known throughout the country for its outstanding reputation, integrity, and reliability. For anyone seriously to question Mr. Harold Sack's best judgment in appraising a piece of American furniture, in my opinion, is foolish. . . . Time after time, in my experience, he has been proven right where others have been wrong."

I had no choice; I had to present it. Besides, Mr. Conger had said it, not I.

Mr. Smith of the I.R.S. stared at the letter on White House stationery for a long moment, eyes narrowed, lips pursed.

Finally he asked, "Why didn't you present all this data beforehand, Mr. Sack?"

"I wasn't required to present this beforehand," I said. "I am only presenting it now because I'm now here to defend something."

Out of the corner of my eye I could see both of Mrs. Moore's attorneys squirming nervously in their chairs. They were afraid I'd gone too far.

Mr. Smith regrouped his forces and moved back into an attack position. He picked up a photo of Mrs. Moore's highboy. "Let me ask you a question," he said. "Just how do you expect to get an appraisal approved of two hundred thirty-five thousand dollars for this highboy when here, in your own description of the piece, you refer to it as *'school of* John Goddard.' That means you're not even saying it was made by John Goddard, you're *attributing* it to his school. Furthermore, it isn't even labeled as such!"

Triumphantly, he threw down my xeroxed appraisal, as if it were a gauntlet.

"Mr. Smith," I said, "there are only two or three such pieces labeled by the maker *anywhere* to be found. Everything in this field has always been by attribution. Furniture of that period does not have to be labeled, or signed, like portraits."

He shook his head. "You said *'school of.'* That's all that matters."

He closed his file.

It was obvious that the hearing was ended. "I'll let you know my ruling," he told us, got up from the table, and left the conference room.

One of Mrs. Moore's attorneys began to tuck away his papers in his attaché case. He sighed. "I'm afraid that man is not going to budge from his position," he said. "If he does, he might go up to sixty-five thousand dollars — but no more, and that will be it, believe me."

"Maybe," I said, "but I'm still of the opinion that Mr. Smith has absolutely no authority in this matter. I know I'm right — in these cases, *anything* over twenty thousand dollars in value is supposed to go right to Washington, where they have panels consisting of professionals who deal with these cases, every six months."

"Mr. Smith doesn't seem to agree with you," he commented.

It was still worth a try. When I returned to my office on 57th Street, I called the head of the arts division of the I.R.S. in Washington. I'd become acquainted with him a few years earlier when I gave classes down there at the Smithsonian on the subject of investing in antiques.

I told him I had no intention of trying to bring his influence to bear on this case, but I did want a definitive answer to my question. Should this case be reviewed in Washington?

"Absolutely," he replied. "Why isn't it being heard here?"

I mentioned Mr. Smith, and the number of the regulation he had cited to us earlier in our conference.

"That regulation has been superseded by another one," said my Washington friend, and he proceeded to read it to me. Sure enough, the wording specifically mentioned that any item in question over $20,000 should be heard in Washington. He promised to send me a copy immediately.

Up came the regulation, which I referred to Mrs. Moore's trustee and lawyers. They were impressed by my persistence, but they were still dubious. "We will not get that man downtown to budge," one of them predicted.

"Let me know what happens," I said. "I'm an optimist."

Several months passed before he called me. "We have a ruling," he announced. "It's as I said. No relief. Mr. Smith has ruled the highboy is worth forty thousand dollars — no more, no less."

Now what?

"If they won't send this case to Washington," said the lawyer, "it's up to us to appeal it. There's an appellate division down there which will hear the case. What we'll have to do is to put together a presentation of all the pertinent material. Would you help us do that? We'll need the entire story of the highboy, its history, its value — the letters from Christie's and Sotheby's, the documentation on your qualifications, sales records, the works."

I agreed to do it. But even I had no idea how imposing a document we'd end up with; a bound presentation, almost one hundred pages long, with photos, letters, appraisals, reprints of articles in magazines and catalogues — it was truly impressive.

When it was finally done, the volume went to the appellate court.

After a careful study, the appellate court sent it back to the local Manhattan district office of the I.R.S., with instructions to send this case down to Washington, D.C.!

Months later, the head of the I.R.S. panel on early American furniture got in touch with me, and asked if I would meet him at the Metropolitan. There we would join Mr. Morrison Heckscher, the curator of American Decorative Arts, and we would officially examine Mrs. Moore's highboy.

Which we did.

After another waiting period, Mrs. Moore and her lawyers received an official notice from the Internal Revenue Service. The figure of $235,000 was completely acceptable.

Years back, in 1909, when Mrs. Russell Sage bought the Eugene Bolles collection, that same assemblage which my father had helped Mr. Bolles amass, it would become the nucleus for the Metropolitan Museum's American Wing. But over the years, my father's contributions remained anonymous. That omission has happily been erased. When Berry Tracy of the Metropolitan suggested we endow three rooms in the new American Wing to be named after Israel Sack, the honor to our father was one we could not possibly refuse.

And now, in a marvelous bit of irony, today, proudly displayed at the Metropolitan, that Goddard-Townsend highboy my father sold to Admiral Moore stands only a few feet away from those three Israel Sack rooms.

Upon reflection, I've come to the opinion that my original appraisal, which induced such a battle with the I.R.S., was, in fact, too low.

If another highboy showed up for sale today, of equivalent quality and perfection, I'd pay a lot more for it.

How much more?
. . . That, I'm afraid, is a trade secret.

THIRTEEN

Authentic or Fake?

IT's one thing to develop sufficient expertise to be able to examine a fake antique when it's brought to you, and to recognize it as such — and in my lifetime, I dare say I've seen many more fakes than I have the real thing — but it's quite another thing to commit yourself, and to pass judgment on that fake.

Truly a Hobson's choice. Consider: you tell an owner that that family heirloom he's presented you with is not at all what he's fondly considered it to be all these years, or you tell the dealer that that table or chair he invested so heavily in last week is of no interest to you because his eye didn't catch a replaced drawer or the cunningly faked carving — and you instantly open up a vein of anger, pain, and disappointment, usually accompanied with hostility.

Or, you can turn away, noncommittal, and shrug, smile politely, and ignore that fake, knowing that by doing so, you promptly become an accessory after the fact — because that piece now has a renewed life-span, and might go on to be sold as legitimate to some other hapless buyer.

It's a choice with which I'm constantly confronted, and as much as I dislike to do so — because I know it's a no-win situation — I usually speak my mind, and let the chips fall where they may.

And oh, how they do fall.

* * *

I learned that lesson very early on. It was brought home to me with enormous impact during our first days in the 442 Madison Avenue store, on a day when a dealer named Jake Margolis walked in, carrying a Chippendale stool which he wished to offer to my father.

My father, as usual, was out, so I took over.

Jake was a brother to Nathan Margolis, a cabinetmaker up in Hartford. One summer I'd been lucky enough to have a temporary job with Nathan in his shop, and I'd learned a great deal about construction techniques from him. Nathan's work was equal to the best of the eighteenth-century craftsmen; local people who loved the great forms of the early periods but did not have the passion or the funds to accumulate originals could and did buy beautiful reproductions from him. His brother Jake, however, dealt only in antiques and their restoration, and over the years had built up a reputation as an authority. Often New York collectors would use Jake, and a few others of the same status, as "experts," to verify the authenticity of some other dealer's wares. Sometimes that "verification" could be used to batter down the hapless dealer's price. Such tactics could rarely be used against my father; his integrity and knowledge were above question.

But Jake's reputation as an expert was also impressive in the trade, and as such, he expected the proper respect and attention, especially from some young neophyte such as I was. He handed over the stool and said, "Here, I'm leaving this for your father to examine. Have him call me if he wants to buy it."

I stared at the Chippendale stool, and I felt my heartbeat increase. Something inside me was flashing a steady warning signal. I knew I was looking at a fake.

It was only logical to me. Stools were an English form, and represented the seats for the lower classes. The Colonies, however, were not class conscious, and any form which smacked of such class distinction was taboo. Therefore, American stools were rare indeed, and any such stool must be so readily authentic that there could be no question it had been made or assembled from old chair parts. All inner surfaces must be what is called "clean and untampered," and if the form is one requiring a slip seat, theoretically this would also have to be totally original, to mitigate against the possibility of conversion from other parts.

This particular stool was *not* early American.

Without hesitating, I blurted out what I thought.

The great Jake Margolis, the authority, flew into a rage.

"Who the hell are you to say I handle fakes?" he yelled. "What do *you* know? Forget it — I'll only deal with your father!" He stamped out, taking his stool with him.

He left me standing there, embarrassed and chagrined. I, a mere youngster in the business, had defied, possibly insulted, this gray-haired maven.

When my father returned, I told him the story. He merely shrugged, and then went over to Jake's place to examine the stool for himself.

When he returned, he was beaming. "You were right," he said. "Very sharp of you."

And did not add one word to chide me for my audacity in having challenged the great Jake Margolis. He didn't have to. I'd learned my lesson. Expertise is one thing. Tact is quite another. Even after you have acquired your status as a maven.

In the years which followed, I've had many other experiences with fakes, some dismaying, others hilarious.

In the early 1960s, a young lady came in to see me, bringing a photograph of a Philadelphia ball-and-claw-foot Chippendale wing chair which her grandmother had bought at auction in Buffalo back in the 1880s. A local decorator in her town had been urging her to sell it. "When she offered me a thousand dollars, I became alarmed," she said, "and I thought I'd better have some professional advice." The local historical society had recommended that she bring her photo down to us, for our opinion.

I studied the photo carefully, and then I said, "I really can't tell you much from this. Either it's a genuine eighteenth-century chair, which is very unlikely, or it might be a Philadelphia reproduction, of the sort that was made for the Centennial."

"How would I know?" she asked.

"You couldn't tell, but we could," I told her.

"Well, if it *is* eighteenth century, how much could we get for it?" she asked.

"Off the top of my head," I said, "at least four thousand dollars."

She was quite surprised. "That much?"

"Yes," I said, "but remember, it's based on our examining it and passing on it."

"Whew," she sighed. "I'd better discuss this with my husband."

"Let us know what you decide," I told her, and she left.

Monday morning, bright and early, she was back. She and her husband had discussed the situation and come to a decision. "We want to sell it," she said.

When could she bring in the chair?

"We have," she said. "It's downstairs, on the street, in our station wagon."

Up came the wing chair, and it went into the back room, where we could study it.

A beautiful chair, covered in a nineteenth-century velour fabric, yes, but underneath, absolutely right. We tore away at the worn fabric at salient points and checked out the frame beneath, and we could immediately see that this chair was one-hundred-percent original.

"Still interested?" asked the young lady.

"Absolutely," I told her.

She heaved another sigh and grinned. "Then you'll buy it?" she asked.

"Come into the office and I'll give you a check," I told her.

When I handed it to her, she said, "I'm delighted — and I hope you sell it for a big profit, because you've been so decent about the whole thing."

"You're welcome," I told her. "So do I."

We put our new acquisition upstairs in a side room, and waited for a customer.

A few weeks later, a customer came in and introduced himself. His name was Jenkins and he was looking specifically for wing chairs. I showed him the ones we had on display. Did we have any others? Yes, we did, a new acquisition as yet not recovered, but a beauty. I took him upstairs and showed it to him. He bought it immediately, at a very good price indeed. "Does the price include reupholstering?" he asked. It did. Fine, he would send in his wife the following day with the material to be used, and then the chair would go down to Mr. Lonano, whose shop did all such work for us.

A few days later the chair and the fabric went to Mr. Lonano's shop, where it was carefully stripped down to the frame. Mr. Lonano called and asked me if I would like to see it in its original state, and I invited Mr. Jenkins to come down and see it with me.

We examined the two-hundred-year-old frame, and it was, as we'd originally assessed it, perfect, an authentic piece in every respect.

"Very impressive," said Mr. Jenkins. "I have another wing chair, which I plan to place beside this one. Would you mind if I brought it down here and had it stripped and reupholstered here?"

"Not at all," I said.

Several days went by, and then he called me to report that Mr. Lonano now had both chairs in his shop, both stripped, and before they were reupholstered, I might like to go down and see his.

When I went down to look at the two chairs, side by side, another warning bell went off in my head.

Mr. Jenkins's chair was obviously not authentic. It was a fake.

Now, how was I to tell him?

I went back to my office and pondered the situation for some time. Then I made a decision. No matter what ensued, I had to tell Mr. Jenkins the truth about his chair.

So I called him. "Mr. Jenkins," I said, "I've been thinking about this all day, and I had to call you, to tell you — without beating about the bush — in *my* opinion, your wing chair is a fake."

Mr. Jenkins burst out laughing.

"Don't sound so agitated, Mr. Sack," he said. "I know it. I had it made by an old Swedish cabinetmaker up on Cape Cod, near where I live in the summer. He used all the old woods to make the frame, and he said, 'Not a man in America would know whether this is a fake or not!' But he didn't know about you, did he?"

I keep a photograph of the old Swede's chair, side by side with the authentic Philadelphia Chippendale ball-and-claw-foot chair.

Beware when something is too much of a bargain. Fakes and spurious designs are often offered at forty to fifty percent less than what they should bring. Take, for example, the famous Brewster chair, which ended up, some years back, at the Henry Ford Museum in Dearborn, Michigan.

That "Brewster" chair, a tour-de-force of spindles, was purchased in 1970 as a rare original of the Pilgrim period. But it wasn't a three-centuries-old masterpiece, not at all. No, it was the work of a clever Rhode Island craftsman named Armand La Montagne, who had carefully made the chair, and then seen to it that his artful creation would later be carefully "planted" on a Maine back porch. There it was inevitably discovered by a progression of fallible antiques dealers, and passed from hand to hand until the final owner, a dealer from Exeter, New Hampshire, purchased it and then sold it to the Henry Ford Museum for the reported price of nine thousand dollars.

That whopping price didn't accrue to Mr. La Montagne. He never made a cent for his work. The chair took him, by his own estimate, two months to complete, and cost him some two dollars in basic materials. So what could have been his motive in creating such a superb fake version of an early Pilgrim chair? In published reports of his coup, he is quoted as having said, "I carried off the entire affair merely to prove how fallible museum people can be."

There's nothing really new about what this Rhode Island craftsman accomplished. Faking has been going on ever since some early cabinetmaker discovered there was money to be made by duplicating someone else's masterwork.

But what should have been the tip-off that the "Brewster" chair was a phony was its price. Since there are only a scant few of such chairs extant, one at the Plimouth, Massachusetts, Plantation, and the other at the Metropolitan Museum in New York, an authentic Brewster chair would have brought at least ten times the price.

Somebody once asked my father how one can tell a genuine piece. "Simple," said my father. "A genuine piece radiates its own authenticity." What I saw at the Ford Museum did not speak to me.

And then there are times when being called in to authenticate someone's treasured heirloom calls for even more diplomacy than is asked of a senior member of the Foreign Service.

I will never forget what happened to me some years back when I was called down to Tennessee to pass judgment on a treasured and rare old antique highboy.

It was during the early 1970s, and a committee down there had decided to redecorate and restore the governor's mansion. As it was reported to me, one of the then-governor's friends and backers, an elderly gentleman named Carbeau, owned a great Philadelphia highboy and had generously offered to donate it to the restored mansion. Since such a donation would involve a large tax deduction, and would inevitably come under the scrutiny of the I.R.S., someone in Tennessee decided it would be prudent to secure an airtight appraisal, and I was approached to fly there and handle it.

I was met at the Nashville airport by a lovely blonde lady, the governor's wife; with a motorcycle escort of state troopers racing us through town, we proceeded to the mansion, where we dined, and then back to the airport we went, always escorted, boarded the governor's private plane, and flew off to Chattanooga. "I'm so thrilled by this whole thing!" said the governor's lady. "Promise me one thing — when we unveil that wonderful antique highboy at the mansion, you'll be our guest!"

I promised I would.

We arrived at the Chattanooga airport, and were met by another corps of state troopers. Motorcycle sirens screaming, we drove out of town and up to a range of mountains; up and up we climbed until we came to the home of the generous donor. We were met at the front door, welcomed in, and led through the front hallway, across to where there stood that fabled Philadelphia highboy. It was my turn to appraise it.

Up to now, the trip had been exciting. But now I was in a dreadful spot.

Yes, the highboy was a fake. A Centennial reproduction, reworked but obviously nothing more.

Everyone was waiting for my reaction. What could I do, or say?

"Excuse me," I said, and took out a pad and pencil. "I really must spend some time here alone, and make a few notes. . . ."

Everyone withdrew and left me alone with that excellent reproduction.

I continued to "examine" it. I was conscious of people peering in from other rooms, watching as I did my studies.

Finally, my hostess could no longer restrain herself, and she came into the room. As she stood by, I asked, "How long have you had this?"

"Oh, quite a long time," she told me. "Since we were married. We bought it at some antiques shop, in New Orleans."

"I see," I told her. "Well, if you don't mind, I believe I'll have to go back to my office in New York and do a good deal more research on it. These matters can often be quite complicated."

"Oh, I do understand," said the Tennessee lady, graciously. "It's really such an honor having you come all this way to appraise our antique!"

Finally we departed from the home, and with the sirens screaming, the state troopers escorted us back to the airport, thence to Nashville, and eventually I was back in Manhattan, where I could sit quietly, without the sirens of those state troopers, and with no anxious politicos staring over my shoulder, to write my candid opinion of the Philadelphia highboy.

What could I say? Only the truth. With a certain amount of trepidation, I wrote my Tennessee host and hostess. "I'm truly embarrassed to have to tell you that your highboy is not a genuine antique," I told them.

A few days later, I received an answer. "Dear Mr. Sack," it read. "No wonder you have such a good reputation in your field. No one else could have handled such a situation with so much tact and diplomacy. Please know how grateful we are to you, and enclosed please find our check for your services."

I'd never before received a fan letter for destroying anyone's expectations so completely.

And I never did get to that gala reception at the governor's mansion, either.

Dealing with a fake at state level is tricky enough; when the problem reaches presidential status, the ramifications are even worse.

Some years back, when Bill Elder was the curator at the White House, a generous western lady offered a Baltimore ladies' writing desk of Hepplewhite design, with eglomisé panels on the crest. Eglomisé is a term for painting on glass. The desk was a beautiful piece, almost identical with another Hepplewhite example in the Metropolitan Museum. But when it arrived in Washington, Bill, who was later to become curator at the Baltimore Museum, questioned its authenticity. He was well aware that in the late nineteenth century, Baltimore had a group of craftsmen who were busily copying eighteenth-century designs, complete with eagle-inlaid motifs, and effectively passing them off as authentic antiques.

It was a ticklish situation, but Bill stuck by his opinion. He was able to prove that the piece was a Centennial reproduction, and regretfully, the proposed donation was tactfully refused.

At that time, we had been writing articles for the *New York Telegram and Sun* on the subject of antique faking, and how authenticity can be determined. Subsequently, we developed an extensive library based on this comparative study. Imagine our surprise when we were put to the acid test, and by no less than the Metropolitan Museum itself!

Fearful that their own example of the Baltimore ladies' writing desk might also be Centennial, of 1876, the Met people disassembled their example and requested me to examine it.

I studied it, and determined that the desk was completely authentic — with one small proviso. The center panel of the eglomisé decoration had been restored. Those three panels were backed by paper — and an examination of the panel by the Met's own expert corroborated my suspicion. The paper wasn't of the period. A small enough flaw! The desk went back on display at the Met — and we all sighed with relief.

It's a long time since Jake Margolis brought in that so-called Chippendale stool, and I confronted him with the assumption that it was a fake.

Since then, I've seen my share of fakes, and my eye has become so educated to the various tricks employed by deft fakers that I can, and often do, give a lecture, cum slides, to try and educate you on how to spot them.

But I'm fallible, too. A few years back, I was at a symposium at the Metropolitan Museum, and the moderator, Robert McNeill, himself quite knowledgeable about antiques, asked me about the possibility of making mistakes in purchasing them. "Tell us, are you infallible in spotting them?" he asked.

"No, I'm certainly not," I told him. "Nor could anybody else be."

"Have you ever bought anything which proved to be less than what you'd expected?" he asked.

"Sure I have," I said. "Who hasn't?"

"Then tell us," he asked, "what do you do with your mistakes?"

"I take them out of the showroom and put them in my house," I told him.

FOURTEEN

The Washington Tables

C ONSIDER the remarkable saga of two gaming tables, which involves high stakes, separation, disappearance, and finally a triumphant reunion, in a complex chain of improbable circumstance which would tickle a Victor Hugo, intrigue a Charles Dickens, and might even gratify a Dashiell Hammett.

To introduce the two major characters, examine first the tables. Diminutive in size, only about thirty-two inches wide, very attractive with their elegant ball-and-claw feet, they began their existence as a pair. But not just any pair, no indeed, sir. These are actually the smallest known such Chippendale-era tables, and as a pair, unique. Their value? Inestimable, sir. . . .

Such gaming tables are one of the very few successful forms of pre-Revolutionary New York furniture. New York was then a very small place, and its supply of fine furniture during the Chippendale period, unlike that of other Colonial cities, was sparse.

Over two hundred years ago, General George Washington presented this demure pair of tables to Judge and Mrs. Berrien, of Rocky Hill, New Jersey, in gratitude for their hospitality in permitting the Father of Our Country to use their home as his headquarters while Congress was in session at nearby Princeton. In this same house, Washington sat for his "most natural likeness," for Joseph Wright, the painter, in 1784.

Now that we have such authentic history for a background, consider the plot. Somehow, long ago, Washington's pair of gaming tables became separated. How? That is still part of a long-term jigsaw puzzle. For over a hundred and fifty years, the two tables were separated, and no one had the faintest idea of where they might be. But, thanks to a complex series of circumstances involving me, my brothers, and a good friend and collector named Lansdell Christie, the two tables have been brought together for a happy ending, and the baffling jigsaw puzzle is complete.

The probabilities of our cheerful third-act curtain, the odds against its happening in real life, would certainly confound any mathematician.

First piece of the puzzle.

Consider the advertisement, illustrated from *Antiques* magazine, in 1945. It obviously indicated that a George Washington gaming table was available if it were to go to a museum or some appropriate collector "in a manner appropriate to its historic importance."

As discreetly as the ad appeared, so did the Washington gaming table vanish from sight. And for the following fifteen years, nothing was heard again about it.

Then, in 1960, piece number two. The curator of the Philadelphia Museum of Fine Arts came in and wanted to see pictures of New York gaming tables. I permitted him to browse through our extensive files. He looked them over, thanked me, and that was that.

Six months later, another piece. I was walking up Madison Avenue and ran into Bernard Levy of Ginsburg and Levy. He asked me, "Did you get the call from the Philadelphia museum on the sale of the New York gaming table and the Hadley chest?" I had not. He informed me they'd been offered for sale, and he'd bid on them, but that obviously he'd lost them to a Wilmington dealer named David Stockwell.

Now I could put two and two together, and the reason why the curator from Philadelphia had so casually dropped by our place to look at photos of New York gaming tables became clear. The museum had obviously bought the one shown in that first advertisement.

*　　　*　　　*

We'd had previous experience with New York gaming tables.

Some years earlier, there had been an auction at the Plaza Galleries, in which such a table had been offered. Subsequently, my father sold it to James Lewis, our landlord at 5 East 57th Street, who lived in Cornish, New Hampshire. Mr. Lewis paid him $6,250 for the table; the profit my father made was minuscule.

Years later, in the 1960s, I had a son at Dartmouth, which is quite near Cornish. As I drove down from Hanover, I decided to drop by and visit the Lewises, whom I had not seen for some time. It turned out to be a very sad visit. Jim had just been at the hospital, where his wife, Betty, was ill with a very rare paralysis. Doctors from all over the world were being consulted, but so far, there was no treatment. Jim envisaged tremendous medical expense, and told me he'd decided to sell a few pieces of his fine collection.

"One of the things my wife has never really enjoyed is that New York gaming table I bought from your father," he said. How much did he want for it? Ten thousand dollars.

I thought that was a very high price. New York tables had never yet received the same appreciation among knowledgeable collectors as had their more elegant Philadelphia counterparts. But since I knew he would be calling in other dealers shortly, I decided to accept Jim's asking price, provided he would give me thirty days to pay. He agreed, and the table came down to New York again.

I put it up for sale for $14,000.

Shortly afterward, another ad appeared in *Antiques*. This time it offered the New York gaming table purchased from the Philadelphia museum by David Stockwell. Described as historic, one of a pair presented by Washington to Judge and Mrs. Berrien, there it was, just as Bernard Levy had told me about it. Mr. Stockwell, it seemed, was asking $12,000 for it.

A family genealogy would accompany this table, written by a gentleman named Rodenbaugh. It detailed the family history, and in it was a drawing of the table Mr. Stockwell was offering for sale.

Very interesting. If this was the same table shown in that 1945 advertisement, it had to be one of a pair. That is what the advertisement stated. Then where was the *other* George Washington table?

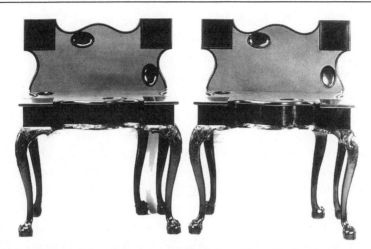

Pair of Chippendale mahogany card tables, New York, circa 1760–1770. This pair belongs to that group of card tables for which New York is famous, one of the rare instances of superior design by New York cabinetmakers to their Philadelphia counterparts in the pre-Revolutionary period. The carving of this group is usually similar, but the aprons sometimes have a grape design rather than the standard gadroon carving, The fifth leg swings to support the hinged top when folded flat for playing. The squared corners are for candlesticks, and the scoops are for the use of chips.

No one knew.

We put our table for sale in our customary monthly advertisement in *Antiques* magazine. Lo and behold, we had a phone call from a dealer in Boston. He supplied another piece of the puzzle.

"Mr. Sack," he said, "I see you have a gaming table you say is New York. I know where there's one that looks like that, but I thought it was English. It's supposed to have a Washington history, but you know those Washington histories," he said, scornfully. "Everybody's got one. Anyway I offered five hundred dollars for this table because it was English, but the man who's got it has two stepdaughters who don't want him to sell it."

Was it possible? The second of the pair?

We said, "Look, go back. Get it. Give them a bigger price, but see if you can buy that table."

It was such a far-fetched possibility that this might be the second of that original pair . . . such a fleeting thought which passed through our minds, that we dismissed it.

But the fact that he'd described the table as small intrigued us. And we were willing to gamble a small sum to find out if it was the same as the other table.

A couple of days later the Boston dealer called my brother Albert with the news he'd been successful. We had the table. But the bad news was the price he'd had to pay. Would we agree to $3,000? The answer was yes, sight unseen.

Shortly afterward, the table arrived in our place. It was a beautiful little piece, but in its construction there was an idiosyncrasy. Most of the gaming tables of this type have an oak gate in the back, solid, straight across, in a horizontal manner. For some reason, this one was scalloped out, in what we call a cymacurve shape, in the back. Done for no good reason by its maker, obviously a whim, most unusual, and totally original. We'd never seen such construction before.

We tucked it away in a closet, and my brother Robert took off for the New York Public Library, to see if he could find a copy of the Rodenbaugh family genealogy which Mr. Stockwell had referred to in his advertisement for *his* table.

Now we had two New York gaming tables, one small, and one larger. But we had no idea of the genealogy of the one we'd purchased from Boston, with its possible Washington connection.

Enter a new character, Mr. Lansdell Christie, a good friend and collector.

He lived in a large estate in Muttontown, Long Island. Once a cadet at West Point, he had not graduated, but he had served in the Air Force as a major. During World War II, he had frequently flown over Liberia, in Africa. There, he'd noted that the plane's compass dipped in certain areas, because of magnetic forces below. After the war, he'd explored that area and discovered rich deposits of iron ore. He began mining it, and by putting his miners on a profit-participation basis with himself, became very successful. He sold all the ore he could produce, and soon amassed a fortune.

Lansdell Christie.

For the first few years of our acquaintance, Mr. Christie politely avoided all of our great offerings. He was busy collecting eighteenth-century French antiques and priceless Fabergé jewelry, which was later displayed at the Corcoran Gallery in Washington, and then at the Metropolitan Museum. Lately, however, he'd begun to take an interest in early American, and we'd become very close. His taste leaned toward Rhode Island pieces, and we kept in touch even when he went out of town.

Several days after acquiring our second table, we had a tremendous snowstorm. I was about to drive to New York from my home in Rockville Center, but the roads were bad. I went to try for a train, but they were all too crowded. I had almost decided to go home when I ran into Ceil Sternberg, Mr. Christie's private secretary, on her way into New York from the same station. She persuaded me to join her; we managed to squeeze into a train and headed for New York. Along the way, she told me her boss was on vacation in Arizona, and was quite bored. Did I have anything interesting in New York which might interest him?

I told her the story of Mr. Stockwell's gaming table, and of the one we'd just purchased, in Boston, and I speculated on the wild possibility that these two might, just might, be a pair.

She was as fascinated as we were, and she asked me if she might tell this story to her boss. It would obviously interest him as well.

I finally got to my office. Shortly afterward, the phone rang, and it was Lansdell Christie, in Arizona, calling about the gaming table. Could he have a photograph of it, and whatever information we had to supply?

Off it went to Arizona. "But I have to warn you," I said, "this is a very far-fetched thing. We don't have much information on this table, we're researching it, but we need to know more."

When he'd received our photos, he promptly called back. How much were we asking for our table?

"I'm not sure this is the missing member of the pair," I said, "but since Stockwell is asking twelve thousand dollars for his, I'll let you have ours for ten thousand dollars. But you have to remember, this is a highly speculative matter — we're not sure of anything."

"Fine," said Mr. Christie. "But let's tie down that other table, too. Shall I try Stockwell? I've done a lot of business with him."

I suggested I try first. I called Stockwell and asked if he would sell me his table at the price he'd offered it, $12,000. But it wouldn't be quite that easy. It seemed Mr. Stockwell had another customer for it, and he'd agreed to hold it for that buyer, pending his decision.

I reported this news to Mr. Christie, in Arizona.

In conversation, he revealed that he'd shown my letter to another couple who shared the same dining table in the Arizona resort where he'd been staying. They'd been very interested in the story and seemed quite knowledgeable about American antiques. I pricked up my ears. Their name? "It ended in a *dash*," he remembered.

"Taradash?" I asked.

"That's it," he said. "How'd you know that?"

I had merely taken a chance. "If it's the Taradash I think it is," I told him, "he's a collector, and we'd better move fast. I've tried working on Stockwell, now it's your turn. And meanwhile, we'd better lock up our gaming table, and tuck it away where nobody else can spot it — at least until you get the other table away from Stockwell."

Mr. Christie agreed, and said he'd be flying home from Arizona promptly, and he'd meet me at his Muttontown home where we could hold a council of war.

The following day, while I waited to hear from him, into our shop, ever so casually, came Mr. Robert Goelet, who previously had been in several partnership deals with Mitchell Taradash. He wandered through our place very slowly, examining everything in sight. Just as casually, we asked him if there was anything special he might wish to see. No, no, he assured us, he was simply browsing.

The gaming tables stayed safely locked in the closet.

By the end of the day, I had a triumphant call from Mr. Christie. "I think I've got the table!" he said, happily. "At the price he quoted, twelve thousand dollars."

"Get a bill of sale," I instructed. "And make sure it has a complete description."

I waited.

The following day, he called with bad news. Evidently Mr. Stockwell had insisted that his partner in the deal, whom he hadn't mentioned before, be taken care of. "He's upped the ante to fourteen thousand dollars," Christie reported. "Isn't that awful?"

"Sure it's awful," I agreed. "But grab it. He has an obligation to you. And make sure he brings the table to your house, and that you pay him on the spot, and get yourself a signed, sealed invoice. When he does that, you call me, and we'll bring the two tables together, and compare them."

He agreed to do so.

Time passed while I waited to hear from him.

Finally his call came. He'd successfully concluded the deal at $14,000, and Mr. Stockwell had left the gaming table in Muttontown, along with a detailed bill of sale!

"I hope you didn't let the cat out of the bag," I said.

No, no, he assured me, he hadn't said a word about a second table. "The only thing I couldn't resist asking him was — if the missing table of the original pair ever did turn up, what such a restored pair of historic pieces might be worth."

And what had Mr. Stockwell replied to that?

"He said if that remote possibility ever happened, the pair would be worth a minimum of seventy-five thousand dollars," reported Mr. Christie, "but that would be almost an impossibility. Absolutely nobody knew where that second table could be!"

I took the second table out of the closet, and hurried out to Muttontown.

It was time for the third-act climax of this puzzle scenario. Would the last two pieces of the jigsaw fit?

There in his home stood Mr. Christie's latest acquisition, table number one from Philadelphia. And now, beside it, we placed the table we'd bought from the dealer in Boston.

Side by side, the pair together. We examined them from every possible aspect.

They were an exact pair.

Each the same in every detail of construction, size and execution, even to that back gate, with its scallop design in a cymacurve!

The puzzle was complete.

But . . . how to establish the genealogy?

Before I went to Muttontown, my brother Robert had returned from the New York Public Library, with a genealogy of the Rodenbaugh family, the one mentioned in Mr. Stockwell's advertisement. He had culled names from that list, one of which, remarkably enough, was still in the Boston telephone directory, with a listing on Louisburg Square.

If that family home was where the second table had come from, then we'd established beyond challenge that it *had* stayed in the family all these years, even though separated from its mate!

I called the dealer we'd bought it from, in Boston.

"If you say yes to the information I'm going to give you," I told him, "I will send you five hundred dollars. That gaming table you sold us — remember? You bought it from Mr. So-and-so, who lives in Louisburg Square, correct?"

There was a pause, and then the dealer finally said, "How the hell did *you* know?"

Jackpot!

He forwarded a letter containing the name and place where the second table had been purchased, and now we had proof positive—these two were the same tables George Washington had presented to Judge and Mrs. Berrien, all those years ago. And they had been restored to their rightful place in American history.

The story was complete, the ending happy.

But every triumphant finale should have an afterpiece.

The two tables were exhibited by Mr. Christie at the Metropolitan Museum in 1966, at a private loan show of American masterpieces. The proud owner — who'd previously said to me, "I never had so much fun for twenty-four thousand dollars in my whole life!" — was pleased with the catalogue of the Metropolitan show. He'd sent copies to all his friends and relatives, including his daughter's husband's mother, who lived down South.

Several days later, she called him and asked, "Lansdell, don't you know I'm a direct descendant of the Berrien family?"

"Good Lord!" said Christie, delighted. "That means those two tables are back in the Berrien family — by proxy!"

My friend Lansdell is gone now, and his great collection of early American, which we were proud to have helped him assemble, was sold at auction several years ago. I'd appraised it the year before, and my final sum came within a few thousand dollars of the million dollars it brought.

But those two George Washington gaming tables never went to auction. Lansdell saw to it in his will that they should never again be separated. They're still back in the family, where they belong.

The Antiques
and the Moderns

THERE'S a somewhat apocryphal story about an antiques dealer traveling through the backroads of New England who stops at a farmer's house to ask directions. There, on the porch, he spots a tabby cat, lapping up milk from a bowl. But not just an ordinary bowl . . . this particular bowl is a piece of fine Oriental Export china, a veritable treasure.

"How much for that cat?" asks the dealer, ever so casually.

"Oh, fifty bucks," says the farmer.

The two men argue over price, and finally strike a deal.

"Now," says the dealer, just as casually, "how much for the bowl?"

" 'Tain't for sale," says the farmer.

"But I'll need it for feeding my cat," says the dealer. "She's accustomed to that bowl. How about ten dollars for the bowl?"

"You crazy?" drawls the farmer. "I have to hang on to that Oriental Export bowl. How do you suppose I sell my cats?"

Years later, that story was reenacted for me, right here in Manhattan.

A young Boston man who'd stopped by to look for chairs for his dining room had taken my advice and gone browsing on Third

Avenue because he couldn't afford genuine ones. Later, he called to report that he'd gone into a particular antiques shop, bought some chairs, and had spotted something he thought might be worth looking at. "I think it's quite good," he said. "It's a chest on chest, and you probably ought to check it out."

Eventually, I asked my brother Albert to go down to survey this possible Remarkable Discovery. He was on the phone shortly afterward with incredible news. "You wouldn't believe it!" he exulted. "In the middle of this junk shop — there's this genuine bonnet-top Philadelphia chest on chest!"

Did he buy it? No. Why not?

Albert, it seemed, had ever so casually offered to buy it from the owner, a dealer named Corti.

"Not for sale," said Mr. Corti.

"Oh, everything's for sale," said Albert. "Put a price on it. Maybe I can change your mind."

Eventually, he persuaded Mr. Corti to change his tune, and the dealer finally said, "How about sixty-five?"

"Tell you what," said Albert. "Suppose I give you my check for five thousand dollars right now?"

"Five *thousand*?" said Mr. Corti, with infinite scorn. "That is a genuine Thomas Affleck signed chest on chest, and it's currently being researched by the people from the Philadelphia Museum of Fine Arts. I mean sixty-five thousand dollars!"

Needless to add, we did not manage to buy the Affleck chest on chest from Mr. Corti.

But a few years later, after his death, it came up for sale at Sotheby's, and before the auction, I spotted it. This time, we finally acquired it — for almost the price he had asked Albert. Like that legendary New England farmer, Mr. Corti understood value.

And his notion of price was also sound.

Throughout the 1960s and on into the '70s, my friend Ralph Blum's earlier prediction about the future upward spiral in early American prices would prove remarkably prescient.

Consider one example.

Back in 1915, my father bought an en suite Queen Anne match-

1915 Invoice listing a Whittier purchase. Note absence of descriptions or dating.

ing highboy and lowboy, of Massachusetts origin, dating from 1730–1740. They had belonged to the Gay family, of Suffield, Connecticut, and at a sale of family effects, my father paid $350 for the pair. Each piece is graced with its original brass handles and escutcheons, and both are of masterpiece quality.

My father brought these prizes to Boston and sold them to Albert Whittier for about $550. Albert's brother, E. Ross Whittier, with whom he had a real estate partnership, thought Albert should be committed for such a wild extravagance.

In 1956, the Whittier collection, which Albert had willed to brother Ross's family, came up for auction at Parke-Bernet, and we promptly brought back into our fold that beautiful pair of Queen Anne pieces for $4,500. By the 1960s, we'd found a new buyer for them, diminutive and dynamic Mr. Joseph Hirshhorn, who was not only a great collector of modern art, but was also captivated by American furniture. Joe was a hard bargainer, but he finally forced himself to part with the exorbitant sum of $10,000 for the pair.

After Joe passed away, his furniture was sold at auction, and we bought back that same matched pair in 1981, this time for $209,000, thereby setting a new price record. Subsequently, the two pieces went off to Houston, where they are now installed in the home of two very knowledgeable contemporary collectors. Five years have passed, and the price of the two Gay pieces has continued to spiral upward.

Whittier Queen Anne matching highboy and lowboy, New England, circa 1730–1750. That these are early pieces is illustrated by the shaped apron retaining some of the early William and Mary influence. The early veneers were very thick, and the figured elements were applied on a straight-grained wood to keep from warping. Veneered pieces of either crotch (as here) or burl walnut are prized very highly and, as opposed to the modern concept of veneering as being ersatz, this is a work of distinction. Very few early matching highboys and lowboys are extant. This pair originally belonged to Reverend Gay of Suffield, Connecticut.

Will it come down? I wouldn't bet on that.

Joe Hirshhorn also acquired a beautiful grandfather's clock from us for $3,750, made by the master of American clockmakers, Simon Willard. The clock, a tall and stately piece, was in flawless condition. Inscribed for the original owner, it had Simon Willard's original paper label behind the case door, along with Willard's set-up instructions.*

* Once properly balanced, American tall clocks keep excellent time. They have striking mechanisms rather than chimes. A few musical varieties are known, which play contempo-

Simon Willard tall clock, Boston, circa 1800–1810. The Willard
family (Simon, Aaron, Benjamin, and Ephraim) are the supreme
names in New England clockmaking. Simon, the eldest brother,
was the inventor of the banjo clock (patented in 1802). This
clock is a combination of the arts of clockmaking,
cabinetmaking, and painting of the eglomisé panels. This style of
clock originated in Boston and is uniquely American. These
clockmakers were the first contractors, taking orders from their
customers and subcontracting the cases to local cabinetmakers,
many of whom worked in the best style.

rary tunes. The cases, as to be expected, vary in design details unique to each of the Colonial
regions. Prior to the Revolution, brass or silvered dials with Roman numerals were common,
later giving way to the enameled painted and decorated dials chiefly imported as standards
with adjustable brackets for inclusion with the brass works, which later in the nineteenth
century were replaced with wooden works.

Joe loved his clock. Having been divorced and remarried several times, he always called us before the fact to arrange for us to store his clock in the warehouse. Upon remarrying, he would then call for his clock to be redelivered. That clock was part of the same Parke-Bernet sale in 1981, and when the catalogue was circulated, I heard from my old friend Ben David.

Long before Ben had been my original partner on Madison Avenue, years ago, his father had been my father's partner; Ben had now retired to California. He'd spotted that Simon Willard clock which Parke-Bernet had estimated at about $30,000, and he fancied it, so he called and asked me to buy it for him. What sort of a limit should I set as his agent? Ben suggested $50,000 as the absolute limit.

But the bidding turned out to be so spirited that I went on past Ben's limit, and bid on my own, up to $65,000. There was a persistent telephone bidder going against me, and I finally let that beautiful Simon Willard clock go for $70,000. I found out later that the discerning buyer had been Bill Cosby.

Ben was amazed at the price, and kept on discussing it with me. He was ambivalent, for there was something about that particular clock which continued to buzz through his subconscious. "Where did you originally buy it?" he asked.

I didn't remember, but I went back into our files to look it up. Then I was astonished to discover that the Simon Willard clock had actually been purchased by me from Ben's father, Leon David!

"Of *course!*" said Ben. "*Now* I remember — it used to sit in our house!"

He was doubly rueful that we had not been able to outbid Bill Cosby. I know the feeling. That clock was, after all, part of our family. Now it's part of Bill Cosby's, and I hope it will give him as much pleasure.

Over the years, one thing about customers has always mystified me. Call it the Collectors-in-Hold-Pattern. It operates year in and year out. We may arrive in our offices of a Monday morning and the phones won't ring for hours. All day long the showrooms will stay silent and empty. In other words, a "dead" day. Perhaps Tuesday and Wednesday will be the same. In show business, if you are a producer confronted with such an absence of customers, you promptly put up the closing notice backstage. Obviously, we can't do any such thing. What we can do is hold the fort and try to ignore the overhead, ticking steadily away like a Simon Willard clock.

Suddenly, without any warning, there comes a break in the silence. In comes a buyer. The phone begins to ring and continues to do so. Buyers are calling, the floor of our showroom has its visitors, and we are back, on a selling wave, in the antiques business.

What causes these ebb-and-flow hold-patterns? I don't know anyone, least of all myself, who can explain the phenomenon. Sometimes the ebb side can be attributed to the onset of April 15, when the I.R.S. must be paid, or to some period when Wall Street has gone into a temporary tailspin. But, generally speaking, it's difficult to correlate the flow side pattern with anything specific. Antiques are hardly a Christmas gift selection, or an impulse shopping item. What I am left to fantasize is that on some given night, there was a dinner party somewhere, perhaps in the home of a collector, at which several other collectors, in an after-dinner conversation amid the Hepplewhite, the Chippendale, the Duncan Phyfe, and the Frothinghams, all came to the same conclusion — that it's a good time to buy. They went home, tossed and turned all evening long speculating on what items to buy, got up . . . and that morning, our telephone begins to ring.

Which brings me to another puzzling phenomenon — why it is that certain fine antiques sell overnight, and others can sit unsold on the floor long enough that they end up almost seeming like furnishings or fixtures. It certainly can't be a matter of price, nor can it be quality, for we have always dealt in the high end of both. But there seems to be no way of predicting the salability of some pieces.

Years back we had acquired a Hepplewhite Salem mahogany breakfront bookcase. Nearly eight feet wide, it had a pedimented top, beautiful glass panel doors with an interesting design of its mullions, and was almost perfect, should its owners wish to so use it, for the display of porcelains. For almost five years, it lingered on our floor. Its quality and beauty were quite evident, and its price, $18,000, was in the early 1960s a reasonable enough figure.

Christie mahogany breakfront bookcase, Massachusetts, circa 1790.
The American breakfront bookcase is a rare form; while it was
abundant in England, it did not become a popular type in America. It became more prevalent after the Revolution. While there are
known examples of New York origin and a few in Baltimore, the
most beautiful examples are from Boston or Salem, Massachusetts.
The central sections are usually of the butler desk design, with the
drop lid section falling forward as a writing surface along the
cubby hole and drawer sections. It is interesting to note how many
such pieces left the country years ago. Henry du Pont was to acquire a choice Salem breakfront for Winterthur in South Africa!

A lady in Baltimore had always coveted it, and for years she'd
talked of buying it as a display piece for her collection of Doughty
porcelain birds. But as much as she loved it, she could never quite
bring herself to pay our price, and there it sat, unsold.

One day, I had lunch with Lansdell Christie in his home in
Muttontown, and he asked me if I'd make a suggestion about any
item we had I thought he might want to install in his house. What
could improve his collection?

"You can start right here in the dining room," I suggested, "and
replace your English breakfront with that beautiful Salem piece we
have in New York." He'd seen it many times previously. My friend

Lansdell promptly accepted my suggestion, but with one proviso. Since that English piece had been one of his wife's favorites, we had better wait until the day she had a hairdresser's appointment, and then, during her absence from the house, we could make the switch.

When I reached my office, happy to have at last found that great Salem breakfront a good home, I found a message waiting; would I please call Baltimore?

On the phone was the wife of that Baltimore collector. She had wonderful news for me! After all these years, her husband had finally decided to buy the breakfront!

The same breakfront I had just sold.

When I told her that, she broke down and began to sob.

The following day, she and her husband came up from Baltimore, determined to ask if we might persuade Mr. Christie to release his purchase. We suggested to him that he might wish to do so. After all, his wife was fond of that English piece, and perhaps —

"I am delighted with my breakfront," he said. "It's not for sale."

The breakfront never went to Baltimore, but ultimately it did make it to Washington.

When Mr. Christie died, his widow presented that great piece to the State Department, and it now resides in its own special niche, in the redecorated dining room in the State Department rooms, surrounded by choice American furniture of Massachusetts origin. . . . Hardly a fixture.

And then there are the myths about Israel Sack, Inc. which have arisen about us over the years.

Some time ago, a lady arrived in our store and introduced herself. A collector from Houston, she had come to browse. I led her through our third floor, where she admired a beautiful Rhode Island Chippendale secretary-desk we had priced at $40,000, and then we went up to the fourth floor, where she found several other pieces to her taste.

She called back from Houston a week or so later to tell me she'd decided to buy three pieces, and would I please have them sent to her. And what about that marvelous Chippendale secretary-desk which she'd so fancied? "No," she told me. "I've decided against buying that."

Was there any particular reason for her turning down such a fine antique?

She hesitated before she replied, and then, "If you really want to know," she said, "my friends down here told me, 'Don't buy anything on the Sack's *third* floor. The best pieces are all on the fourth!' "

Where do you find antiques?

I've been asked that question for many years, and the best answer I can come up with is — one never knows where the next piece will surface. Nor why.

One morning the phone rang and when I picked it up, I heard what had to be a very old lady on the other end. "Stack's?" she asked. "Sorry, wrong number," I said, and hung up. Moments later, she called again. "I have two numbers here I was given. One is Ginsburg and Levy, and the other seems to be Stack?"

"The name is Sack," I said. "How can I help you?"

"Well, I believe I have some interesting things to sell," she said.

"Such as?" I asked, politely.

"One is a Chippendale lowboy," she said. "It seems to have a brass plaque on it, dated 1754, and it reads 'Made for Polly Riche.' It's been in the family for many years. Then I have some American silver made by a craftsman named Myer Myers and a Philadelphia chair . . . and I wondered if you might be interested."

Chippendale? Myer Myers? The greatest American silversmith? Yes indeed we would be interested. When could we see them?

"Could you come up, say, an hour or so from now?" she asked.

My brother Albert promptly broke every metropolitan speed limit in reaching her apartment.

When he returned, beaming like the Cheshire cat, he had acquired some magnificent wares. And a very satisfied seller.

She called up again a few days later.

"You were so nice, and it's such a pleasure dealing with you," she said. "May I come down and bring you a batch of family papers I've found? They seem to go along with the items you bought."

They were priceless pieces of authenticating material.

How lucky for us that she dialed our number a second time and didn't go on to that of our major competitors.

*   *   *

One of the most beautiful pieces we've ever had in stock was a
Chippendale carved mahogany piecrust tea table, which came from
Mrs. Charles Hallam Keep's collection, and was exhibited at the
famous 1929 Girl Scout Loan Exhibition, at the American Art Galleries in New York.

These tables were made by some of the best Philadelphia craftsmen, and had tops which were mounted on bird cage supports,
which allowed the table tops not only to turn but to tip. Thus the
table could be placed in a corner with its top open and tipped,
revealing its magnificent carved edges.

Every dealer and collector knew about Mrs. Keep's table, and
would have jumped at the chance to acquire it.

Then how did it come to us?

Courtesy of a careless guest.

One morning Mrs. Keep's daughter called us. She'd inherited her
mother's precious table, and was most upset about it. The top of the
table had been maintained in its old "crusty" finish, which the early
collectors prized as most desirable. The night before, at a party in her
house, one of her guests had placed his highball glass on the table,
and the alcohol had left a telltale white ring.

"This might happen again," she said, "and I really cannot stand
the responsibility of maintaining this valuable piece in its original
state any longer. If I sold it, could you replace it with a suitable
English piece that isn't so precious?"

Shortly afterward, we had the famous Keep piecrust in our possession. After much discussion, pro and con, we decided to have
that old "crusty" finish removed. Sure enough, beneath it, as Maxim
Karolik would have predicted, we discovered a magnificent golden
walnut original finish.

It glows in its current setting, in the home of Martin Wunsch,
where careless guests cannot do it any harm.

When it comes to antiques, you must be informed.

In the early 1960s, we had a middle-aged lady customer from
Rhode Island who bought a piece from us, and subsequently began
to research the subject of Newport antiques with a passion.

Chippendale mahogany silver table, attributed to John
Townsend, circa 1770–1780. Galleried silver tables are almost
nonexistent. This example has so far been the only Newport
specimen. The various elements of Townsend design are prevalent here — namely, the cross-hatching, the stop-fluted legs, the
characteristic knee brackets, the pierced cross-stretchers with
gadroon carved molding attached by screws, and the chamfered
edges on the leg bottoms. The pierced fretted gallery unique to
tea tables has a precedent in a galleried Newport, Rhode Island,
urn stand in the Henry Francis du Pont Winterthur Museum.

One day she was taking tea with a friend of hers, a Mrs. Harrison, when she spotted in a corner of the room a Newport tea table. But to her eye this seemed far from an ordinary table; this one had a gallery top, stopped fluting on the legs, and cross-stretchers below with gadrooning. As her hostess had been using it daily, the table was covered with various household items.

"That looks like a John Townsend table," said our friend.

"Oh, yes, absolutely," said Mrs. Harrison. "It's been in our family for two centuries. I inherited it."

The two ladies studied the table. "I've never seen one with a gallery top," said our friend. "This must be unique."

How unique she couldn't possibly know. It was one of a kind, even rarer than the Townsend tea table I would buy years later in Essex.

"Is this insured?" asked our friend.

No, not at all. It had been around for so long, Mrs. Harrison had never bothered to insure it.

For starters, our friend insisted her hostess clear off the top of that rare table. Then, for an insurance appraisal, Mrs. Harrison got in touch with the Metropolitan Museum. When the curator arrived to examine her table, he placed a preliminary valuation of seventy-five hundred dollars on it. And he insisted on an option to buy it for the Metropolitan.

Eventually, when the Met passed on its option, our friend prevailed on Mrs. Harrison to sell it to us.

We promptly got in touch with Henry du Pont, and when he came up to see it, he lost no time in purchasing it for his collection. It is now one of the most valuable treasures in Winterthur.

All because one of our customers bothered to do her research.

One of the purest examples of the kind of happenstance involved in acquiring antiques is a superb antique which is now in the Richard Dietrich collection. It is a carved ball-and-claw-foot Chippendale tea table of Philadelphia origin. The circumstances surrounding our acquisition of that magnificent table vividly underscore the unpredictability of this so-called business.

We had heard of a private collection in a home in Dover, Dela-

Chippendale carved mahogany tea table, Philadelphia, circa 1760–1770. This tea table was made in Philadelphia presumably by Benjamin Randolph for Vincent Louckerman of Dover, Delaware. The account book of Vincent Louckerman lists monies loaned to the cabinetmaker — one of Philadelphia's best craftsmen. As stated previously, most Philadelphia tea tables were circular with tripod pedestals — either plain, dish rimmed, or piecrust carved. This example, the standard shape in New England at this time, is one of the few rectangular Philadelphia tea tables.

ware; the family was the Bradfords, descendants of Vincent Louckerman, a successful eighteenth-century Philadelphia merchant. Louckerman's account books show references to loans of cash to Benjamin Randolph, one of Philadelphia's most gifted cabinetmakers. Since Louckerman had loaned Randolph such sums, it was safe to assume he'd acquired furniture from Randolph. There are labeled examples of Randolph's chairs in the Boston Museum of Fine Arts, and many of Philadelphia's finest pieces have been ascribed to him.

We were preparing the first volume of the American Antiques Library, and in a letter to the Bradfords, we politely expressed our interest in including their legendary pieces in such a work. Their response was politely affirmative, and my brothers Albert and Robert were invited down to their home, to spend time photographing the family treasures. It was a small collection, but choice. In the Bradford home were a set of chairs which finally ended up in the State Department's Diplomatic Reception Rooms, a piecrust carved tea table, a superb chest on chest, and best of all, that carved rectangular tea table.

The photographs my brothers brought back were excellent, and coupled with their glowing descriptions of the family treasures, made my mouth water.

Was anything for sale?

"Not a chance," insisted my brother. "Not the remotest possibility. When we hinted at selling, we were turned down flatly."

So I swallowed my enthusiasm and went on to other pursuits.

Imagine my surprise, a few months later, when Mr. Bradford himself called up from Delaware to ask me if I knew a certain gentleman from Detroit, an antiques collector, who had expressed an interest in his beautiful carved tea table.

"No, I don't know the man," I said, "but how did this question arise?"

It seemed that there had been an open house tour of the Bradfords' historic home, and this gentleman had spotted the tea table and offered Mr. Bradford the enormous price of $25,000 for it, on the spot.

"He's probably going to consult you people later," said Mr. Bradford, "and I don't want to lose such a lush sale."

I was amazed. Hadn't we been told nothing was for sale?

"If you're considering such a sale, to a stranger," I said, "why couldn't we be candidates for the purchase?"

"You'd pay such an extraordinary amount?" he asked.

"No," I assured him. "We'd pay more."

I'd already realized the price was superb, but then, so was that table.

Mr. Bradford hesitated. "I'd better let you know," he said.

I waited, obviously impatient, for his response.

Then he called again. "Thirty thousand dollars and the table is yours," he said.

We closed the deal at $29,000.

That magnificent table came to us. Ours is a small business, and again the word traveled fast. All sorts of collectors dropped in to see that beautiful table. As did our competitors. After seeing it, one of them made certain that the Bradfords were promptly notified of the steep price we had placed on Benjamin Randolph's masterpiece.

One day, Mrs. Bradford herself came in. "May I see the table again?" she asked.

I led her to its place of honor in our showroom.

She stared at it thoughtfully. "I understand you've put a price of seventy-five thousand dollars on it, Mr. Sack," she said.

"Absolutely correct," I told her. And I waited for her angry reaction.

But she surprised me.

"I certainly hope you get that price, Mr. Sack," she said, smiling. "You've earned it!"

We did get our price from Richard Dietrich, and the table is now a jewel of his collection. But none of this would have ever happened had not some total stranger from Detroit, on a house tour in Delaware, offered to buy a table from his host.

By the way, nobody ever heard another word from him.

Wherever he is, I'll always be grateful to him.

Then there are those awkward times when couples disagree violently on matters of taste.

I sold my friend Lansdell Christie one of the finest Newport pieces

Christie Goddard corner chair.

extant, a Goddard corner chair with a leather seat, which we had acquired from its original owners, the Hereshoff family. It promptly became one of Lansdell's special treasures.

One evening I was a guest at dinner, and Mrs. Christie said, "Harold, I have a bone to pick with you. I don't hold it against you personally, but that hideous chair you sold my husband — I simply can't stand it. It's so ugly — I make him keep it in a separate room."

Ugly? I asked her to be more specific.

We examined that beautiful chair together. "That leather seat," she said. "All cracked and sagging. Dreadful."

I carefully removed that original leather seat, in its frame, which contained the inscription "Made for John Brown," from Goddard's workshops. That left us the chair minus any original decor save for its elegant frame.

"Why not have us make you a reproduction frame, and your decorator can pick out a lovely piece of damask, and then you'll have any effect you want," I suggested.

Mrs. Christie accepted my suggestion enthusiastically. "Now I love it!" she said.

Lansdell patted my shoulder. "God bless you, Harold," he murmured.

Mrs. Christie had her reproduction seat covered, but I insisted that the original leather seat be crated and carefully stored away, for it was as valuable as the chair from which we'd removed it.

Years later, after my friend died, and his collection came up at Sotheby's for auction, I examined that superb chair. It was still covered in Mrs. Christie's damask. Where was the *original* seat?

I called the family home in Muttontown. Nobody had seen the crate with its precious contents. "Search for it!" I insisted.

Finally, downstairs in a basement cupboard, it was unearthed . . . and restored to the chair.

Mrs. Christie may have preferred damask, but history respects that original two-centuries-old leather seat.

And then there is "The Lindens."

Many years ago, it was built in Danvers, Massachusetts, for an affluent Yankee named King Hooper. It was actually Hooper's second home; he had another house in Marblehead, which by an odd coincidence was the same building my father restored and used as a showroom for his antiques in the late 1920s.

"The Lindens" was a great Colonial mansion. At one time General Gage, the British commander, used it as his headquarters. Later it became an inn, and over the years it changed hands many times. By the twentieth century, sadly enough, "The Lindens" was in a deteriorating area, and became threatened with destruction. My father heard of the possibility and became quite upset; the Danvers mansion was far more beautiful than the house he had restored in Marblehead. "The Lindens" was still in good condition, so rather than see it torn down, my father and his great friend Leon David bought the house in 1934 for a very modest ten thousand dollars.

Even though none of the locals cared sufficiently to preserve "The Lindens," there ensued a great hue and cry. Two out-of-town antiques dealers had purchased this precious house? What were they about to do with this great remnant of American history?

My father and Mr. David, "the old gents," as my friend Ben David and I referred to them, promptly offered to sell the house at absolutely no profit to any local group which wished to preserve it. No cash was forthcoming, merely loud objections.

"Lindens," originally built in Danvers, Massachusetts, now in Washington, D.C.

At that time, the Kansas City Museum was looking for a Colonial paneled room for its new American wing, which had been endowed by the generosity of the publisher William Rockhill Nelson. The parlor room at "The Lindens" was perfect for such a display; a deal was made, and the paneled parlor was dismantled and shipped off to Kansas City, where it was rebuilt in precisely its original state.

Then the house stood empty. Eventually, a Washington couple, Mr. and Mrs. George Morris, who had traveled throughout the East searching for an old house, by chance encountered Ben David at a Massachusetts auction. When he mentioned "The Lindens," they became quite interested. Eventually, they bought the mansion for a price of fourteen thousand dollars, and engaged a young architect named Macomber, who'd worked at Williamsburg, to tackle the complex job of having the house dismantled and shipped to its new site in Washington, D.C. Under Mr. Macomber's supervision, every single piece of "The Lindens" was carefully labeled and numbered, and then, on railroad flatcars, shipped to Washington. There, at Kalorama Circle, Mr. Macomber reconstructed the old house on its new foundation, and when he had finished, "The Lindens" stood in its imposing glory, exactly as it had for two centuries up in Danvers, including a reproduction of that room which had gone off to Kansas City.

Over the next forty years, Mr. and Mrs. Morris gradually furnished the house with classic early American furniture and decoration. "The Lindens" became a famous showplace, where Mrs. Morris took great pleasure in escorting visitors through the rooms, describing in great detail the ancient history of this great American mansion built in Massachusetts in 1754.

Several years ago, Mrs. Morris became quite ill, and it was evident that the largest part of her estate would consist of her collection of antiques and that fine house. An attempt was made by my friend Clem Conger to arrange a sale of "The Lindens" to a Texas millionaire who had evinced some interest in keeping it all together. I was engaged to appraise the contents, and when I had finished, I'd come up with a figure of approximately $2,200,000 for the furniture. The house itself was appraised at between $1,500,000 to $2,000,000.

Unfortunately, the Texas gentleman lost interest, and after Mrs. Morris passed away, everything went into liquidation by her executors. In 1982, the contents of "The Lindens" went to auction at Christie's, in New York. The sale attracted considerable attention, and when it was over, the total raised came to $2,200,000. My previous appraisal was dead on target.

But thereafter "The Lindens" stood empty, up for sale.

Recently, a couple entered our showrooms unannounced, and somewhat nervously introduced themselves. Their name was Bernstein, and they were from Washington, and they hoped they weren't intruding, but could we possibly answer a few questions?

"Of course," I said. "Why not?"

"Well, you're the most important dealers in the field," said Mrs. Bernstein, "and we don't want to bother you. We don't know too much about early American — up to now we've bought mostly English antiques, and we're afraid we might be imposing on you."

Not at all. What was their problem?

It seemed that Mr. and Mrs. Bernstein had recently purchased "The Lindens" on Kalorama Circle, and they intended to restore the old house to its former splendor. They were keenly aware of the house's history; they had even journeyed to Danvers to interview any descendants of the former owners who might have information on its original state. "Do you think you might have some suggestions on early American furniture that would suit such a famous house?" she asked.

"Mrs. Bernstein," I said. "Our family has been involved with that house for almost half a century. Now that you've bought 'The Lindens' that makes *you* family, too. So tell us, what can any of the Sacks do for you? We're *hamische menschen*" (hometown simple folk).

"Oh, Mr. Sack!" she said, smiling happily. "*Now* we can talk!"

With the invaluable assistance of Mr. Macomber, the very same remarkable architect from Williamsburg who brought the house safely down to Washington fifty years ago, Mr. and Mrs. Bernstein have done a beautiful job of restoring "The Lindens." It gleams and shines with absolutely authentic colors, its paneling is burnished, its stenciled floors restored expertly . . . and as for furniture? We've done everything we could to find Mr. and Mrs. Bernstein the finest pieces.

After all, within the walls of "The Lindens" there is two centuries of history — both American and Sack. For the Bernsteins, and for us, this project has been a true labor of love.

As prices have gone up, so has risen an entirely new group of collectors. Younger, more aggressive, often better educated and more knowledgeable than their predecessors, they are certainly more varied.

They are, as a rule, more aware of the symbiosis between dealers and collectors. Symbiosis, according to the dictionary, is "a living together, a companionship." That is an apt description of the relationships between the Sack family and our customers.

Many collectors who use a dealer prefer to keep the use of his services somewhere in the background, and to make it seem that all the collector had to do was to write a large check, and accept delivery.

Good collections are not assembled on that basis.

A good dealer is a teacher, and enjoys seeing his customer or client reach new plateaus of knowledge and taste. Each of us needs the other. A dealer can provide his customer with expertise, knowledge of availability, and a decent approximation of a piece's market value. You need a knowledgeable dealer who is honest. We need an informed client. Honesty without knowledge is as damaging as knowledge with no honesty.

We keep voluminous photographic files, going back many years, and they have been a priceless source of knowledge to aspiring collectors who wish to learn. With our guidance and teaching, the newer buyers have gained a grasp of the great panorama of early American artist-craftsmen creations.

For years, antique dealers' catalogues have invariably been prestigious showpieces rather than commercially successful marketing tools. Either they lacked illustrations and touted the management's perception, or they overwhelmed the customer with an abundance of chic. We too were guilty of that error — our monthly advertisement on the front cover of *Antiques* magazine was prestigious, but tended to give a rather lopsided impression that everything we carried was excessively high-priced.

One day, while looking through a 1951 issue of that same magazine, I noticed a section devoted to the American collection of the Metropolitan Museum. There were dozens of pieces illustrated on each page, and yet, in spite of the small size of the photos, each was an eye-catcher. How could we use that same technique for a catalogue?

I conferred with a mail-order house next door, and we evolved a technique employing photo offset. Our first venture into such a catalogue proved successful, and captured the imagination of our clients, especially Mr. Joseph Hennage, a commercial printer. He took over the next issue, and we have to date published forty. Mr. Hennage persuaded us our clients would be proud to have their pieces registered, and thus we began to publish hardcover bound volumes yearly, called *American Antiques*. These are now eight in number, and with some four thousand early American pieces illustrated between covers, the catalogue is a reference work used by curators, cataloguers, and dealers.

*   *   *

Some of our pupils have become more apt than their teachers.

In the late 1960s, we began to deal with young William du Pont, the son of Haskell du Pont. He and his brother Richard had an instinctive and native flair for antiques, and they strengthened it with a continuous and serious study of objects, photos, and textbooks, as well as conferences with leading dealers. With a name such as du Pont, they could well become fair game for any unscrupulous dealer, but the brothers were not to be patsies for anyone. They soon weeded out of their activities any dealer who dealt in spurious pieces.

On one occasion, young Bill du Pont amply proved to us the thoroughness of his self-education.

An upstate New York dealer had flashed to us a small snapshot of what appeared to be a bonnet-top highboy. He said he had acquired it in Nova Scotia, and it was probably the property of a Tory family which had fled there during the Revolution. Those loyal to the Crown had a difficult time then, which accounts for so many of our great pieces turning up in Europe, and even in such far-off locations as South Africa.

This dealer, however, was not interested in selling, or so he said at the time. Some months later, during the Winter Antiques Show in New York, I passed by his booth on opening night. There, standing in all its glory, was the same highboy. Was it there solely on exhibit, or was it for sale? The dealer seemed to have changed his mind, and yes, he would consider its sale. Price? "No less than ten thousand dollars," he said. Quickly, I accepted.

The prize was remarkable. It had all the majesty and strength of the finest of New England highboys, and it had a fan-carved upper and lower drawer, a well-proportioned bonnet, double case moldings, and its lower section protruded over the base, as in earlier pieces, a lovely touch. There was also C-scrolled marginal carvings on the well-shaped cabriole legs. The original early brass handles and escutcheons, the rich finish to its mahogany, were truly the icing on the cake.

Young Bill du Pont fell in love with it, and snatched it up at $29,000. A healthy profit for us, true, but a sound and good buy for

Queen Anne mahogany bonnet-top highboy, Massachusetts, circa 1740–1750. The grace and proportion of this highboy illustrate the high achievement of the development of this form in the Colonies. This highboy is also a good example of the design interchange in Rhode Island and Massachusetts during this period. The spiral finials and the fan-carved lower central drawer with the blank upper center drawer are Massachusetts design, the scrolled bonnet and the marginal carved rounded knees and pad feet are of Rhode Island design. The early Queen Anne bat wing brasses and the overhanging lower case molding place this highboy at a very early period, closer to 1740 than most conventional bonnet-top highboys. Below is the recarved replaced upper drawer front.

him. He still counts it among his best treasures, in spite of the remarkable event which took place after he'd taken delivery, and which might well have proved disastrous for all of us.

One day, as I sat staring at the highboy, before it went off to Bill, a slight but fleeting thought went through my mind. That fan-carved drawer on the top section . . . it gave me pause. Something about it bothered me . . . but what?

I quickly dismissed it, and went on to admire that beautiful piece.

But a few weeks later, after we had delivered the highboy to Bill, we had an urgent call from him. He was obviously upset.

"I know it's hard to believe this," he said, "but I think the fan-carved top drawer has been replaced. I've studied it carefully, and I'm certain it's *not* the original."

Now it is true that several of the great New England bonnet-top highboys have an uncarved top drawer, and a fan-carved lower drawer. Such is the case with the signed Benjamin Frothingham piece sold by us to C. K. Davis, which is now in the Winterthur Museum.

But it might have been that someone had decided that a fan-carved upper drawer would be more desirable, and added it to this piece. A horrible thought, as it could mean the entire drawer front was new, *not* original.

My brothers Albert and Robert hurried to Wilmington, and after examining the piece again, they called back with the dismaying news that Bill du Pont was correct in his suspicion. It had to be a replaced drawer front. We had indeed goofed.

I regretted I had not followed through on my fleeting sense of error.

But, due to a bit of luck, and a brilliant piece of deduction on the part of my brother Robert, all was not lost.

The dealer from whom we'd originally purchased the highboy lived in New York state, not far from Robert, and they'd both had the use of an independent cabinetmaker's shop nearby. On Robert's visits to that shop, he'd long since noted that the cabinetmaker did most of the other dealer's work. It was a long shot, but might the cabinetmaker be involved? We all decided Robert should visit the cabinetmaker and find out.

He confronted the cabinetmaker, and let him know we knew the drawer front had been replaced, and that we were proceeding with a court action. If he withheld evidence, we would promptly bring suit.

The frightened cabinetmaker not only promptly confessed, but produced the original drawer front which he had saved!

Robert then visited our dealer friend and told him that we now had the evidence, and if *he* confessed, we'd guarantee him no prosecution. Shamefacedly, he admitted the swap.

We returned the original uncarved drawer front to Wilmington, where it resides still, in company with Bill's other treasures . . . thanks to Bill's educated eye.

There are other collectors to whom price is totally unimportant. More often than not, we encounter them in strange settings. One afternoon, a middle-aged stranger wearing a mackinaw and jeans dropped in and wandered through, eyeing our displays with obvious appreciation. As he passed certain pieces, I heard him comment, "Beautiful . . . we have one like it. . . . Mmm, that one's a lot like mine," and so forth. I had never seen him before, so I had no idea whence his expertise came. Then, as he departed, he said, "Sack, if you're ever in Wilmington, please come visit us. We'd be glad to show you *our* collection."

I thought no more about him until the following year, when I attended the Wilmington Antiques Show. At the end of the long and tiring opening day's activities, as I was about to go up to my hotel room for a well-deserved night's sleep, I encountered my New York visitor. "Delighted you're here!" he said. "Come on over to my house now — my wife's a terrific cook, she'll have something for us to eat, and we'd like you to see our antiques!"

I wasn't too enthusiastic about a late-night jaunt, but I was hungry, he insisted, and finally I agreed. We drove in his car to a very modest neighborhood of small rowhouses. It didn't seem like the most promising locale for an antiques collection, but I was far too tired to worry about that.

We pulled up in front of an unassuming house, and he led me inside to the kitchen. There, his wife, a pleasant lady, was waiting for us with a midnight supper of sandwiches. First we would eat, and then I must look at their collection.

As I ate, I suddenly noticed, beneath the oilcloth cover of the kitchen table, a beautiful inlaid bellflower leg. My eyes widened. The kitchen table at which we were enjoying our supper turned out to be a superb Hepplewhite Pembroke specimen!

We went on through the small house, its rooms filled with furniture. By the dim lights, they showed me as fine a collection of antiques as I'd ever seen before. In one room was a superb Philadelphia highboy. "It's obviously not good enough for you," he apologized. "See, one bale of the brasses is missing."

Not good enough? It was a magnificent piece, of museum quality, as was most of the furniture jammed into that modest house.

How had they amassed this rare collection?

"On a thirty-seven-hundred-dollar-a-year salary, it wasn't easy," he admitted.

It seemed that during the Depression, when he and his wife first married, they'd needed furniture. Since neither of them fancied department store items, nor could they afford them, they'd become customers at a cabinetmaker's shop nearby, where they'd first seen antiques. The cabinetmaker, who worked for Philadelphia dealers, often had pieces for sale, at very low prices. "Even at those Depression prices, all we could pay him was five or six dollars a week, but he was willing," explained my host. "Since we were taken with the highboy, and the table, and all the rest of those things here, we could afford to buy them. Today, of course, we couldn't possibly afford these antiques. . . ."

The operative word behind the assemblage of that remarkable Wilmington collection, which is still intact in that modest house, certainly hadn't been money, then. It was the best motive of all: love.

Over the years, I've run up against some very stiff competition at auctions, but never quite so remarkable as the time I learned I had educated my own opposition.

When I first met him, he was an eleven-year-old. A bright young lad named Michael, he is the son of two of our good customers in

Cleveland. His mother, Inge, has probably read every book and catalogue extant on the subject of early Americana. She fostered this same passionate interest in the subject in her children, thus adding to a new crop of future collectors.

One day the family arrived in our showrooms with their son Michael. According to his mother, Michael's excellent school record had been rewarded in a tangible manner. He had been brought up to New York to claim a prize. The prize? He was to be permitted to choose any item of furniture we had on display, with a price tag up to $10,000.

(Before anyone cites Thorstein Veblen's theory of conspicuous consumption, it would be pertinent for me to point out that I agree with Michael's parents. Other fond parents endow their children with savings bonds, or stocks, or long-term federal securities. I may be prejudiced, but to present one's offspring with a unique piece of valuable early American, one of a kind, seems to me preferable to passing out an engraved piece of banknote paper. Given such a choice, we Sacks have for many years now opted for the furniture every time.)

Michael eagerly sought out his prize. He roamed our showroom the entire day, studying each piece carefully and checking out its fine points. Finally, he settled on a cherry serpentine-front chest of Connecticut origin, which fit into his financial allotment.

But the eleven-year-old's eye was already sharpened to excellence. While going through our inventory, he had spotted another piece, a Massachusetts blockfront chest of drawers with ball-and-claw feet, which we had recently acquired from the museum in Copenhagen, Denmark. Its history was fascinating. Years before, a Danish diplomat, while here in the United States, had married a lady from Salem, Massachusetts. The chest had traveled across the Atlantic with her to Denmark. Now that it had returned to its native grounds, young Michael wanted it. But the price on that chest was $45,000 . . . well over his allowance. Even the fondest of doting parents would not indulge him to that extent. He returned to Cleveland, and his hard-earned Connecticut piece shortly followed him.

But he couldn't forget the Massachusetts chest.

We eventually sold that beautiful blockfront to an executive in

Greenwich, Connecticut, who also found its elegance and its accompanying history irresistible. Sadly, he died several years later; eventually his widow consigned many of their fine pieces to auction at Sotheby's.

When the chest came up, I began bidding on it. I pursued it vigorously, all the way up to $60,000, when I decided to drop out.

On the way out of the auction rooms, I ran into young Michael's mother, in from Cleveland. "Sorry, Harold," she said, smiling. "But I was the successful buyer on that chest."

I congratulated her on her good taste, and reminded her it was the same chest that Michael, as a boy, had been fascinated by. "Oh yes indeed, I remember," she told me. "And this time, I was determined to see that Michael would get it."

Both pieces are now in Michael's collection, and as a young corporate executive, he promises to be one of the elite group of collectors in the future. Every young collector should have such a mother.

SIXTEEN

The Future for the Past

Back in 1969, I lectured at the Grolier Club in New York, and afterward I answered questions from the audience. One young man asked, "Mr. Sack, have prices for antiques peaked? Where do you think they will go in the future?"

"I don't think the future has arrived yet," I answered. "No American piece has yet reached the magic hundred-thousand-dollar mark at auction. We've seen such prices at private sales, but the general public doesn't yet know about them."

I could have gone into detail about one spectacular sale which had already happened. I was referring to a strange encounter I'd had with a beautiful lady, which led to a triumph for us. So inadvertent was this episode that I had to believe there is some mysterious force that directs our actions. Coincidence is not a satisfactory explanation.

She was a very cultured English lady, a total stranger, who walked into our shop one day and introduced herself. She was a shipping broker settled now in London, and she had a commission from a member of the Krupp family in Germany to acquire a Pennsylvania Chippendale secretary.

Since nobody from outside the United States had ever before expressed interest in acquiring such a piece, my curiosity was piqued. Why such a request from Germany? Perhaps it was because Pennsylvania had been primarily a German settlement, and the term Pennsylvania "Dutch" originally was *Deutsch* (German) and not Dutch?

Whatever the reason, alas, we had no such piece available.

The lady and I spent some time chatting. She did not seem inclined to leave. I showed her various photos of other pieces, and tried to give her a crash course in the early American concepts of design. I specifically showed her a photo of a blockfront Newport secretary, embellished with carved convex and concave shells, both on its writing lid and top section. It was one of about only ten or eleven we know exist, all attributed to the Goddard-Townsend workshops. This superb example I showed her was the one belonging to Miss Ima Hogg of Texas. That piece had originally turned up in London, obviously brought to England from Nova Scotia by a Tory family fleeing the Colonies.

No doubt other such fine pieces had arrived in England, and I asked my visitor to take special note of those unique carved shells. They were what made such furniture truly masterworks.

Finally, she left, thanking me profusely for my interest in her quest. I heard no more from her until several years passed.

Without warning I received a photo in the mail from London. She had sent it; it showed a block and shell carved Newport kneehole desk, possibly the most fully developed of this rare and precious group I'd ever seen.

Her letter stated that on the back of one of the drawers could be found inscribed *"Daniel Goddard — his drawer."*

I was far too excited to write, so I immediately called to tell her that if the piece in her photo was authentic, we would without a doubt be willing to pay her more for it than anyone else.

She explained that it belonged to two gentlemen, neighbors of hers in London, and they'd forwarded all the information about the desk to Parke-Bernet in London. "Stay with it — please — and keep us informed," I urged her. She promised she would.

Fortunately for us, the London branch of Parke-Bernet called New York to inquire about "Daniel Goddard." Their New York cataloguer said he had never heard of such a person. Fortunately, we had. Daniel was either the brother or the son of John Goddard, neither of whom was particularly well known as a cabinetmaker.

Goddard mahogany block and shell carved kneehole bureau or dresser, Newport, Rhode Island, circa 1780. These bureaus are among the most costly and coveted prizes in American furniture. The attribution of their makers extends from John Goddard and John Townend to Edmund Townsend and to Daniel Goddard, and the pieces vary in design, some being of the three-shell variety and others of the four-shell variety. A few have writing desk compartments behind the shell carved top drawer.

I sent a good friend of mine, a dealer in the import-export business, to London, commissioned to act as our agent. With great skill, he negotiated its purchase for a good price, and the greatest of all the Goddard-Townsend kneeholes came safely across the Atlantic, back to its homeland . . . a true prize, indeed.

There would be only one collector at that time who had the courage to pay our price, the then-astonishing $250,000. He was a young man who subsequently loaned the piece to the Philadelphia Museum of Fine Arts, where today it takes its well-earned place among the aristocrats of American furniture.

Its value today? Just as I did that day at the Grolier Club, I hesitate to suggest, or even guess at, a price.

But price was not the motive, neither for us, nor for that dedicated collector who bought it. Regaining a buried American masterpiece for our country was.

. . . If that lady had not lingered in our shop, and had not learned about block and shell pieces that day, who knows if it would have happened?

The magic six-figure mark asked about at the Grolier was to be attained publicly at auction, shortly thereafter in 1971. A Rhode Island Queen Anne highboy went for $102,000 at Parke-Bernet, and another Newport block and shell kneehole, at Freeman's in Philadelphia, was purchased by Doris Duke for a restoration project in Newport.

In the next two decades, history has been written and rewritten in each ensuing auction.

Take, for example, the episode of the five Philadelphia Chippendale chairs with the carved hairy-paw feet.

The style derives its name from the carved paw feet executed by skilled craftsmen, an incised tooling which resembles animal paws. They are a variant of the conventional ball-and-claw foot, and while predominantly English in history, their rare appearance in the thirteen Colonies is chiefly found in the Philadelphia region.

Most of the examples we know have a Cadwalader family history. General Cadwalader having been one of Washington's associates, the fame of Cadwalader family furniture has spread widely over the past two centuries.

These five hairy-paw chairs belonged to a Major Fanshawe of England, who had inherited them from a Georgian mansion in Ireland, owned by one of his friends. When he brought them to Sotheby's in London for sale, it was not that unusual for him, as well as the Sotheby's people, to consider them as late George II, and English in origin. But one of the Sotheby's London experts thought he detected a possible American flavor to the chairs, and promptly consulted Ron De Silva of the American department at Parke-Bernet in New York.

Ron is a graduate with an M.A. in American Studies from

Chippendale mahogany hairy-paw side chair, Philadelphia, circa 1770. A group of five chairs, of which this is one, made history in 1974 when it brought $207,000 at Sotheby's auction. In 1984 another chair from the same set was sold for $275,000. There were no doubt at least a dozen or more in the original set. They represent along with Philadelphia sample chairs the highest rococo development in the Colonies.

Winterthur, which is the only official training school we have for future curators. He remembered a similar chair in the du Pont collection and hurried down to Winterthur to check. He soon concluded that these five chairs from England were, in fact, from the very same set as the one in Winterthur! All were the work of Benjamin Randolph of Philadelphia, the great craftsman who had made the desk on which Thomas Jefferson wrote our Declaration of Independence.

An analysis of the wood used in the structural corner blocks confirmed Ron's judgment, and from then on, among potential collectors, there was pandemonium. Everyone wanted one of Major Fanshawe's superb chairs.

Sotheby's in New York did a masterful job of promotion. All the chairs were illustrated in the catalogue of the sale, and a special advance photo was sent out to each and every important collector. The five were scheduled to be sold as a pair, a single, and then a second pair, in sequence.

I had calls from several customers, as well as from the Metropolitan Museum and Colonial Williamsburg. How to satisfy them all required diplomacy and the wisdom of a Solomon. Finally, I informed each potential buyer that I estimated it might take $40,000 apiece on the chairs to prevail over the competition, but even so, because of the order in which the chairs were being brought up for auction, that price was at best a chancy proposal. Therefore, if they would agree to permit me to bid as their agent, and to control the disposition of the chairs for each of the buyers for whom I was dealing at a ten-percent premium, I'd do my best for all of them. They agreed.

The day of the auction came. Sotheby's was packed. It became a nerve-wrenching session for me; I knew the competition would be intense. But when the first pair was sold to me for *under* our limit, I knew I would prevail. I could use the savings I'd just garnered toward the purchase of the two remaining lots. By the end of the sale, the five chairs had been knocked down to us for a total of $207,000.

Each of my customers was satisfied. The Metropolitan got one which contained an upholsterer's label from Philadelphia; Williamsburg got one; and my two clients divided up the remaining three chairs — one acquiring a pair, a rare prize.

A young dealer from Connecticut, David Laughlin, attended that sale, and became so involved with the paradox of these five historic chairs turning up in Ireland and then in England, thousands of miles from their origin, that he would spend the next two years tracing their history. To unearth the complex trail of those chairs from the original Cadwaladers of Philadelphia, to Lord Westmeath's castle in Ireland, thence to Major Fanshawe, and finally back to America was an intricate job of detection, and the book he was to write, *The Case of Major Fanshawe's Chairs*, is as good as any detective story.

Ironically, in 1983, still another chair, a seventh from that same Cadwalader set, turned up even farther away, in Italy. When it came up for sale at Sotheby's, it brought $275,000! In a matter of ten years, a considerable appreciation in price. . . .

Later on, a hairy-paw Chippendale card table, also with a Cadwalader family history, was consigned to Sotheby's. When the bidding stopped at $220,000, and it was ours, I was faced with another problem. I had two customers who both wanted that beautiful piece. We ended up arranging a three-way phone hookup at which it was agreed I would flip a coin in my office, and whoever called it properly would be the successful buyer.

Believe it or not, both the winning buyer and the loser were satisfied with the outcome.

Lately, the publicity evoked by such dizzyingly high prices at auction has tended to encourage owners to send their fine pieces to public sale. So onward and upward has been the result.

But there has also been quite a controversy here in New York over the process of auctioning off valuable items, with questions raised about the entire machinery.

As a dealer, I'm often asked for my opinion about auction houses. How do I feel?

In my opinion, the auction house is an antagonist to the dealer, on one hand, and, on the other, an ally. As the new head of Sotheby's recently declared, he has the best of all possible worlds. He is a retailer, with no inventory.

To which I would respond that there is some truth in his statement, but not necessarily *all* the truth.

Being a retailer who does not teach, who does not clearly define what he is selling, who sells only to the buyer who bids the highest, and who thereby puts all his customers into open competition, who does not render all the services which a good dealer renders, who does not stock items when a customer needs them, who charges his customer extra for conditioning, transportation, and insurance, who does not render a scholarly referenced invoice, who does not buy back an item, who does not finance a purchase at no charge to the buyer — all of which is what auction houses do *not* do, and we *do*— simply means to me that auction houses are getting paid for being retailers . . . but without our overhead.

Certainly, there's no question that auction houses can perform a total function for an estate, say, which no dealer, especially specialists such as we are, can perform. None of us dealers has the public relations department to generate that excitement and publicity that a good auction house can. And for some buyers, the anonymity of buying at auction, rather than the chance of being snubbed at some dealer's showroom, is quite welcome.

But the truth is, much as the dealer may malign the auction

house, or the auction house play down the dealer, we need each other. The auction house covets a dealer's consignments, and depends on his inventory for its goods. The dealer, conversely, needs the auction house because not only can he buy there, but his own customers know that the auction house is a ready marketplace, should the buyer need to liquidate in large amounts in the future.

Therefore, as one nation, though unfriendly, needs the other, so neither side — auction house or dealer — is alone unto himself.

Half a century ago, my father cautioned his customers, "If you can afford the best, buy the best."

Beneath which, he added, "The slogan 'A good antique is a good investment' is absolutely true."

But even he would have not been prepared for the world record we set in 1983 with the Gibbs family block and shell desk, also attributed to John Townsend, at auction.

At this point, our organization had expanded to the third generation of Sacks, when my brother Albert's son Donald, who had served in the Vietnam war, came home and joined us. In the years to follow, he became a very competent expert, and our younger customers gravitated to him as they had to me when I was his age.

By 1983, public consciousness of early American had truly been raised. The Bicentennial sparked an additional interest in our heritage, and seemed to add momentum to the already thriving interest. The new American Wing of the Metropolitan, in which the Israel Sack rooms were installed, was under way. Yale had hosted a superb loan exhibit under the direction of Charles Montgomery, assisted by Pat Kane, who had been given a full professorship after leaving Winterthur. In addition, selections from that Yale exhibition were flown to the Victoria and Albert Museum in London — quite a tribute, at long last, from the Mother Country, to the arts of her ex-colonies. The Museum of Fine Arts in Boston, under the direction of Jonathan Fairbanks and Wendy Cooper, organized a comprehensive exhibition with a superb catalogue by Wendy Cooper, entitled "Paul Revere and His World." And our firm, in cooperation with Lawrence Fleischmann, organized a joint exhibition of both

Harold Sack and the Gibbs kneehole desk, purchased for a record price of $687,500 in 1983. The upward spiral of this recordbreaking Newport form commenced in 1950 when Jess Pavey, then a young Birmingham, Michigan, antiques dealer, paid the then unheard-of price of $16,000 at the Norvin Green sale at Parke-Bernet auction gallery in New York City.

paintings and furniture, on the theory that great American furniture should be shown in the company of great American painting.

When that magnificent Gibbs desk came up at auction, we had been commissioned to purchase it for one of Donald's clients, a young man who had been making a good deal of money on Wall Street. He had agreed with us before the sale that the piece was absolutely supreme, and warranted an all-out bid, with no limit.

However, a few days before the sale, that all-out bid was scaled down to $500,000, and we had agreed to represent him at a ten-percent commission. That would be his absolute limit.

Came the actual sale, and once again, I was under great tension. I began to bid.

There, beneath the lights, stood that beautiful desk, its fabulous decorative shells gleaming, its elegance obvious to everyone in the auction room.

Up and up went the price. And then, we were past $500,000.

Then, it was $520,000, which in itself was a new record for any American piece. I advanced it to $525,000.

Back came another bid: $550,000.

I had no idea where the competitive bidding was coming from, but it was my turn. Since I was no longer bound by our agreement with Donald's client, I was strictly on my own from here on.

I was perspiring, and around me, there was an awed hush.

I advanced the bid to $575,000.

Was the competition still coming?

Obviously it was, because suddenly Mr. Marion, of Sotheby's, announced, "I have six hundred thousand dollars!"

Mr. Marion is president of Sotheby's for good reason. He is a masterful auctioneer. His cadences and expressions would serve any Broadway leading man, and he commands the auction scene with authority. He turned and stared long and hard at me.

It was my turn.

I glanced at my brother Albert, who sat beside me. We both had the same impulse. He nodded. We would go for broke.

In a loud and clear voice, I said, "Six hundred and twenty-five thousand dollars."

Silence.

Mr. Marion raised his gavel and waited for a response.

Still, silence.

"Come *on*, John!" I said aloud, involuntarily.

Down came his gavel. "Sold!" he announced.

Around me, the silence dissolved into applause, and congratulations.

Including Sotheby's ten-percent premium, we had set a new record price for an American piece: $687,500.

Next morning, Rita Reif reported the story in the *New York Times*, and the story was picked up by all the media, to be sent all over the world. Our photographs were taken, posed behind our prize.

When the bill arrived the next morning, however, there was no applause; we were alone. What would my father have said?

A few weeks later, Donald's customer, for whom we had originally been empowered to bid, could not stand it any longer. He wanted that desk still, and he came for it. We struck a fair deal with him whereby the beautiful Newport piece is now in his home, the jewel of his rapidly growing collection.

But even the astonishingly high price that the Gibbs piece achieved had not prepared me for what happened on January 25, 1986, a mere three years later, when a superb Philadelphia tea table was sold at auction to a New Hampshire collector, Mr. Edward Nicholson, for $1,045,000!*

We were well aware of the quality of that particular piecrust table, with its scalloped edge top, fluted columnar base, and ball-and-claw feet. My brother Albert had purchased it in 1953 for $7,000 — in those days, an extremely high price. My father had subsequently sold it for $15,000. But when the Christie's auctioneer knocked that magnificent piece down to Mr. Nicholson, I ended up the under-bidder.

Why hadn't I continued to bid, and secured it for my own client?

Simply because I'd been instructed to exercise my own best judgment on price, and when we reached those dizzyingly high six-figure numbers, I recognized that Mr. Nicholson, my opponent in this auction, had every intention of doggedly staying with me until he secured the prize. Since the multiples we were bidding were now $50,000, when he topped my bid of $990,000,** I behaved prudently and withdrew.

Rap! and that great table was his.

When the applause died down, I told Mr. Nicholson: "It's worth more. You got a bargain. A bargain means value — not price."

Later on, he was quoted in the press as saying, "I think there is an exhilarating feeling in owning masterpieces. That table, for example; it is not really mine. I am just holding it as a fiduciary trust."

What will happen now?

I told Rita Reif of the *Times* that I believe this new price record will serve to attract a lot of other high-quality pieces out of their present hiding-places into the market. It has the same effect as when the four-minute mile record was breached. These days, whoever runs the four-minute mile comes in last.

But one irony remains constant.

We never would have arrived at such a time as now, when early American furniture and decorative arts have achieved such status and appreciation among our countrymen, were it not for the intu-

* Including a ten percent buyer premium.
** Including a ten percent buyer premium.

ition and good taste of such immigrants as my father, a late American who loved early American.

Nowadays, the new generation of curators and appraisers can be taught by rigorous academic method. We have recourse to all sorts of scientific techniques by which antiques, real or not, can be appraised and authenticated. But remember, men like Israel Sack did it all by feel. Their equipment? A sharp eye, a native shrewdness, and the secret ingredient, deep abiding response for what they loved. "It speaks to me," said my father. That was his science.

He was a true pioneer, and as a result of his efforts to raise American consciousness to the value of our own native crafts, he became, like Maxim Karolik and other contemporary dealers, a valued teacher.

Certainly, today's prices for fine pieces are astronomic, compared to those of past years. But how does one properly assess the value of the unique works of the Frothinghams, the Willards, Paul Revere, the Duncan Phyfes, the Randolphs, and the rest of those brilliantly creative artist-craftsmen?

And if we are all of us more aware of their worth today, it's because of my father and all those Lowell Street pickers, hardy explorers who journeyed out of the city each day with horse and buggy, to scour the countryside and to bring back hard-won treasures to their candlelit basement shops.

For me, it is a very long distance from those days when I was a boy, bouncing up and down in the back seat of my father's open touring Buick, traveling with him through a rural landscape populated by hostile farmers and their wives, most of whom may have subscribed to the occasional sign I can remember which warned "No Dogs — No Jews." Yankees who believed that this jovial, Old Testament–quoting Israel Sack from Boston had to be truly crazy for wanting to hand over his good cash money for some dusty old relic which had been hidden away in the back parlor for years. . . .

Even in his wildest fantasies, my father could not have foreseen the eventual prices achieved by those same relics he unearthed. But knowing Israel Sack as well as I did, I am certain the prices in 1986 wouldn't have impressed him all that much. For he had that other

Harold Sack in front of a Massachusetts Chippendale blockfront chest-on-chest.

motto which he was fond of quoting. No matter what the price was he'd achieved for some one-of-a-kind Hepplewhite this, or Chippendale that, once it had left the shop, he'd sigh and say, "Sell . . . and repent."

Even though he was a dealer, he hated to see them go.

All he did, throughout those years, was to let the furniture speak to him.

Loudly, and clearly.

And so it continues with me and my brothers, the sons of Crazy Sack, today.

SEVENTEEN

The Fabulous Nicholas Brown Secretary

E VERY so often, someone will ask whether I think there are any buried treasures of early American antique furniture, still waiting to be unearthed.

Being an optimist—in this business, what else can one be?—I certainly hope these treasures exist.

But if they don't, I will always be satisfied that I was the successful high bidder on the greatest of American decorative masterpieces, the Nicholas Brown Goddard-Townsend six-shell secretary.

Not that this superb example of Newport's finest, which dates back to the 1760s, was precisely a buried treasure as, since 1814, it had been in daily use by the Brown family in their home in Providence, Rhode Island.

The John Nicholas Brown Center, created in 1983 by the Brown family of Providence, Rhode Island, is dedicated to the study of American civilization. The Center is headquartered in the 1814 Nightingale-Brown House, thought to be the largest wood frame house to have survived from eighteenth-century America. In this grand Georgian mansion, the last five generations of the Brown family, who helped settle Providence in the 1630s, have been closely intertwined with the cultural, political, and economic development of the state and nation. As a living laboratory of

The Nightingale-Brown wooden frame house built in 1814, Benefit Street, Providence, Rhode Island, occupied by the Brown family since the early nineteenth century. The secretary was moved in 1814 to the Nightingale-Brown house, where it resided until it was sold on June 3, 1989.

American culture—rather than as a house museum or collecting institution—the John Nicholas Brown Center serves as a resource for visiting scholars, the region's academic institutions, and other organizations active in the study and practice of art, architecture, history, and historic preservation. Through its residence program, seminars, publications, sponsorship of original research, and the use of its own archives, the center acts as a catalyst in furthering the study of American civilization. (As stated in the Christie's New York catalog of the sale.)

For centuries we'd known of the secretary's existence, but there had never been a hint that it might possibly come to market.

Illustration of the Nicholas Brown secretary in the Nightingale-Brown house along with Brown family furnishings.

There were originally ten such desks and bookcases, with their distinctive block-and-shell treatment in both the lower and upper sections, made by the Goddard-Townsend craftsmen. Two of them can be seen at the Museum of Fine Arts in Boston, and two are in the Rhode Island School of Design. There are other fine examples at the Rhode Island Historical Society, at the Metropolitan Museum in New York, another is at Winterthur, one at Bayou Bend, and in the Garvan Collection at Yale.

But this secretary, which was originally made for Nicholas Brown by John Goddard himself, is the most impressive of all. It is nine feet, four inches high, a towering and beautiful creation.

I was privileged to see and admire it closely several years back, in 1982, in a very hush-hush manner. One of my customers, a most tasteful collector, called to invite me to join him on a trip to examine a very special item. When he called, he sounded as if he might have been working for the CIA. "Please—don't discuss this with anyone," he cautioned. "It's a secret. I'm asking you for your evaluation. Meet me in Boston, and I'll drive you to take a look."

My interest was piqued. But when we drove up to the old Nightingale-Brown house in Providence, I was truly astonished. What could we possibly be doing *here*? Well, it seemed that the collector had been discussing the possibility of purchasing some of the Brown family pieces.

What he explained to me was that he had offered to buy some antiques from the family, which would provide them sufficient funds to operate as a historic study institution. The furniture involved in such a deal would be left on the premises, on display, so as not to disturb the decor of the Brown house. Very large sums of money were involved.

Amazing. I had heard nothing about such an arrangement. This was even more remarkable in the early American antiques business, where the grapevine crackles with lightning speed whenever such an opportunity arises.

This, then, was my first opportunity to examine the fabulous Nicholas Brown block-and-shell secretary, about which I'd heard all my life. The four sons of Nicholas Brown—Nicholas, John, Joseph, and Moses—were each given a block-and-shell secretary. Three of the desks survived—Nicholas', John's (which is in the Garvan Collection in Yale), and Joseph's. Moses' desk was presumed destroyed in the nineteenth century in a fire at his farm. This secretary, which is the tallest of the group, was presumedly made for the older brother, Nicholas.

There it stood, an awesome piece towering above us. There are few private homes anywhere that could actually house this secretary; it has a statuesque, almost religious feeling to it. The more one examines it, the more one is struck by its fantastic quality. With regard to the quality of the mahogany that was used in its construction, I've never seen its equal.

Before their children came of age, the Brown family sent their ships to the Indies. There, the finest mahogany was selected and brought back to New England, to await the time when it would

Nicholas Brown block-and-shell carved secretary made by John Goddard of Newport, Rhode Island, circa 1760–1770, sold at Christie's for $12,100,000 on June 3, 1989.

be used. One must assume that the tree from which this mahogany was taken stood high up on some mountain, a towering tree imposing enough to be used for this specific piece.

It was a joy to examine it close up. The feet presumedly appeared to be in excellent condition, but it was impossible to up-end the piece to examine the understructure.

My instinct, on which I usually rely, told me that this wonderful piece was in excellent shape, considering the amount of daily

use it had been put to for the past two centuries, and is a tribute
to its maker.

I was delighted to put my blessing on it.

Subsequently, the Brown family and the collector could not
come to terms. The complex deal he had proposed did not go
through. As for that amazing Nicholas Brown secretary, it
remained in the Providence house.

Silence descended, and then, seven years later, I received
another phone call. This time it was from Ed Nicholson, of New
Hampshire, that same collector who'd bought the Philadelphia
piecrust tea table in 1986 and had broken through the million
dollar mark, thus making quite a name for himself in the small,
but intense, network of major antiques collectors.

Even though Ed had bested me at that particular sale, he'd
rarely purchased pieces from us, but we'd kept in touch on a
friendly basis. However, on this day, I was surprised when he
passed on some very interesting news. "One of my friends in
Rhode Island just tipped me off," he said. "He's heard that the
Brown family had a meeting in which they'd decided that the six-
shell secretary is going to be sold, in order to raise the money to
restore the Nightingale Brown house."

Indeed, important news.

How much would be involved? "They need enough to restore
that old house properly. Your guess is as good as mine; maybe
several million?"

Or perhaps even more. As it turned out, the family also wished
to create and endow a Brown Foundation for the Study of
American Culture.

Ed was obviously anxious to be a potential buyer. He wasn't
ready to make an offer, but he certainly was interested in finding
out whether I'd be his competitor.

I thought over this information he'd just passed on . . . if the
Brown family had not been able to agree with my old collector
friend on a private sale back in 1982, then obviously there would
be only one means by which the various Brown family members
could be satisfied. That great nine foot tall secretary would have

to be sold at auction, where it would be open to public bidding.

"Neither you nor I can make a private bid," I told him. "There has to be an auction." I explained my thinking to him. "You're probably right," said Ed. "Which auction house?" Good question. "I wish I knew," I told him. "If you hear anything, will you let me know?" he asked. "Only if you agree to call me, " I said.

We both laughed. Competitors always!

After we'd spoken, I thought about this amazing situation. I realized one thing immediately. Whether the piece came up for sale at Sotheby's or Christie's made little difference to me. What mattered to me was that Israel Sack be the one to buy it—the only Goddard-Townsend secretary left in private hands, and it certainly was the greatest example of that Newport workshop's creations. Never again in my lifetime would such a prize come up for sale, of that I was certain. For me, a Sack who's spent most of his life searching for the finest early American antiques, wasn't that sufficient reason to send me off in pursuit of it?

In the days that followed, I simply could not get that secretary out of my mind. If it went to auction, and I had to bid against all my competitors, who knew which of them would have the most resources? It might be a museum, or some as-yet unrevealed foundation, anxious to acquire this prize; perhaps affluent Japanese, who always looked for the best and rarest, but who as yet had not purchased an American piece.

Assuming I managed to buy it for our firm at such a potentially high price, what would I do with it? Find a buyer who'd be willing to pay us an even higher price?

That seemed unlikely. What was my alternative? I needed a buyer ahead of time. Someone with deep pockets, heavy resources of his own, who would permit me to act for him.

Luckily, I thought I had someone who could possibly be that person.

A few years earlier, a young man and his wife had appeared in our salesroom, unannounced. Modest and unassuming, he wished, as he still does, to remain anonymous. All I can say about him is that he is a successful financier, and that he and his wife had decided to remodel a house in which the furniture would be early American antiques. They had collections in other areas, but American furniture was new to them. I later found out that they had consulted, among others, Morrie Heckscher, curator of the American Wing at The Metropolitan Museum of Art, for guidance on obtaining an education. They wanted to learn about American antiques and I was only too glad to help them. They listened, they learned, they asked questions, and eventually, they began to buy.

I soon realized that neither he nor his wife were interested in the politics of the antiques business, nor could they care less about the gossip, the in-fighting among dealers and collectors, as well as the various games that fill our days. What they wished to accomplish was to assemble a collection of the best available, the very best. I soon noticed that his wife had a discerning eye for quality.

How my father, Israel Sack, would have enjoyed knowing them!

I called my prospective client, and I told him, "The greatest piece of early American furniture I've ever seen is going to come on the market."

"That's a very large order," he said.

"The largest," I said. "Nine feet worth." He listened while I described the provenance of the Nicholas Brown secretary. Then I went on to tell him of its beauty: the skill of the craftsman who'd made it, that amazing mahogany, those beautiful hand-carved shells. . .

"You sound as if you're in love with it," he said.

"Absolutely," I said. "I haven't been able to sleep for the past couple of nights, just thinking about it."

"What do *you* have to decide about it?" he asked.

"Where it goes," I said. "It will certainly be sold by either Sotheby's or Christie's, and the auction will be in six or seven months." I took a deep breath. "It seems to me that this wonderful piece should go to someone who appreciates it, *and* deserves it—*and* can afford it."

"I agree," he said. "Such as?"

"You," I said. "You deserve it. I'd like to see that you get it, and if you agree, I'll act for you, and I'll do everything I can to make certain that you're the buyer."

He didn't even pause to think about my offer. "I'm with you," he said.

Remarkably enough, we'd settled the major problem. I could pursue the Nicholas Brown secretary on his behalf and make certain that it go to his collection. Now we'd have to sit back and wait for whatever developments arose as the piece moved toward its eventual auction.

Word circulated soon enough that it would be up for sale. People kept coming into the shop, dropping by for ostensibly other reasons, but always, the same question kept cropping up. . . "What about the Brown secretary?"

Some of them were good customers, others were connected with museums as trustees; whoever they were, they all were busy trying to find out what would happen.

As was *I. I* was trying to find out what sort of competition *I* could expect. Might it be a museum, such as the Chicago Art Institute, where a new wing had recently been installed? Certainly they'd like to have the Nicholas Brown secretary. Could they put together sufficient capital from their supporters to swing the purchase of such an expensive piece?

Then there was the matter of dealing with collectors. They were now accustomed to ever-rising prices as I had predicted previously. In January 1987, a Philadelphia easy chair with hairy-paw feet, made for John Cadwalader, had set a new auction record at $2.75 million! In November of that year, at Sotheby's in London, an elegant Marie Antoinette console table, made for Versailles by Louis XVI's cabinetmaker Jean-Henri Riesener, sold for $2.9 million (a world record for furniture)! Certainly, this Brown piece could go higher, but if so, how many collectors could afford such a price?

It dawned on me that perhaps Doris Duke could. For years now, she had been working to bring authentic Newport antiques back to that city, to restore them to the homes she'd been preserving. Certainly that lady was capable of paying such a price—would she be my competition?

So far, we did not even know which auction house would be handling the sale. Then, one day, one of the Sotheby's executives called to inform me that he had heard the Brown family had lately received some private offers for their secretary! "I just thought you'd like to know," he told me.

I thanked him, and promptly called my client. "If there are private offers being made," I said, "perhaps we ought to get in line and make one ourselves, wouldn't you agree?"

"Certainly," he said.

"It should be an offer that will knock them dead," I said.

"Fine," said my client. "Make one."

At that particular moment, I was calling him from an airport phone. "Such as?"

"What do you think it will take?" he asked. "Who knows?" I said. "A piece like this is unique. I think it will bring over eight at least, but if there is competition, it could go anywhere," I replied. "I think there would be a lot of bidders between five and eight, but above that, it gets rather thin. It may bring ten, maybe more," I said.

"What do you think of an offer of eleven? I would value a private sale, and the seller would avoid the auction house fees," my client said.

"I think that would be very tempting to the seller," I said.

"Go ahead," said my client.

I'd certainly picked the right one!

I finally made the call to Providence, where I reached Mr. Emlen, the curator of the John Nicholas Brown Center for the Study of American Civilization, now the owners of the secretary; he was the man in charge of selling the family heirloom. I told him I knew he'd received private offers, and that I was now prepared to make one of my own. "Eleven million dollars, plus or minus a little, either way," I said.

Mr. Emlen laughed.

"May I ask you what's funny about that?" I inquired.

"Nothing," he said. "Only that it's so much more than any of the other offers we've had," he told me. "But I'm very glad to hear such amazing figures. Even so, it has been decided to sell the piece at public auction. No private sale, no matter how impressive your offer is . . . and it *is* impressive."

Shortly afterward, Christie's formally announced that the sale of the Nicholas Brown secretary would take place in June 1989 at their auction gallery in New York.

Christie's, which very much wanted the prestige of such a sale, had obviously offered all sorts of extra bonuses to the consignors. They'd promised a handsome special-bound catalog, endless amounts of publicity, and worldwide news of the sale to customers in Europe. They produced a videotape of the piece with historic background, etc., and sent this video to a select group of potential buyers. They'd also contracted to construct an imposing display case in their New York galleries, in which the huge Goddard piece would be displayed. Its doors would open during the day, and then close at night, under constant security, of course. The entire sale would be treated as a media event, which it certainly proved to be.

But surprisingly enough, before Christie's put the piece on display, we at Israel Sack were to get the secretary first!

Temporarily, of course.

Since our workshop is well known for its high standard of expertise and craftsmanship with which our people repair and restore precious antiques, Christie's had the Brown secretary trucked down directly to us from Providence. In our shop, the piece would be carefully and lovingly inspected, to make absolutely certain that everything was in optimum shape before the sale.

It arrived, and finally, I had a chance to be alone with Goddard's masterpiece, to go over it in daylight, without any interference or distraction.

We walked into our workshop, and there it was. Inches away, silent, gleaming, splendid. Now we could examine all its subtleties of design and construction.

My old friend and customer from Boston, the late Maxim

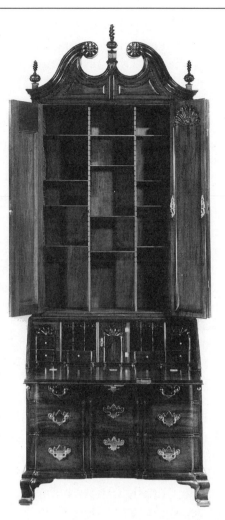

Nicholas Brown secretary illustrating the hinged folding door
arrangement in the upper section. Michael Moses, in his book,
Master Craftsmen of Newport; the Townsends and Goddards, said,
"the brilliance of achievement" can best be appreciated by
understanding the solution of the problem of extending the three-
panel blocking of the drawers into the upper case section. The
solution is ingenious. One door is formed of two blocked panels
capped by shells—one concave, the other convex—hinged to form
one door. The opposing door has a single convex panel capped by a
shell. "It is very dramatic and entirely American," said Moses.

Karolik, whose collection at the Museum of Fine Arts, Boston, is reputed to be one of the greatest, is supposed to have commented about this towering piece, "One more inch and it would have been a freak. As it is, it is perfection."

Later, in the thoughtful analysis that he would write for the forthcoming June sale, Dean Failey, who is the head of Christie's American furniture department, would write ". . . it is the quintessential piece of American furniture. It has always been considered a masterpiece. It ranks as the most important piece of furniture ever to be sold publicly."

I agreed with them both.

Since it was imperative that I finally see the underside, our men gently laid the secretary on its back, and thus I had an unobstructed view of it from below. Amazingly, after all those years of use, all was in first-class shape. Such a fine tribute to those early Newport craftsmen. How fortunate I was to be totally alone with it for the days it was in our shop.

Finally, the piece was checked over and trucked to Christie's on Park Avenue. We were sorry to see it go, but we were also relieved to be free of that awesome responsibility.

At Christie's, it was installed in its new display cabinet with the folding doors. There, each morning, the doors were opened, and the Nicholas Brown secretary went on display for potential buyers or for spectators drawn to this rare sight.

Outside, on Park Avenue, the traffic roared by in busy, stressful Manhattan, but inside Christie's showroom, as collectors came in to admire this piece, there was silence, an almost reverential awe. All day, visitors, myself included, came back often to stand and marvel at this remarkable achievement. . . this tangible evidence of the craft of the early Americans, brought out of its Providence home for the first time in two hundred years.

Each week that spring brought more publicity, and with each story in the media, there was enhanced excitement.

People were still constantly trying to find out what I knew. I, of course, was engaged in precisely the same practice.

I worried. I calculated. I speculated. Who would be our competitors? How high could they bid to secure this prize?

I had another conference with my client, and we reviewed strategy. "Assume I'm at the sale, representing you," I said. "You won't be there, so I need your mandate now. Suppose you call me up afterward, and ask me how I did, and I have to tell you we lost it because I bid up to ten million, and then somebody topped me."

"Don't stop at ten, then," he replied. "Keep going."

"But to where?" I asked.

"I see where a Jackson Pollock painting just sold for seventeen million," he reminded me. "This should be worth as much, if not more."

Amazing!

A week or so later, the air was buzzing with even more rumor. Again we spoke. "Supposing somebody goes *over* seventeen?" I asked. By now, we were both on edge. "Do we lose it because I should have gone higher?"

"If somebody else thinks that it is worth more, I wish them well," he said. It had always been his practice to bid to buy, but not to regret being topped.

Now, at least, I was absolutely certain I could top any other bidder.

But if the bidding reached those levels, I wanted to make certain this sale would be properly publicized. Since we were bound to raise the price of American decorative arts to a new plateau, it was time to have the entire world look to us with proper admiration.

I called Dean Failey of Christie's, and asked him at what time his firm would be scheduling the sale that Saturday. "We've been thinking of 4 p.m.," he told me.

"You'd better change it," I said. I'd already spoken to my good friend Rita Reif of *The New York Times*, who writes about antiques, among other things, and I passed on her advice. "If you want to make the front page of the *Sunday Times*, not the metropolitan edition, which only reaches the East, but the *national* edition, which covers the country, then the news has to be in by noon, or 12:30 at the latest, on Saturday."

"I see what you mean," said Dean, "I'll look into it."

Shortly afterward, the auction of the secretary was scheduled for Saturday, June 3, at Christie's, at 11:30 a.m.

That Saturday morning, I was in my seat.

The salesroom was crowded. TV crews were covering the event; press people were everywhere, and in front, auction house people were manning the telephones for out-of-town bidders.

In the crowd of onlookers, I could see quite a few other dealers and collectors, all waiting for that moment of truth!

Rap! went the gavel. The auction began.

The first bid was two million.

The auctioneer stared at us. I heard "Five million."

From behind me there came another bid—"Seven."

Ed Nicholson dropped out at nine million.

By now there were only two contenders left. Myself, and a bald-headed man whom I didn't recognize.

"*Ten!*" was his bid.

I raised my paddle. "Eleven," I told the auctioneer.

Silence.

My heart was racing; I waited for another bid. Would the bald-headed man go higher?

Obviously not. *Rap!* "*Sold!*" said the auctioneer.

The Nicholas Brown secretary had been bought by Israel Sack.

Amazingly, the entire sale had not taken much more than two or three minutes!

Bedlam broke out! The TV reporters and the press all crowded around, congratulating me, excitedly commenting on this new record we'd set, and demanding to know the name of the successful buyer I represented.

All I would say was that it had been bought for a couple who'd been seriously collecting American antiques. Name? No name.

Mr. and Mrs. Anonymous, they were, and still remain.

I'd been waiting for the real action to begin after my last bid—after all, I had many millions in my head—and now, it seemed I'd bought that magnificent piece for my young client at the price of eleven million, plus a one million, one hundred thousand dollar buyer's premium—$12,100,000.

ANTIQUES
And The Arts Weekly

★★★★★★★★★★★★★★★★★★★★★★★★ June 9, 1989

Newsstand Rate 70¢ Copy
Outside Connecticut $1.25   **Published by The Bee Publishing Co., Newtown, Connecticut**   Subscription Rates
See Page Two

46 — Antiques and The Arts Weekly — June 9, 1989

Shell Shocked!

NEW YORK CITY — The market for American decorative arts was put to its most important test in decades with Christie's sale of the Nicholas Brown desk-bookcase for $12.1 million on June 3.

The memory of earlier salesroom triumphs was eclipsed at approximately 11 am when the Newport casepiece became the most expensive piece of furniture sold at auction. Its price was four times that of Marie Antoinette's console table; twice that of a Gutenberg Bible; and more than any example of sculpture.

Just before the sale began at 10 am the descendants of Israel Sack, their friends and associates entered the auction hall. Christie's American furniture specialist Dean Failey and Robert P. Emlen, director of the John Nicholas Brown Center for the Study of American Civilization, escorted the clan to the front of the room where it settled into the first few rows of seats on the left. A younger generation of the Browns of Providence, owners of the desk-bookcase until late last year, sat to the Sacks' immediate right.

By 11 am the sale room was packed. Christie's president Christopher Burge announced lot 100, the bookcase, and asked for an opening bid of $2 million. Portsmouth, N.H. dealer Ron Bourgeault stepped forward with a bid of $5 million.

Bidding proceeded in $1 million increments. The room was still, except for the flicker of gold pen above the second row and the motions of an American collector seated midway on the aisle. The collector had never bid at an American furniture sale before.

Christie's sells Brown Bookcase for $12.1 Million

New York dealer Harold Sack had the clients.

Story and Photos by
Antiques and The Arts Weekly
Laura Beach, Assoc. Editor

Part of the press publicity that was buttressed by radio and TV coverage of the record-breaking price of the Nicholas Brown secretary.

A new record, certainly, but lower than I'd expected to have to pay. Ironically, assuming Christie's waived the seller's premium to get the business, the seller received exactly what we had been prepared to offer earlier for a private sale. I was overwhelmed. This was my moment and I was so happy to share it with my brothers and my family.

Harold Sack standing next to the Nicholas Brown secretary in the Israel Sack, Inc., showrooms after its sale at Christie's on June 3, 1989.

Harold Sack with his bidding paddle, number 912. The paddle used
to bid on the Nicholas Brown secretary was retired by Christie's
and given to Harold as a gift on his eightieth birthday.

Later on, I learned that my bald-headed opponent had been
bidding on behalf of Doris Duke, the one collector I'd feared.
Obviously, she'd set him a limit beyond which he could not go.
Her loss, our gain.

We went back to the Israel Sack showrooms and had a celebra-
tory brunch, with champagne. Later, on my eightieth birthday,
Christie's sent me the bidding paddle I'd used that memorable
June morning. Number 912. Their birthday note said they'd
retired my paddle and wanted me to have it as a fond memory of
the day I'd set a new record for American antique prices.

How did I feel? Marvelous! And when my client called that
morning and got the good news, he and his wife were delighted.

After all, he and his wife now own an integral part of our American history.

When their new home is finished, and the Nicholas Brown secretary is moved into it, I can only hope that it gives them as much pleasure as it did me.

After all, to encourage a man to spend so much money, I had to have an inner feeling of great affection for that splendid piece. The fact that the Nicholas Brown secretary made a new record, however, is not as important to me as the effect the sale had on public attitude toward Americana in the decorative arts. In 1990, this sale was recorded in the Guinness Book of World Records. Remember, when my father started in this business, back in 1903, the American decorative arts was truly a stepchild. No longer. It's not the money the piece commanded that pleases me, it's the respect that went with it.

I have been in the antiques business for more than half a century, but in retrospect, June 3, 1989, at Christie's, is the high point of my entire career. I confess that from that first day in January, when word came that the Nicholas Brown secretary would appear on the market, I secretly prayed each night that I might live long enough to see the day when it came up for sale, in order that I might achieve the honor of Israel Sack being its buyer.

Now that a Sack has set a new record for an American piece of that quality, one that still stands, I realize nothing can ever approach my exhilaration of that Saturday morning.

And, oh yes, the sale, plus news of the record we set, *did* make the front page of Sunday morning's national edition of *The New York Times*!

Not a bad morning's work.

Colonial American Desk Is Sold for $12.1 Million

By RITA REIF

An elaborately carved 18th-century American desk was bought yesterday by a New York antiques dealer for $12.1 million, the highest price ever paid for an object other than a painting.

The sale of the Newport relic with an enviable pedigree catapults antiques and decorative arts to a new plateau. The auction, at Christie's in New York, is the most recent in an overheated market in which records are toppled almost daily for an increasing number and variety of artworks.

This year 11 paintings and this desk, a secretary, have each brought more than $10 million at auction, a level that was first surpassed in 1983. Until yesterday, no work of the decorative arts had sold at auction for more than $3 million.

"Not all masterpieces hang on the wall," said the purchaser, Harold Sack of Israel Sack Inc., after Christopher Burge, Christie's president in New York, brought his gavel down on the purchase. Mr. Sack said he was representing a young man with a variety of business interests who "is forming a superior collection" of American furniture.

Starting at the Top

"He and his wife are just starting as collectors," Mr. Sack said. "They have been collecting for a relatively short time — it can't be more than three or four years."

One interesting aspect of this couple's antiques collecting that Mr. Sack said is increasingly common is that they have just come into the market and are starting at the top, buying the finest antiques. "These people who are at that level are not buying out of disposable earned income," he said.

No piece of furniture auctioned over the last several decades has aroused as much interest as this bonnet-topped mahogany secretary, robustly carved with a block-and-shell front, which was probably made by John Goddard, a master Rhode Island cabinetmaker of the pre-Revolutionary period. It is the tallest, at 113 inches, of the nine six-shell Newport secretaries known to survive, most of which are in museums.

This desk-bookcase, the tallest surviving example of what was a status symbol for merchants in Colonial America, eclipsed the $3 million level which was reached only last month. It was then that a diamond-encrusted Russian enameled Easter egg, made in 1890 by Peter Carl Fabergé, was auctioned for that figure at Christie's in Geneva. The highest sum ever before achieved at auction for a piece of furniture was $2.97 million, paid in November at Sotheby's in London for a Louis XVI console table that once belonged to Marie Antoinette.

Many Historical Associations

Mr. Burge said he did not expect many works of the decorative arts to sell for the price that the desk brought at auction. "There is always going to be a premium paid for the fine arts," he said. "It is possible to see $100 million for the right picture, but it will be a long time before we see $50 million for any work of the decorative arts."

Mr. Burge said the price for the desk was at least $7 million more than anyone at Christie's thought it would be. But even some American antiques collectors had suggested a much higher price might be paid.

"The desk has so many historical associations," he said. "It is the only such desk available, and it is probably the best example of a six-shell Newport secretary. If you are going to buy a great and soaring piece of American furniture — this is it."

The market for American furniture is very strong, Mr. Burge said. "But big prices, on the whole, are paid for very few pieces, and only Americans buy

> 'Not all masterpieces hang on the wall.'

American furniture. In French furniture, you have many more people going for much higher prices — an awful lot sell for $300,000 or $400,000."

'Bound to Be a Ripple Effect'

The pedigree of the Rhode Island secretary auctioned yesterday is as impressive to many American furniture collectors and museum curators as French furniture made for royalty. "It had descended in the family of the original owner, Nicholas Brown of Providence, who was in shipping and commerce, producing candles from whale oil," said Dean Failey, who heads American furniture sales at Christie's. "Brown University took its name from the Nicholas Brown family of Providence."

Mr. Sack said there was bound to be a ripple effect in the antiques market that will cause prices to increase on the finest-quality pieces. "I also think that this new plateau will bring out a lot of great pieces of furniture that are still in hiding."

Until yesterday, the only object other than a painting to sell at auction for more than $10 million was the 12th-century Gospels of Henry the Lion, an illuminated manuscript, which was sold in 1983 for $11.9 million at Sotheby's in London.

Mr. Burge said he attributed the high prices for art and antiques to "the availability of money and the enormous new wealth many people enjoy."

At least one dealer in American art and furniture decided before the sale not to bid. "I can't see myself buying a piece of furniture for more than I would pay for a painting," Alexander Acevedo, a Madison Avenue dealer, said after he paid a record $5.23 million for Frederic Edwin Church's "Home by the Lake," the highest figure paid at auction for a pre-20th-century American painting. He said he was sure the secretary would go for more than $10 million. "To me, it is no longer an investment; it's a tombstone."

The desk had remained in the family of Nicholas Brown since it was carved in the 1790's. In December, a descendant and namesake of the original owner, Capt. Nicholas Brown, executive director of the National Aquarium of Baltimore, donated the desk to the 175-year-old wood-framed Nightingale-Brown House of Providence, which is endangered. The residence, where he grew up, now houses the John Nicholas Brown Center for the Study of American Civilization. The center is named for Captain Brown's father, an Assistant Secretary of the Navy in the Truman Administration.

The New York Times/Dith Pran

$12.1 Million Desk

An 18th-century American desk, which sold at a price usually paid for famous paintings. Page 36.

The June 4, 1989, *Sunday Times* announcing the record-breaking sale of the Nicholas Brown secretary.

Index

About the Authors

Harold Sack is the president of Israel Sack, Inc. He is an adviser to the White House and Department of State collections of Americana, and a member of the furniture committee of the Metropolitan Museum of Art. He has also lectured at numerous museums and colleges on the subject of American antiques.

Max Wilk is a theater, television, and film writer, theatrical historian, and novelist. He is the author of more than twenty books, including his most recent novel, *A Tough Act to Follow*.